Learning, Food, and Sustainability

Jennifer Sumner
Editor

Learning, Food, and Sustainability

Sites for Resistance and Change

palgrave
macmillan

Editor
Jennifer Sumner
University of Toronto
Toronto, Ontario, Canada

ISBN 978-1-137-53903-8   ISBN 978-1-137-53904-5   (eBook)
DOI 10.1057/978-1-137-53904-5

Library of Congress Control Number: 2016947968

Cover illustration: © simon Jonathan webb / Alamy Stock Photo

Printed on acid-free paper

This Palgrave Macmillan imprint is published by Springer Nature
The registered company is Nature America Inc. New York

Dedication of book to Cathleen Kneen

This book is dedicated to Cathleen Kneen, a contributor to this work. She was an educator, activist and friend whose spirit continues to guide us in our work on food system transformation.

Contents

LIST OF FIGURES

LIST OF TABLES

AUTHOR BIOGRAPHIES

Peter Andrée is an associate professor in the Department of Political Science at Carleton University in Ottawa. His research focuses on the politics of food and the environment, and he practices, and teaches, community-based participatory research methods. He is co-editor of *Globalization and Food Sovereignty: Global and Local Change in the New Politics of Food*, which examines social movements the world over seeking to build more sustainable and just food systems.

Donna Appavoo has a background in human nutrition and teaches in the Chang School at Ryerson University in Toronto, as well as being an administrator and researcher with Appavoo Medicine Professional Corporation. Her interests include food systems, health systems, food security, gender, sustainability and ecohealth.

Deborah Barndt is a professor emerita in the Faculty of Environmental Studies at York University in Toronto and an artist and activist around environmental and social justice issues in the Americas. She is the author of *Tangled Routes: Women, Work, and Globalization on the Tomato Trail*, and has written numerous book chapters and articles on food, arts-based education, and the global food system.

Sharon Brodovsky holds a Master's in Business Administration from the University of Toronto and works as a social impact strategist. She leads a consulting practice that supports social sector organizations, foundations and private companies to design, develop and implement social impact strategies, plans and evaluative tools to monitor, demonstrate and communicate impacts.

Abra Brynne grew up on a farm in the Okanagan Valley and, as part of a family of 13, learned the value of co-operation, good food, and hard work from an early age. Abra has worked closely with farmers and on food systems for the past twenty-five years, with a priority on place-based food systems and the regulatory regimes that impede or support them. Most recently she has been incorporating Indigenous food sovereignty and sustainable fisheries into her work. She is a founding member and special advisor to the Canadian Biotech Action Network, and a founding member of both Food Secure Canada and the BC Food Systems Network. She is currently the Director of Engagement and Policy at the BC Food Systems Network.

Angie Carter has a PhD in sociology and sustainable agriculture from Iowa State University and teaches at Augustana College. Her research interests include power and social change within agricultural systems, social justice, and gender. She is also a board member of her local food co-operative and the Women, Food and Agriculture Network.

Phil D'Adamo-Damery is a postdoctoral research associate in the Department of Agricultural, Leadership and Community Education at Virginia Tech. His work is focused on exploring the politics of community education and strengthening possibilities for social justice and food systems change.

Sarah Goldstein is a trained chef, volunteer youth food educator and recent graduate of York University's Master of Environmental Studies program. Her research centered on reclaiming the food system through sustainability and education, with a focus on how to build a sustainable food system, alternative food movements in sustainability and culture, and strategies for food education and food literacy education. During the course of her master's program, she worked with Evergreen Brickworks and their Green City Adventure Camp, where she developed and implemented food programming for elementary-aged children.

Kristiina Janhonen is a doctoral student working in the Department of Teacher Education at the University of Helsinki. She received her Master's degree in Education in 2009 from the University of Helsinki. Her PhD dissertation examines adolescents' food education through quantitative and qualitative methods.

Lauren Kepkiewicz is a PhD candidate in the Department of Geography and Planning at the University of Toronto. Through her research, she aims to understand the ways that food connects people to land in the context of the Canadian settler colonial state. Lauren is also employed as a research assistant for the Community First: Impacts of Community Engagement (CFICE): Community Food Security Hub and has worked for organizations such as Irvine Creek Organic Farm, Katimavik, and Africa Youth for Peace and Development.

Cathleen Kneen was a veteran of the peace, social justice, women's, and food security movements. Since 1980, she and her husband Brewster Kneen co-published *The Ram's Horn*, a monthly newsletter of analysis of the food system. She chaired Just Food Ottawa for eight years and was the Chair of the newly formed Ottawa Food Policy Council, while continuing to represent Food Secure Canada in several capacities, including the Technical Committee for the Canada Organic Standard and the North American committee of the Civil Society Mechanism for the FAO Food Security commission.

Pamela Koch is the executive director of the Laura M. Tisch Center for Food, Education and Policy at Columbia University. She has a doctorate in Nutrition Education and is also a registered dietician. She conducts research and creates resources that are at the intersection of food systems, nutrition education, and public policy.

Charles Levkoe is the Canada Research Chair in Sustainable Food Systems and an Assistant Professor at Lakehead University. He is the principal investigator of a research project focusing on the role of non-wage labour on small-scale ecologically oriented farms and also the academic co-lead on CFICE: Community Food Security Hub, a major cross-Canada initiative exploring community campus engagement. His broader research focuses on the role of grassroots organizations in relation to sustainable food systems, their connection to place, and their ability to mobilize across sectors, scales, and places.

Susan Machum has a PhD from the University of Edinburgh and holds a Canada Research Chair in Rural Social Justice at St. Thomas University in Fredericton, New Brunswick. Her research explores the relationship between rural and urban communities, food systems and women's contributions to agriculture. She uses a participatory action research model to engage rural communities and activists in theoretically informed social change agendas.

Johanna Mäkelä is Professor of Food Culture in the Department of Teacher Education at the University of Helsinki. She has previously worked as the head of food research at the National Consumer Research Centre. Her field of expertise lies in sociology and food and consumer studies.

Mary McKenna is a registered dietician and a professor in the Faculty of Kinesiology at the University of New Brunswick. She has written extensively in the areas of school nutrition, and is a member of Food Secure Canada, Farm to Cafeteria Canada, the Canadian Child and Youth Nutrition Program Network, Dietitians of Canada and the New Brunswick Minister's Roundtable for Agriculture.

Christopher Murakami is a PhD candidate in the Department of Learning, Teaching and Curriculum at the University of Missouri, where he works as a graduate research assistant and the manager of the MU Children's Learning Garden. He has a teaching credential in secondary science education and has written both popular and scholarly articles on science education.

Kim L. Niewolny is an assistant professor in the Department of Agricultural, Leadership and Community Education at Virginia Tech. Her areas of scholarship interest include participatory forms of adult, extension and community-based education, community and rural development, and action research and community-based participatory research.

Päivi Palojoki is Professor of Home Economics Pedagogy in the Department of Teacher Education at the University of Helsinki. She has a background in education and food science, and her expertise lies in research on the relationship of food choice and nutrition knowledge and the development of home economics pedagogy on different levels of schooling. She is the leader of the Food, Culture and Learning research group at the University of Helsinki.

Claudia M. Prado-Meza has been a professor at the Faculty of Economics, Universidad de Colima, since she graduated with a PhD in Sustainable Agriculture and a certificate in Social Justice in Higher Education from Iowa State University in 2013. Her interests are local food systems, transnationalism, social justice and gender. She is also the president of the non-governmental organization PROCEDER AC that looks for ways to creatively teach about human rights to high school students from Colima, Mexico.

Wayne Roberts is a leading policy analyst and practitioner in the areas of food, public health and urban planning. He managed the world-renowned Toronto Food Policy Council for many years, and has served on the boards of the Community Food Security Coalition, Food Secure Canada, FoodShare and the Unitarian Service Committee of Canada. He is the author of *The No-Nonsense Guide to World Food* and a recipient of the Queen's Jubilee Medal in recognition of his contribution to community service.

Tammara Soma is a PhD candidate in the Department of Geography and Planning at the University of Toronto. Her research interests include food security, food systems planning, sustainable agriculture and food waste. Her thesis focuses on household food consumption and waste in urban Indonesia.

Jessica Soulis is a food systems and sustainable agriculture consultant who graduated from Iowa State University with an MS in sustainable agriculture and sociology and a certificate in Social Justice in Higher Education. Her research interests include social justice, food access and health, and food sovereignty. She serves on the board of the Iowa Food Systems Council and was a founder and editorial board member of the *Journal of Critical Thought and Praxis*.

Jennifer Sumner teaches in the Adult Education and Community Development Program at the Ontario Institute for Studies in Education at the University of Toronto. Her research interests include food and food systems, co-operatives, globalization, sustainability, rural communities and critical pedagogy. She is the author of *Sustainability and the Civil Commons: Rural Communities in the Age of Globalization* and co-editor of *Critical Perspectives in Food Studies*.

INTRODUCTION

Jennifer Sumner

Learning and food are central to human existence. Learning helps us to survive and evolve as a species, while food provides us with the glue that holds our survival and evolution together. In tandem, they form a dynamic combination that has fueled change for millennia.

In spite of their centrality to human existence, learning and food have seldom been addressed at the same time. Those who study learning have not often turned their gaze toward food, while those who study food have generally overlooked the learning associated with it. And yet, food is not only an object *of* learning but also a vehicle *for* learning (Flowers and Swan 2012). In essence, food is inherently pedagogical, and eating is a pedagogical act (Sumner 2008a) as is producing, processing, distributing, purchasing, and disposing of food. What we learn, and do not learn, by engaging in these human endeavors has deep and enduring implications for the sustainability of our food systems and our world.

This book explores the complex intersection of learning and food in the home and community, in the classroom, in social movements, and into the future, all within the context of contributing to more sustainable food systems.

LEARNING

Learning is the process of gaining new knowledge, of synthesizing acquired knowledge, and of rejecting knowledge that is no longer fit for purpose. It is much broader than education and refers to any elements that combine to produce a change in mental constructs or behaviors (Spencer and Lange 2014). As such, learning is also a lifelong process, from babies learning to use eating utensils and adolescents learning to cook for themselves, to adults learning to feed a family, and seniors learning to link nutrition and healthy aging.

While learning is lifelong, not all learning is positive. Spencer and Lange (2014) raise this issue when they discuss people learning how to use cocaine or how to con pensioners out of their savings. In the same vein, people can also learn to see frozen microwaveable dinners as the food of the future, to consider fast food as comfort food, or to equate the consumption of junk food with freedom. All of these examples highlight the fact that "learning defies easy definition and simple theorizing" (Merriam and Caffarella 1999, 248).

Learning is generally divided into three main categories: formal, non-formal, and informal learning (Hrimech 2005), all of which have close associations with food. Formal learning takes place in classrooms at all levels—from nursery school to graduate school. While often didactic, it can also be collaborative, with teachers and students learning together and from each other. Primary students learning about basic nutrition, secondary students learning about food and water issues, culinary students learning how to incorporate local food into their menus, and university students studying the political economy of food are all examples of formal learning.

Non-formal learning occurs in planned situations outside the classroom such as retreats, seminars, and workshops. This kind of learning is actively chosen by participants who are seeking expertise in a desired area, such as composting, pickling, or permaculture. One form of collective non-formal learning that evolved from the Danish folk schools is kitchen-table meetings. For example, the Ecological Farmers of Ontario hold kitchen-table meetings at designated farms during the winter months as a forum to teach each other about specific aspects of organic farming (Sumner 2008b).

Informal learning takes place through everyday encounters and self-teaching. Though the most common form of learning, it is also the least recognized. In spite of this lack of recognition, people learn all the time as they go about their daily lives—working, shopping, playing, traveling, watching television, surfing the internet, meeting friends, and dining with family. Reading the ingredients on a food label, talking to your neighbor about allotment gardens or setting aside a day to teach yourself how to make bread are all examples of informal learning.

Crosscutting these traditional divisions are particular types of learning, such as experiential learning, embodied learning, and transformative learning. Experiential learning links life experiences and learning, keeping in mind that "experience can be very problematic" and people may have to unlearn experiences of racism or abuse (Spencer and Lange 2014, 9). Boud (2005) maintains that experiential learning is commonly used in two different senses: it describes the prior learning that is brought to a new experience, and it refers to learning processes in which the learner's experience provides the prime source and stimulus for learning. School gardens, cooking classes, and worm composting all offer opportunities for experiential learning.

Embodied learning reminds us that we not only learn with the mind but also the body. "Embodied learning is a way of recognizing that we know with our bodies as well as our minds, to reclaim our wholeness as learners" (Clark 2005, 210). The story of French author Marcel Proust biting into a madeleine and feeling an explosion of memories is a prime example of embodied learning.

Transformative learning occurs in the face of a disorienting dilemma and results in a fundamental shift in worldviews. Unlike other forms of learning, it involves a "deep, structural shift in basic premises of thought, feelings and actions" (TLC 2015). Watching a film like *Food Inc.*, eating food you have grown yourself or going to a slaughterhouse can result in transformative learning.

In essence, learning occurs every day, in many ways, and one of the greatest catalysts for all sorts of learning is food.

FOOD

Food has always been associated with learning, from our earliest ancestors learning how to grow food instead of hunting and gathering it, to modern shoppers learning how to navigate competing messages in the supermarket: Local or global? Conventional or organic? Fair trade or free trade? The answers to these questions, and many more, highlight the overwhelming complexity of food. In the words of Welsh and MacRae (1998, 242):

> Food is a nexus for industry, rural/urban relations, global trade relations, domestic and social life, biological health, social belonging, celebration of community, paid and unpaid work, expressions of care, abuse of power, hunger strikes, fasts and prayer. Food is part of daily life at least as much as we are consumers and possibly more as we labour for either love or money.

Clearly, food is much more than simply fuel for the body—it carries deep social, cultural, economic, and environmental implications that people experience every day. And because food has long been associated with wealth and power (Friedmann 1993), it also intersects with questions of gender, race, class, ethnicity, and imperialism. For all these reasons, food engenders learning, whether we learn to adapt to eating nutritionally compromised industrial food (see Winson 2013) or whether we learn to demand food that is healthy, green, fair, accessible, and affordable.

The growing interest in food has created a whole new vocabulary to learn, such as food miles, food deserts, food systems, food justice, and food pedagogies. Food miles represent the distance that food has traveled from field to fork. The concept emphasizes the relationship between the calories available in the food and the energy expended to transport it to the place where it will be consumed, as well as the oil and carbon emissions associated with this transportation. In a global economy, food travels enormous distances. For example, Xuereb (2005) estimates that food items sold in southern Ontario, Canada, have traveled, on average, about 4500 kilometers from the place they were grown or raised. Learning to eat "closer to home" helps to reduce food miles and supports the local economy.

The evocative concept of food deserts was developed by food policy researchers in the UK to characterize human settlements lacking access to a variety of healthy and affordable foodstuffs (Winson 2004). Highlighting the fact that access to food is not only limited by income but also by such factors as geography and distribution, food deserts are areas with insufficient numbers of stores and other food-related facilities that provide access to fresh and healthy foods (Koç et al. 2012). They are often found in low-income and/or minority urban communities but can also be found in rural communities, schools, universities, bus stations, airports, and along major highways. Communities in food deserts can learn to create food oases by opening a food co-op, participating in a food-box program or lobbying policy makers to address food desert issues.

Food systems are interdependent webs of activities that include the production, processing, distribution, retailing, consumption, and disposal of food (Sumner 2012). Like all systems, food systems are interconnected in such a way that they produce their own pattern of behavior over time (Meadows 2008). This behavior affects both humans and the environment in positive or negative ways, depending on how the system is organized and who benefits from this organization. For example, the current global food system is organized to benefit large multinational food corporations, not the one billion people who go hungry every day. A sustainable food system would be organized to benefit the majority of people in the world by ensuring everyone was fed within the ecological limits of the planet (Sumner 2012).

Food justice is associated with a growing social movement of food activists who emphasize production that is not only environmentally sustainable but also socially just, taking into account workers in all sectors of the food system (Koç et al. 2012). These activists bring an anti-oppression analysis to the question of food system transformation, linking anti-racism, feminism, and Indigenous rights movements to the food movement. Learning to participate in boycotts and buycotts—that is, deliberately choosing not to purchase or actively choosing to purchase a product—is one of many ways to work toward food justice.

The concept of food pedagogies brings the realms of food and learning together in a novel combination that evokes engagement and transformation. Food pedagogies have been described as:

> Congeries of education, teaching and learning about how to grow, shop for, prepare, cook, display, taste, eat and dispose of food by a range of agencies, actors and media; and aimed at a spectrum of "learners" including middle class women, migrants, children, parents, shoppers, and racially minoritised and working class mothers. (Flowers and Swan 2012, 425)

For these authors, food pedagogies encompass either intended or emergent change—whether in behavior, habit, emotion, cognition, and/or knowledge—at a range of levels, from the individual, through the family to the group and collective level. Following the tenets of critical pedagogy (e.g., Finger 2005), critical food pedagogies entail a range of approaches that are not just concerned with any type of change but with change that addresses power and injustice (Sumner 2015). Brazil's new dietary guidelines are an inspiring example of critical food pedagogy because they encourage people to avoid fast-food restaurants and processed food and warn about the propaganda inherent in food advertising.

All in all, as Roberts (2013) contends, food is a hot topic—for two reasons. First, many people have come to realize that food cannot be taken for granted any longer. And second, many people have also become excited about food projects that "help them find their voice and satisfy their desires for a meaningful, engaged, empowered and authentic life" (11). Such a life will only be fully realized within a framework of sustainability.

SUSTAINABILITY

Sustainability is a word that is commonly used but seldom understood. It came to prominence with the publication in 1987 of the Brundtland Report—*Our Common Future*—which promoted the concept of sustainable development. A vague and contested term sustainability has been associated with a bewildering range of ideas, from the Dow Jones Sustainability Index to Deep Ecology (Sumner 2007). But its appropriation by self-serving interests should not disqualify it from use. Originally associated with environmental problems, it has expanded to cover social and economic issues as well, making it ripe with learning opportunities and ideal for analyzing food.

In its most undeveloped form, sustainability entails the ability to meet present needs without compromising the ability of future generations to meet their own needs (Koç et al. 2012). While this adaptation from the Brundtland Report has gained familiarity, it does not define the term "needs" and is premised on ever-expanding economic growth, which global warming is currently teaching us to question. A recent definition involves a more focused approach, linking it with the concept of the civil commons—co-operative human constructions that protect and/or enable universal access to life goods such as water, shelter, education, health-care, and, of course, food (Sumner 2007). Linking sustainability to the provision of life goods addresses the problem of needs and does not depend on economic growth—it could thrive in a steady-state economy. In short, building the civil commons by providing more life goods makes us more sustainable; enclosing the civil commons by providing fewer life goods makes us less sustainable. Nowhere is this clearer than in the realm of food. And given that sustainability doesn't come naturally—but has to be learned (Sumner 2007)—linking learning, food, and sustainability brings together three vital aspects of our future as a species.

PUTTING IT ALL TOGETHER: LEARNING, FOOD, AND SUSTAINABILITY

Interest in food has burgeoned over the last 20 years for a number of reasons, beginning with the consolidation of the global corporate food system. This consolidation has resulted in growing corporate control over what we eat, the pervasive commodification of food, and the spread of the so-called Western diet—highly processed foods laden with salt, sugar, and fat. Under this system,

> Food is no longer viewed first and foremost as a sustainer of life. Rather, to those who seek to command our food supply, it has become instead a major source of corporate cash flow, economic leverage, a form of currency, a tool of international politics, an instrument of power – a weapon! (Krebs 1992 in Millstone and Lang 2003, 11)

In reaction to the increasing corporate control of this vital life good, a number of social movements have coalesced around the subject of food. For example, the local food movement questions the distance that food now travels and champions food close to home. The food justice movement condemns the injustices associated with the global corporate food system. And the food sovereignty movement demands that peoples and nations should be able to choose their own foodways, instead of being forced (through supra-national mechanisms such as trade agreements) into the global corporate food system.

Hot on the heels of these food movements have come popular books and articles dedicated to food, led by authors like Michael Pollan, Marion Nestle, Eric Schlosser, and Raj Patel. These publications have been followed by scholarly interest in this rising phenomenon. A number of academic disciplines have already recognized the importance of food—including sociology, geography, planning, and history—spawning a host of textbooks, conferences, special journal issues, and courses on the subject.

In short, food is one of the fastest growing areas of study in many fields, but education is just beginning to grapple with what Belasco (2007, 5) described as this "edible dynamic" (e.g., Sumner 2008a, 2013a, b; Flowers and Swan 2012; Swan and Flowers 2015; Walter 2013). Such engagement is crucial, given the mounting evidence that our global corporate food system has become massively unsustainable. Goodman et al. (2014, 4) describe the glaring and multifaceted contradictions of this system and "the exploitative trading relations embedded in the global supply chains that support its growth and (expanded) reproduction." They go on to describe the food insecurity and malnutrition of over one billion people, the interrelated ecological and livelihood crises, the growing global resource constraints on our intensive, fossil-fuel-dependent agriculture, and the disease crises associated with Western lifestyles and diets focused on animal fats and highly processed industrial food, more accurately referred to as "edible food-like substances" by Michael Pollan (2008, 1). Faced with a suite of environmental, social, cultural, and economic problems associated with the global corporate food system, it is time to ask: What is the role of education? Does it merely promote adaptation to this unsustainable system or can it encourage the kind of learning experiences that will contribute to much-needed change?

This edited volume will be the first to address these questions by exploring the intersection of learning and food at the interface with sustainability. Taking a broad pedagogical approach to the question of food, it will focus on learning, resistance, and change in a number of key sites—homes, communities, schools, and social movements—while also looking to the future. The ultimate aim of the book involves *learning our way out* of our current unsustainable food system and *learning our way in* to more sustainable alternatives.

All the chapters in this book link learning, food, and sustainability in creative and instructive ways. Within the home and community, Chapter 1 focuses on one of the most intimate links between food and learning—breastfeeding. Susan Machum explains how breastfeeding involves a steep learning curve for mothers and newborns, including the move from abstract knowledge to praxis. After briefly reviewing breastfeeding practices over the last century, she explores the options available to families, particularly within the larger context of the tensions between initiatives that support breastfeeding and the concurrent backlash against it. She concludes that providing mothers with emotional and financial security are some of the parameters of a sustainable food system.

Learning to prevent food waste at home is the topic of Chapter 2. With the global issue of food waste as a backdrop, Tammara Soma looks at women's unpaid foodwork in Indonesia and how children are taught to eat all their food through folktales and the Islamic concept of "mubazir," meaning acts of wasting and being excessive, which are considered sinful. These pedagogical tools help to reduce or prevent food waste and contribute to a more sustainable food system.

Chapter 3 visits community health-care settings with Donna Appavoo, where the educational tools used by professionals ignore the interdependence of food systems and health systems, and focus narrowly on biological markers and daily energy requirements. An emerging narrative is challenging this focus on the nutrient constituency of foods by prioritizing community food security—described by Hamm and Bellows (2003, 37) as a "a situation in which all community residents obtain a safe, culturally acceptable, nutritionally adequate diet through a sustainable food system that maximizes community self-reliance and social justice." By broadening the focus to include "local sustainable food" and "sense of community," this alternative narrative uncovers and supports the many facets of the interconnections between food systems and health systems, and facilitates addressing complex inter-systemic issues such as diabetes.

Schools provide another site where learning, food, and sustainability connect and inspire. In Chapter 4, Pamela Koch looks at the school curriculum, arguing that food-based education needs to both consider larger food system issues and fit into the practices of the current education system. Ultimately, food-based education would encourage students to know which foods are healthy, ecologically sustainable, and socially just. In this way, students would be equipped with the critical knowledge and analytical skills to make challenging decisions about food in the future.

Learning gardens are the topic of Chapter 5, in particular the process of developing a children's learning garden at a Land Grant University in the USA. While seemingly a reasonable and straightforward idea, implementing it became a learning project in itself as Christopher Murakami and fellow university students in the preschool and teacher training program had to negotiate the politics, policies, and culture of a large institution. The result was a compromise that straitened their original goals but nevertheless created a bridgehead that helps children develop a healthy relationship with the food, nature, and community.

Chapter 6 continues the focus on schools with an investigation into the development of food education in the Finnish comprehensive school setting. Finland has a long history of engagement with healthy food. For example, the provision of tax-paid, nutritious, hot school meals has been part of health promotion in Finnish schools for over 60 years. Kristiina Janhonen, Johanna Mäkelä, and Päivi Palojoki make a case for taking students' agency and participation as premises for educating about food and eating. As well as promoting personal well-being and health, food education is seen as a medium for understanding the complexities of the world and for supporting sustainable lifestyles embedded in everyday practices.

The next section hones in on social movements as sites of resistance and change. Chapter 7 examines alternative food movements and the role of narratives in community food work. Beginning with the idea of education as cultural work, Kim L. Niewolny and Phil D'Adamo-Damery illustrate the educative role that narratives can play in engendering political praxis and new possibilities. In particular, they look at the Appalachian Foodshed Project to show how narratives and storytelling can open up ways to humanize the "wicked problem" of food insecurity while creating new possibilities in the everyday work of resistance and learning.

Chapter 8 proposes campus-community engagement as a means to strengthen the food sovereignty movement. La Via Campesina, a world-wide peasant organization that is the largest social movement in the world (Friedmann 2012), coined the term food sovereignty, which entails the right of peoples and governments to determine their own agriculture systems, food markets, environments, and modes of production. Using community-service learning, Peter Andrée, Lauren Kepkiewicz, Charles Levkoe, Abra Brynne, and Cathleen Kneen consider how movements for food sovereignty and community–campus engagement can work together to provide academics with important training for critically engaging with food systems, to encourage knowledge sharing between social movement actors and academics, and to support social movement organizations working toward more just and sustainable food systems.

Chapter 9 rounds out the social movement section by considering the food justice movement through a certificate course offered by the Coady Institute at St. Francis Xavier University in Antigonish, Nova Scotia. Deborah Barndt reflects critically on the challenges associated with two shifts: one from dominant notions of food security to a consciousness based on food justice and food sovereignty and the other from dominant educational models to popular education methods that valorize Indigenous knowledges and holistic ways of knowing.

The final section of the book looks toward the future. Chapter 10 investigates food literacy, in particular among young people. Although food education programs have grown in popularity in recent years, their outcomes are unclear. Are they contributing to a food-literate population and, if so, what kind of food literacy is being achieved and what are the prospects for food system change? Sarah Goldstein studied food education at The Stop Community Food Centre in Toronto and discovered that by focusing on individual behavior modification, the program primarily facilitates the dominant food literacy paradigm based on neoliberal consciousness. For this reason, it does not necessarily lead to wider food system change, thus raising the question of what is the best form of food education for the future if we want a more critical and engaged food literacy and a more sustainable food system.

School food and nutrition policies as tools for learning and change are the subject of Chapter 11. Mary McKenna and Sharon Bodovsky propose that teaching about such policies in schools moves them from the hidden curriculum—part of the unspoken academic, social, and cultural messages communicated to students—and makes them explicit. This move changes students from being passive recipients of policy to active participants in all aspects of the process. As a result, students gain greater understanding of school food environments, become engaged in a personally relevant topic, and enhance their development as future citizens.

Chapter 12 of the book involves learning to transgress—that is, learning to ask how we can learn our way out of our current unsustainable food system and learn our way into more sustainable alternatives. Angie Carter, Claudia M. Prado-Meza, and Jessica Soulis were students in a sustainable agriculture program at a public, land-grant university in the USA. They used their experiences as both students and agents of social change to better understand the unlearning and relearning process and the creation of community as a transformative space. They also inquired how their experiences can inspire others as they collectively unlearned their way into more sustainable food systems.

The Afterword by Wayne Roberts sums up the importance of learning and food. After highlighting the invisibility of food in educational systems and society at large, he vividly describes a number of potential and actual transformative exceptions where food is not only visible but also front and center. Using illustrations from his own broad food experience, he outlines how schools and communities provide permeable sites where people can learn resistance and change and realize that a more sustainable food system is possible.

Together, these chapters offer an opening to a world made more sustainable by the conscious recognition of the connections between learning and food. In their study of alternative food networks, Goodman et al. (2014) observed that food is a realm of knowledge. "Growing and eating are both practices imbued with ways of knowing the world, and with knowing the ways to construct the kind of world we want to inhabit" (44). The kind of world most people want to inhabit is more sustainable than our current one. The chapters in this book show how learning about food and broader food issues can make us more sustainable and inspire us to begin constructing that world.

References

Belasco, W. (2007). *Appetite for change: How the counterculture took on the food industry* (2nd ed.). Ithaca/London: Cornell University Press.

Boud, D. (2005). Experiential learning. In L. M. English (Ed.), *International encyclopedia of adult education* (pp. 243–245). New York: Palgrave Macmillan.

Clark, M. C. (2005). Embodied learning. In L. M. English (Ed.), *International encyclopedia of adult education* (pp. 210–212). New York: Palgrave Macmillan.

Finger, M. (2005). Critical theory. In L. M. English (Ed.), *International encyclopedia of adult education* (pp. 165–168). New York: Palgrave Macmillan.

Flowers, R. & Swan, E. (Eds.). (2012). Special issue on food pedagogies. *Australian Journal of Adult Learning, 52*(3), 532–572.

Friedmann, H. (1993). After Midas's feast: Alternative food regimes for the future. In P. Allen (Ed.), *Food for the future: Conditions and contradictions of sustainability* (pp. 213–233). New York: John Wiley and Sons, Inc.

Friedmann, H. (2012). Changing food systems from top to bottom: Political economy and social movements perspectives. In M. Koç, J. Sumner, & A. Winson (Eds.), *Critical perspectives in food studies* (pp. 16–32). Toronto: Oxford University Press.

Goodman, D., Dupuis, E. M., & Goodman, M. K. (2014). *Alternative food networks: Knowledge, practice and politics.* New York: Routledge.

Hamm, M. W., & Bellows, A. C. (2003). Community food security and nutrition educators. *Journal of Nutrition Education and Behavior, 35*(1), 37–43.

Hrimech, M. (2005). Informal learning. In L. M. English (Ed.), *International encyclopedia of adult education* (pp. 310–312). New York: Palgrave Macmillan.

Koç, M., Sumner, J., & Winson, A. (Eds.). (2012). *Critical perspectives in food studies.* Toronto: Oxford University Press.

Meadows, D. H. (2008). *Thinking in systems: A primer.* White River Junction: Chelsea Green Publishing.

Merriam, S. B., & Caffarella, R. S. (1999). *Learning in adulthood* (2nd ed.). San Francisco: Jossey-Bass.

Millstone, E., & Lang, T. (2003). *The Penguin atlas of food.* New York: Penguin Books.

Pollan, M. (2008). *In defense of food: A eater's manifesto.* New York: The Penguin Press.

Roberts, W. (2013). *The no-nonsense guide to world food.* Oxford: New Internationalist Publications Inc.

Spencer, B., & Lange, E. (2014). *The purposes of adult education: An introduction.* Toronto: Thompson Educational Publishing.

Sumner, J. (2007). *Sustainability and the civil commons: Rural communities in the age of globalization.* Toronto: University of Toronto Press.

Sumner, J. (2008a). Eating as a pedagogical act: Food as a catalyst for adult education for sustainability. *Kursiv: Journal fuer politische Bildung, 4*, 32–37.

Sumner, J. (2008b). Protecting and promoting Indigenous knowledge: Environmental adult education and organic agriculture. *Studies in the Education of Adults, 40*(2), 207–223.

Sumner, J. (2012). Conceptualizing sustainable food systems. In M. Koç, J. Sumner, & A. Winson (Eds.), *Critical perspectives in food studies* (pp. 326–336). Toronto: Oxford University Press.

Sumner, J. (2013a). Food literacy and adult education: Learning to read the world by eating. *Canadian Journal for the Study of Adult Education, 25*(2), 79–92.

Sumner, J. (2013b). Eating as if it really mattered: Teaching *The Pedagogy of Food* in the age of globalization. *Brock Education Journal, 22*(2), 41–55.

Sumner, J. (2015). Waging the struggle for healthy eating: Food environments, dietary regimes and Brazil's dietary guidelines. *Local Environment.* DOI: 10.1080/13549839.2015.1087480

Swan, E., & Flowers, R. (Eds.). (2015). *Food pedagogies.* London: Ashgate.

TLC. (2015). *About the transformative learning centre, transformative learning centre.* Retrieved September 20, 2015, from http://tlc.oise.utoronto.ca/About.html

Walter, P. (2013). Theorising community gardens as pedagogical sites in the food movement. *Environmental Education Research, 19*(4), 521–539.

Welsh, J., & MacRae, R. (1998). Food citizenship and community food security: Lessons from Toronto, Canada. *Canadian Journal of Development Studies, XIX*, 237–255.

Winson, A. (2004). Bringing political economy into the debate on the obesity epidemic. *Agriculture and Human Values, 21*, 299–312.

Winson, A. (2013). *The industrial diet: The degradation of food and the struggle for healthy eating.* Vancouver: UBC Press.

Xuereb, M. (2005). *Food miles: Environmental implications of food imports to Waterloo region.* Region of Waterloo Public Health. Retrieved November 28, 2015, from http://chd.region.waterloo.on.ca/en/researchResourcesPublications/resources/FoodMiles_Report.pdf

PART I

Learning, Food, and Sustainability in the Home and Community

CHAPTER 1

Learning and Food at the Mother's Breast

Susan Machum

Introduction

Shortly after learning I was pregnant in early 2000, I headed to the bookstore and promptly purchased *What to Expect When You are Expecting* by Murkoff, Eisenberg and Mazel (1998). This book is one among many adorning local bookshops offering advice to the soon-to-be mother. Now in its fourth edition, I owned the expanded and revised second edition published in 1998. What this book and others like it do is guide the first-time mother through the month-by-month changes their body is experiencing as their baby grows inside them. While its intention is to reassure, inform and advise the first-time mother on how to handle various situations, the book's detailed attention to what can go wrong in pregnancy was sometimes unnerving. Nevertheless, this book was constantly referenced and read throughout my entire pregnancy as I engaged in what sociologists call an **anticipatory socialization** process. Even though I was not yet a mother, I was anticipating motherhood by learning what my new role involved and preparing for life with my newborn child. In effect, as a pregnant woman, I was already preoccupied with the responsibilities of caring for a child, and this book helped me navigate both the prenatal and postnatal phases of my pregnancy.

S. Machum (✉)
Department of Sociology, St. Thomas University, Frederiction, NB, Canada

J. Sumner (ed.), *Learning, Food, and Sustainability,*
DOI 10.1057/978-1-137-53904-5_1

The truth is this book was just one among many. Before my first child was even born, I read well over a dozen books on pregnancy, breastfeeding, motherhood and parenting—and since then dozens more parenting books have been added to my bookshelves—while pretty well all of my books on the early years of childrearing have been re-gifted to first-time mothers and fathers. In fact, many of my first childcare books made their way onto my bookshelf via friends and colleagues whose children had outgrown their advice. What I have come to realize about parenting is that the learning curve is steep, and what you need to know and do is ever changing. Quite simply, the advice on how to parent, teach and guide your child is highly dependent on your child's stage within the life course.

During the prenatal phase of a baby's life, the primary agenda is to carry a healthy baby to full-term. To this end, most expectant mothers are learning to transform their lifestyles, diets and exercise habits to meet the needs of the growing baby. In effect, mothers' bodies are being 'given' over to and being 'taken' over by the unborn child. And if you opt to breastfeed—which I did—this process can last much longer than three trimesters. As Bendefy (2012, p. 25) argues 'breast-feeding is … the "fourth trimester" in terms of [a] baby's brain growth and development'.

Even if the production of breast milk is a biologically, evolutionary and ecologically sound infant feeding strategy that 'naturally' follows childbirth, for many mothers and newborns, breastfeeding involves a steep learning curve. It is a skilled activity that requires a significant amount of patience, trial and error and effort on the part of mother and child. Not all mothers and newborns take to breastfeeding easily. And while mothering books may teach pregnant women and new mothers the benefits and mechanics of breastfeeding, until you actually start breastfeeding your knowledge remains purely theoretical. It is when you start nursing your newborn that you begin to apply your abstract knowledge—some nursing mothers may experience instantaneous success, while others may experience a series of challenges, and still others may, for a number of reasons, never succeed at breastfeeding or never attempt to breastfeed. This relationship between theory and practice is referred to as **praxis**.

Praxis captures what we do, and how our everyday activities create and re-create the social world, cultural patterns and social expectations. Social policies, including health policies, are closely related to praxis in that a policy lays out a governmental plan of action (Lightman 2003). But policymakers cannot ascertain in advance to what extent a policy agenda will succeed. Likewise, during pregnancy, mothers may plan to initiate breastfeeding, but whether or not they do, and the duration they nurse, can only be measured after the child is born and infant feeding is proceeding.

This chapter explores infant feeding, in particular the first months of life before solid foods are introduced. It does so through a sociological lens and the use of **autoethnography**. Sociologists study the relationships between an individual's life experiences and the larger social world in which our biographies unfold. Autoethnography reflects on the relationship between one's individual life and the larger social context in which it is lived. This agenda fits well with sociology, which aims to recognize that **personal troubles** and decision-making processes are embedded in larger social contexts or what C. Wright Mills (1959, 2000) called **public issues**. This is certainly the case when it comes to breastfeeding. As this chapter will illustrate, a mother's decision on how to feed her infant child is not simply a private matter; throughout the last decades, breastfeeding has become a public health issue that pits human milk against formula, breast against bottle and 'nature' against science.

The chapter begins with a brief overview of breastfeeding practices over the past century. Then it considers the range of options available to families to meet the nutritional needs of their newborn. The third section reflects on the larger socio-economic, political and cultural context within which infant feeding decisions are made—specifically it considers policy initiatives that support breastfeeding and the concurrent backlash against breastfeeding. The chapter concludes with a discussion of the role human milk plays in supporting and building a local, sustainable, food system.

Breastfeeding Practices During the Last Century

At the beginning of the twentieth century, breastfeeding was the norm with more than two-thirds of mothers' exclusively breastfeeding their infants (Wright and Schanler 2001, p. 421S). But between 1930 and 1960, breastfeeding in North America declined dramatically from one decade to the next (Fomon 2001, p. 409S), and breast milk was steadily replaced with cow's milk and infant formulas. Interestingly, this replacement of 'natural' milk with 'artificial' milk occurred during first the Depression years, then the war years, and finally as women increasingly entered the paid labor force. Even so, as Fomon (2001) documents, commercially prepared formulas were available at the end of the nineteenth century, but the uptake was not there at that point in history.

Formula or 'artificial' feeding options fell into two categories—there were home-made formulas and commercially prepared ones. In fact, between 1880 and 1930, many corporations were making and perfecting infant formulas as alternatives to breastfeeding. They sought to create a product that was nutritionally equivalent to breast milk, but they found that formula-fed babies sometimes had poorer health and lacked nutrients when compared to breastfed babies (Fomon 2001). However, as science improved and formulas better met the needs of newborns, its adoption for infant feeding began to take off in the 1950s. At the same time, Fomon (2001, p. 412S) observes:

> considerations of convenience began to supersede considerations of cost, and the popularity of commercially prepared formulas increased dramatically … [no doubt] accelerated by the introduction in 1959 of iron-fortified formulas and the vigorous promotion of these formulas by the formula industry and by pediatricians.

It was five years later, at the height of formula and bottle-feeding, that I was born. My introduction to food was corn-syrup-laced Carnation milk, and I am convinced it is responsible for the incredible sweet tooth I harbor to this day. But as my mother says, 'I was just doing what the nurses and doctors told me to do. Everybody I knew was bottle-feeding'. According to a source in Olver's (2004) food timeline, in 1964, 'one baby in five, usually those past three or four months of age, [was getting] whole cow's milk. [While] only one in 10 [were] breastfed [even though breastfeeding was described as] still the safest, most convenient and least expensive method of nourishing an infant'.

Breastfeeding did not, however, match the ideological framework of the day, which supported the strong belief in scientific intervention and 'better living through chemistry'. It is perhaps no coincidence that this is the same historical moment that the green revolution is gaining ground and dramatically transforming food production from small-scale family-oriented farms to commercially oriented, industrial farms (Roberts 2008). Nevertheless, by the 1970s, a pendulum shift occurs and breastfeeding once again starts to gain momentum. Fomon (2001, p. 415S) reports it is hard to identify the exact impetus for this swing back toward breastfeeding but notes it is a grassroots movement rather than one led by 'health professionals, and may have been in part associated with negative publicity directed against the formula industry'. It was during this period that North Americans and Europeans were learning of the negative impact aggressive marketing of infant formula in developing countries was having on infant mortality rates there (Fomon 2001; Brady 2012). It was also a period of Keynesian economics and the rise of the welfare state so policies were coming into play that supported breastfeeding. For example, it was in 1971 that Canadian women who had banked at least 20 weeks of insurable earnings could apply for 15 weeks of maternity leave benefits (Marshall 2003). At the same time, the World Health Organization (WHO) did, and continues to, recommend exclusive breastfeeding for at least the first six months of a child's life (Heymann et al. 2013).

The global impact of these processes was more breastfed babies; even so the WHO (2015) would still like to see more babies breastfed for longer periods of time because of the positive outcomes of breastfeeding on infant health. In Canada, there was a steady increase in the number of women initiating and exclusively breastfeeding. Health Canada (2012) reports that in 2003, 37.3 percent of new mothers exclusively breastfed for the first four months, while 17.3 percent were continuing to do so at six months of age (whereas in 2009–10, the figures were 44.2 percent at four months and 25.9 percent at six months). So clearly supplementary feedings are often being introduced after the fourth month despite recommendations to continue exclusive breastfeeding until six months of age. Personally, I remember being pressured by family and friends to introduce solids earlier than six months, and while I did not do this for my first child, I think I did in the case of my second, in part because he seemed more interested in eating solid foods.

INFANT FEEDING AND BREAST MILK PRODUCTION

Feeding a newborn involves two sets of decisions based on prior learning. First, parents must decide what kind of milk the child will consume—will it be human milk or formula, or some combination of both? Second, parents must decide how that milk will be delivered—by breast or by bottle or by both breast and bottle? How these questions are answered presents a range of possibilities for feeding the newborn. At one end of the spectrum sits the newborn who is exclusively breastfed. In this case, the infant drinks human milk directly from mother's breast. On the other end of the spectrum is the newborn who is exclusively bottle-fed with formula.

In the middle, you have babies who are exclusively fed human milk by both breast and bottle. As well there are babies who are fed both human milk and formula from both breast and bottle, and still others who might be fed breast milk or formula exclusively by bottle. In short, a range of options prevails for meeting the nutritional needs of the newborn baby, but the choices made will depend on the parents' knowledge frames, their social situation, and the larger social support network in which their lives are embedded.

There is an extensive self-help literature available for expectant mothers to consult on the dynamics of successful breastfeeding. *The Nursing Mother's Companion* (Huggins 2015), *Breastfeeding Made Simple* (Mohrbacher and Kendall-Tackett 2010), *The Womanly Art of Breastfeeding* (Wiessinger et al. 2010) and *Work. Pump. Repeat.* (Shortall 2015) are just a few titles sitting on the bookstore shelves today, giving advice and information on breastfeeding from birth onwards. During my first pregnancy, I relied on Neifert's (1998) *Dr. Mom's Guide to Breastfeeding* to understand the breastfeeding process and overcome breastfeeding challenges.

Overwhelmingly, these books explain how a mother's body produces milk—that is, the relationship between giving birth, the release of hormones and the various stages of milk production. All emphasize that breastfeeding is a natural and normal part of human evolution. Humans are mammals and mammals have evolved to produce and consume mother's milk in infancy. For example, Wiessinger, West and Pitman (2010, p. 62) write, 'your body and your baby have instincts and abilities not just for birth but for breastfeeding as well'. Mohrbacher and Kendall-Tackett (2010, p. 14) argue, 'babies and mothers are hardwired to breastfeed'. Yet as noted above, many women opt not to breastfeed.

Those mothers that do decide to initiate breastfeeding are advised to do so within the first two hours of giving birth. Ideally, the baby and mother are able to make skin-to-skin contact because this promotes latching. During the first feeding, the newborn baby is greeted with **colostrum**—a 'liquid gold' that is easy to digest because it is low in fat and sugar but high in protein and full of antibodies that are 'capable of attacking harmful bacteria' (Huggins 2010, p. 41). In the first few weeks of birth, babies require frequent feedings; first because their stomachs are small and second because it is the very act of nursing that establishes the milk supply. Put simply, the more milk a baby demands, the more a mother's body produces. What is more, a mother's body quickly becomes completely in-tune with the baby's feeding patterns.

I certainly found this to be remarkably true. Most of the parenting books I read, the health care professionals teaching the prenatal classes, and lactation specialists at the hospital recommended feeding for 10–15 minutes on one breast then switching to the other. But Neifert's (1998) advice was to nurse exclusively on one breast during a feeding and then to switch to the other breast for the next feeding. She argued this pattern would maximize caloric intake by giving baby access to both foremilk and hindmilk at every feeding. As Mohrbacher and Kendall-Tackett (2010, p. 88) explain, during a feeding:

> The first milk a baby gets (sometimes called *foremilk*) is lower in fat (in some cases like the 1 percent cow's milk we might buy from the store). As baby continues to feed, the milk increases in fat (more like 2 percent milk). As the baby continues to drain the breast, the fat content increases until it is as fatty as whole milk, then half-and-half, then cream (sometimes called *hindmilk*).

What amazed me as a nursing mother was how my body produced milk according to this pattern—one breast would be full and ready to feed while the other was empty whenever my child wanted to nurse. I did feed on demand, responding to my child's indications that he was hungry, and I do remember being remarkably tired during the first six weeks of his life. In part I was sleep deprived, and even though he was gaining weight and doing well, I was obsessed with keeping a feeding log as advised by the health care professionals. It was a visit from my sister, who had successfully breastfed her daughter into toddlerhood, that finally really helped me learn to relax and gain confidence as a nursing mother. Her advice: 'You are doing fine. Stop making yourself crazy with this breastfeeding log. Just feed your son when he's hungry'. Until she spoke these words, I did not have the confidence to ignore the books and lactation experts and follow my child's lead. In the end, we were able to exclusively breastfeed until he was six months old and we continued breastfeeding until he reached three and a half years of age.

But not all mothers want, or are able, to follow this pattern of infant feeding. Infant nutrition is, in fact, very much influenced by what McMullin (2009) calls CAGEs—that is, the interconnections between a person's social class, age, gender and ethnicity. Personally in relation to breastfeeding, I am drawn to the idea of maternal CARE rather than CAGEs as class, age, the region of the globe in which women live, and their ethnicity have significant impacts on breastfeeding practices.

Nevertheless, gender remains a dimension of breastfeeding experiences. To start, fathers cannot breastfeed, but they can learn to feed their infant mother's milk from a bottle. Maher (2015, p. 195) concludes gender is an important but often neglected dynamic of breastfeeding because

> husbands and fathers are important in permitting, enjoining, or limiting breastfeeding, in determining the way in which it is done, by whom [for example, by mothers or wet nurses], and the time of weaning.

In my case, my husband supported breastfeeding, but it would seem he was unable to master the art of bottle-feeding (Bendefy 2012, p. 29) given my son refused to consume the milk I pumped and left for him. However, our family was incredibly privileged because even though I was working full-time, we live in a small city and my work offers somewhat flexible hours, so I was able to drive home between classes and meetings, nurse my child and then come back to the campus. Sometimes women are able to bring their young infants to work with them and this facilitates breastfeeding, and still others have generous paid maternity leaves. Those who do not have the capacity to stay at home, come home during the day, or take their child with them to work but want to continue feeding their child human milk can start pumping, storing and transporting their milk from work to home on a daily basis (Shortall 2015). This represents incredible dedication to both breastfeeding and the value of human milk in an infant's diet.

For some mothers, their socio-economic situation and working conditions are much more precarious, and they may not have the opportunity to work and pump, so formula feeding becomes the most practical option. The decisions that we learn to make are embedded in the larger social context we find ourselves in. Our social class position, our age, our geographic location and cultural expectations surrounding appropriate infant feeding strategies all play a role in our infant feeding practices. We need to recognize that maternal health is directly related to breastfeeding success. As Mohrbacher and Kendall-Tackett (2010, p. 220) note, ' stress can inhibit milk release, slowing milk flow'. Likewise, food insecurity and poor nutritional health for mothers can directly impact children's health and nutrition (Food Banks Canada 2015). This is especially true for breastfed babies, given their mothers are the direct producers of the milk they consume.

Breastfeeding is the ultimate form of reproductive labor in the Marxian sense of the term, in that the milk production of nursing mothers falls outside the purview of paid labor while at the same time it is directly contributing to the reproduction of the next generation of workers. Maher's (2015) discussion of the rise of milk banks and milk exchanges may provide exceptions to this case. But in general, lactation remains an unpaid and undervalued form of work. Yet advocates of breastfeeding would argue lactation and infant feeding is a critical dimension of socially necessary labor time and should be recognized as making a significant contribution to infant health. In reality, all infant care falls under the umbrella of reproductive labor.

Breastfeeding can be understood as a form of self-provisioning; but of course, mothers usually need to meet their own nutritional needs through the market. Thus, the breastfeeding mother is embedded in and consuming from a larger global food system—which may or may not be socially sustainable for her depending upon her resources and food choices—but by breastfeeding, she directly acts as a shield and mediator between her child and the global food system. Understanding the social context and the historical moment within which families learn to make infant feeding decisions is critical for understanding their choices.

Breastfeeding: A Public Issue

Over the last few decades, there has been a concerted effort on the part of health care professionals and governments to support breastfeeding initiatives. In fact in many countries, public health policies and changes in work legislation have facilitated breastfeeding, especially among working mothers. This section provides a brief overview of policy initiatives that support breastfeeding; but it also recognizes the growth of a public discourse that is undermining these very same policy efforts.

Policy Initiatives That Support Breastfeeding

The WHO (2015) notes that on a global scale, approximately 36 percent of infants aged 0–6 months are exclusively breastfed, and they report that infants who are breastfed are generally healthier than those who are not. Yet the capacity to breastfeed is greatly influenced by the CARE nursing women experience, especially given that one's region or place of origin dictates the social, economic and health policies that govern their lives. For example, Bendefy (2012, p. 19) reports:

> Provincial Human Rights Codes in Canada protect a woman's right to breastfeed in public, as does the Charter of Rights and Freedoms. Some provinces specifically address the right to breastfeed in the workplace. These laws generally outline ways that employers should accommodate a woman who needs to pump breast milk during business hours—for example, supplying a secluded place near an electrical outlet where a woman can plug in her pump and express milk undisturbed.

Shortall (2015) reviews US legislation and state laws that support expressing breast milk while working. She indicates that only 24 states 'have laws that relate to women in the workplace. They range from amazing … to totally toothless' (Shortall 2015, pp. 60–61). She further notes (p. 62) that

> Many women who are discriminated against or denied the ability to pump at work don't pursue legal recourse, because they need the job and are scared to lose it, can't afford the legal fees, or simply don't have the energy. So they just suffer discrimination at work, move on and find a new job, or stop breastfeeding to make the problem go away.

Obviously, living in a country or region where breastfeeding is encouraged will see higher rates of uptake than ones which do not.

Kam's (2015) story of how Cambodia increased exclusive breastfeeding from 11 percent to almost 74 percent in one decade reveals how effective strong public health policies and education campaigns can be at totally transforming a nation's breastfeeding culture. According to Kam, Cambodia succeeded in changing infant feeding culture through a barrage of media campaigns and interpersonal communications with new mothers. As part of their Baby-Friendly Community Initiative, they established mother support groups and retrained health care professionals to transform cultural traditions surrounding breastfeeding practices.

Since 1991 Canada and its provinces have also been developing, implementing and monitoring Baby-Friendly Initiatives (Breast Feeding Committee for Canada 2012). A key mandate of the national initiative has been to develop policies that promote breastfeeding anywhere, anytime. Specifically, they have sought to implement

evidence-based practices [that] create environments that support and protect breastfeeding and family-centered care which ensures that the family unit learns about healthy eating practices from birth. (Breast Feeding
Committee for Canada 2012, p. 11)

And while such agendas are laudable and critical for long-term breastfeeding success, public opinion is still very much divided over the benefits and
need to breastfeed.

Public Backlash Against Breastfeeding

In August 2015, BBC radio host Alex Dyke was temporarily suspended
from broadcasting for saying on-air that 'breastfeeding is unnatural. It's
the kind of thing that should be done in a quiet, private nursery'. He was
offended that a rather 'large' woman started breastfeeding her infant toddler on a bus—witnessing a toddler being nursed in public embarrassed
him and he argued the nursing mother was guilty of placing him in an
awkward situation. He further added, 'I know it's natural, but it's kind of
unnatural. We don't want it in public. It was OK in the Stone Age, when
we knew no better' (Johnston 2015, p. 17).

Meanwhile, a month earlier, in Wiarton, Ontario (200 kilometers
northwest of Toronto), a nursing mother was asked to leave a restaurant because she began breastfeeding her baby on the patio rather than
in the women's bathroom. How exactly things unfolded in this situation
is unclear. But that women who opt to breastfeed in public are shunned,
called out, or asked to 'cover up' remains a consistent message among
breastfeeding women (see CBC News 2015).

This public backlash and shaming of women who breastfeed in public
is emerging at the same time that a pro-bottle-feeding movement is gaining momentum calling for the cessation of stigma associated with women
who opt for formula feeding. The pro-bottle feeding activists, some feminists and some members of the scientific community have been steadfastly
questioning and outright challenging the positions and benefits of breastfeeding. Situated firmly in this camp, Wolf (2011, p. xiii) posits:

In the absence of compelling medical evidence, how have scientists, doctors,
powerful interest groups, and the general public come to be persuaded that
breastfeeding is one of the most important gifts a mother can give her child?

Thanks to neoliberalism, argues Wolf, science, motherhood and public health authorities have a collective interest in framing breastfeeding as the best method of infant feeding. These three institutions essentially ignore any evidence that challenges the benefits of breastfeeding by 'restrict(ing) the kinds of questions asked, or the potential risks (of breastfeeding) worthy of investigation' (Wolf 2011, p. 67). It is the position that 'breast is best' that Wolf has the greatest aversion to and her position throughout the book is the 'public health message about breastfeeding is out of sync with both the infant-feeding science and the realities of many women's lives' (Wolf 2011, p. 146). Her final conclusion (p. 148) is

> Breastfeeding [advocates reinforce] traditional notions of women, their bodies and their 'natural' orientation toward caregiving; [breastfeeding] keeps women tethered to their babies and creates risks for them in a market that demands total commitment from 'ideal workers'.

Jung's (2015a) recently published book, *Lactivism*, contributes to the public backlash against breastfeeding by arguing that breastfeeding and breast milk are oversold as infant feeding strategies. But her position is rather interesting in that she lays out just how insidious the global food system has become with corporations creating and promoting the use of an extensive range of breastfeeding paraphernalia. In effect, in the world of infant feeding, one group of corporations is pitted against the other. According to Brady (2012, p. 529), corporations selling formula have annual sales exceeding US $31 billion, while Jung (2015b) notes, 'companies that manufacture breast pumps ... and ... breast-feeding accessories ... like clothes, pillows and nutritional supplements' also represent big business. What this means is that regardless of what side of the debate the public is on, there are corporations on each side with vested interests in influencing and promoting particular scientific research programs.

What is striking about the unfolding public debate over bottle and breast, formula and breast milk, artificial and natural infant feeding practices is how both sides are feeling shamed and stigmatized in their efforts to learn how to feed their babies. Public breastfeeding is being framed as a cultural taboo—something insidious, 'unnatural', threatening, awkward and uncomfortable to witness. Breastfeeding is framed as exhibitionism. Lactating mothers who have their nursing children in tow are expected to set up feedings at mother-baby 'feeding stations' usually located in public washrooms. Is that where you want to eat your dinner? On the other hand, women who choose formula and bottle-feeding feel that they are being publicly branded as 'bad mothers' who do not care about the health and well-being of their young children. Paradoxically, bottle-feeding a child in a public space never meets with the same reprisal as breastfeeding—in short, bottle-feeding is a perfectly acceptable, publicly sanctioned activity.

CONCLUSION

Even though health, medical, socio-economic and political reasons may cause women and newborn infants to opt for bottle-feeding, it is utterly nonsensical to argue that breastfeeding is 'unnatural' or that it belongs in the Stone Age. While infant formula and bottle-feeding may offer viable alternatives to breastfeeding, it is illogical to promote formula and bottle-feeding as the best approach for meeting an infant's nutritional needs. While no significant differences in long-term health outcomes *may* be present between bottle and breastfed babies in the developed world, Brady's (2012) and the WHO's (2015) overview of the situation for children in the developing world paints a different story. Rosen-Carole (2015) contends that rather than pit bottle versus breastfeeding mothers against each other, it would be a far more useful public debate to establish what social, economic and political conditions prevent women from around the world doing what is physiologically normal—in short, what are the obstacles to breastfeeding?

This is a very critical question for educators and social scientists interested in building a sustainable global food system because the production and delivery of human milk to newborns and young children represent the very core of human existence. To live, humans need clean air, water and food. Breastfeeding represents the absolutely shortest possible food supply chain. By learning to breastfeed or pump and feed human milk to her infant child, a mother directly acts as a shield and mediator between her child and the larger global food system. As noted earlier, how well fed the baby is depends in part on how well fed the mother is. Using bottles to deliver pumped breast milk does allow a third person to be involved in infant feeding, but the mother needs to remain in close physical contact— or have stored sufficient milk—for a prolonged absence to maintain the feeding pattern. While away, she must pump regularly to sustain her milk supply.

Despite the growth in breastfeeding paraphernalia, at least in theory, breastfeeding represents the least amount of technological implements and tools for feeding infants. Of course, to be truly implement free (i.e., void of breast pumps) nursing mothers need to be enmeshed in social and economic policies that support them staying home with their newborns. When lactating mothers and nursing children are in public, they need to be able to feed and eat without reprisal. Despite public opinion to the contrary, breastfeeding is a *natural process* that is biologically and ecologically sound. Normalizing breastfeeding is an essential step in building a sustainable food system.

The public cloaking of breastfeeding has led to the loss of tacit knowledge and the invisibility of breastfeeding mentors. Breastfeeding is not something that women can practice before birth, but once their child is born, they have multiple opportunities for learning and perfecting the feeding technique. As the WHO (2015) notes:

> While breastfeeding is a natural act, it is also a learned behaviour. An extensive body of research has demonstrated that mothers and other caregivers require active support for establishing and sustaining appropriate breastfeeding practices.

I would argue that my journey with breastfeeding was successful because I was embedded in a strong support network—both at home and in terms of labor policies and maternity leaves which gave me the opportunity to be at home with my newborn and later to navigate home and work as they grew older. Also thanks to my socio-economic position, I had access to a plentiful supply of nutritious foods. This sense of emotional and financial security meant stress and anxiety were minimized; so my milk supply was never in jeopardy. I was able to breastfeed without fear of reprisal, and I never felt that nursing my children was threatening or undermining my sense of self or career goals. I would argue that these lessons—learned while breastfeeding my children—are the parameters that any global food system needs to achieve, if it is to be sustainable.

References

Bendefy, I. (Ed.). (2012). *Baby day by day* (Canadian Edition). London: DK Publishing.

Brady, J. P. (2012). Marketing breast milk substitutes: Problems and perils throughout the world. *Archives of Disease in Childhood, 97*(6), 529–532.

Breast Feeding Committee for Canada. (2012). *The baby-friendly initiative (BFI) in Canada: BFI status report.* http://breastfeedingcanada.ca/documents/BFI_Status_report_2012_FINAL.pdf. Accessed 25 Aug 2015.

CBC News. (2015). *Breastfeeding mom asked to leave Ontario restaurant.* http://www.cbc.ca/news/trending/breastfeeding-mom-asked-to-leave-ontario-restaurant-she-claims-1.3148210. Accessed 14 July 2015.

Fomon, S. J. (2001). Infant feeding in the 20th century: Formula and beikost. *The Journal of Nutrition, 131*(2), 409S–420S.

Food Banks Canada. (2015). *Hunger count 2015.* Mississauga: Food Banks Canada.

Health Canada. (2012). *Trends in breastfeeding practices in Canada (2001 to 2009–2010).* http://www.hc-sc.gc.ca/fn-an/surveill/nutrition/commun/prenatal/trends-tendances-eng.php. Accessed 25 Aug 2015.

Heymann, J., Raub, A., & Earle, A. (2013). Breastfeeding policy: A globally comparative analysis. *Bulletin of the World Health Organization, 91*(6), 398–406.

Huggins, K. (2015). *The nursing mother's companion.* Boston: Houghton Mifflin Harcourt.

Johnston, I. (2015, August 14). DJ suspended after complaining about 'unnatural' breastfeeding. *The Independent,* p. 17.

Jung, C. (2015). *Lactivism: How feminists and fundamentalists, hippies and yuppies, and physicians and politicians made breastfeeding big business and bad policy.* New York: Basic Books.

Kam, R. (2015). *How one country went from 11% to 74% exclusive breastfeeding.* www.bellybelly.com.au/breastfeeding/country-from-11-to-74-exclusive-breastfeeding/. Accessed 25 Aug 2015.

Lightman, E. (2003). *Social policy in Canada.* New York: Oxford University Press.

Maher, V. (2015). Women and children first? Gender, power, and resources, and their implications for infant Feeding. In *Ethnographies of breastfeeding: Cultural contexts and confrontations* (pp. 187–208). London: Bloomsbury Acadmic.

Marshall, K. (2003). Benefits of the job. *Perspectives on Labour and Income, 4*(5). The on-line edition. http://www.statcan.gc.ca/pub/75-001-x/00503/6515-eng.html. Accessed November 15, 2015.

McMullin, J. A. (2009). *Understanding social inequality: Intersections of class, age, gender, ethnicity, and race in Canada.* Toronto: Oxford University Press.

Mills, C. W. (1959, 2000). *The sociological imagination.* New York: Oxford University Press.

Mohrbacher, N., & Kendall-Tackett, K. (2010). *Breastfeeding made simple: Seven natural laws for nursing mothers.* Oakland: New Harbinger Publications.

Murkoff, H., Eisenberg, A., & Mazel, S. (1998). *What to expect when you're expecting.* New York: Workman Publishing.

Neifert, M. R. (1998). *Dr. Mom's guide to breastfeeding.* New York: Plume Books.

Olver, L. (2004). *The food timeline—Baby food history notes.* http://www.food-timeline.org/foodbaby.html. Accessed 25 Aug 2015.

Roberts, W. (2008). *The no-nonsense guide to world food.* Oxford: New Internationalist.

Rosen-Carole, C. (2015). Promotion without support: A reply to editorials that attack breastfeeding advocacy. *Breastfeeding Medicine.* https://bfmed.word-press.com/2015/10/18/promotion-without-support-a-reply-to-editorials-that-attack-breastfeeding-advocacy/. Accessed 20 Nov 2015.

Shortall, J. (2015). *Work. Pump. Repeat.* New York: New York Abrams.

Wiessinger, D., West, D., & Pitman, T. (2010). *The womanly art of breastfeeding.* New York: Ballantine Books.

Wolf, J. B. (2011). *Is breast best? Taking on the breastfeeding experts and the new high stakes of motherhood.* New York: NYU Press.

World Health Organization. (2015). *Maternal, newborn, child and adolescent health: Breastfeeding.* http://www.who.int/maternal_child_adolescent/top-ics/child/nutrition/breastfeeding/en/. Accessed 28 Nov 2015.

Wright, A. L., & Schanler, R. J. (2001). The resurgence of breastfeeding at the end of the second millennium. *The Journal of Nutrition, 131*(2), 421S–425S.

CHAPTER 2

The Tale of the Crying Rice: The Role of Unpaid Foodwork and Learning in Food Waste Prevention and Reduction in Indonesian Households

Tammara Soma

INTRODUCTION

There is an old tale wherein a farmer heard a sobbing sound coming from her field. She looked around the rice paddy only to find that the source of the sound was a handful of unharvested rice plants that were left behind during the harvest.

Interviews conducted with women who are in charge of household food provisioning in Bogor, Indonesia, regarding their strategies on reducing food waste, revealed that they often recount this folktale to their children. Many of the women still admonish their children not to waste food in their households by repeating the following *pepatah* (saying): "finish all your food or the rice will cry." The West-Java tale of the Crying Rice is one of many examples of the unpaid foodwork whereby Indonesian par-

T. Soma (✉)
Department of Geography and Planning, University of Toronto,
Toronto, ON, Canada

© The Author(s) 2016
J. Sumner (ed.), *Learning, Food, and Sustainability*,
DOI 10.1057/978-1-137-53904-5_2

19

ents (predominantly women) pass down **traditional knowledge** to their children to instill moral values and the need to respect and value food.

This chapter is based on a study the author is currently conducting to understand the impacts that **retail modernization** (supermarket revolution), **urbanization**, and globalization of food consumption have had on the generation of **food waste** in Bogor, Indonesia. During this fieldwork, the author discovered alternative forms of intergenerational learning employed by women of the households to reduce and/or prevent food waste. This chapter will demonstrate that "unpaid foodwork," which is generally associated with practices such as the producing, procuring, and the serving of food in the home, is also implemented in the sharing of folktales, the sharing of traditional knowledge, and the teaching of religious messages on matters of eating, including the cooking and wasting of food. As demonstrated in a study on the Guji people of Ethiopia, the sharing of folktales is a process of knowledge transmission, and for parents, a way of educating and disciplining children (Jirata 2012). While "unpaid-work" is not considered to be part of market-based labor work, it is an invaluable educational tool with the potential to make environmental contributions.

The chapter will begin by exploring the larger picture of unpaid foodwork and **food literacy** in the home through a historical lens by employing Strassers's (1999) analysis of the social history of trash and interviews conducted with households in Bogor, Indonesia. In the subsequent section, the definition of "unpaid" in the concept of "unpaid foodwork" will also be challenged. This challenge is based on the view that the devaluation of non-market-based foodwork (i.e., unpaid foodwork) hinges upon putting a higher value on work that is tied to monetary compensation (i.e., the market) while devaluing social reproductive work in the domestic sphere. It will then discuss the concept of informal learning and environmental knowledge transmission through alternative methods such as storytelling, religious teaching, and the imparting of traditional knowledge on food provisioning by the family. By drawing on a case study of 21 households from the author's fieldwork in the city of Bogor, Indonesia, the chapter will go on to provide an overview of the phenomenon of food waste and analyze the role of unpaid foodwork in more sustainable food provisioning practices such as through the prevention and reduction of food waste. This chapter argues that sharing folktales, such as "The Tale of the Crying Rice" in Indonesia, has the potential to serve as a useful tool for informal learning and can be mobilized by households to prevent or reduce food waste. The understanding of traditional knowledge may entail knowing how to process leftover foods into a new meal, knowing how to use ingredients commonly thrown out such as offals, or how to make food last longer (e.g., through pickling, salting) which then leads to the prevention or reduction of food waste. Finally, the chapter will demonstrate that alternative forms of knowledge transmission, such as unpaid (non-market-based) foodwork and storytelling, are predominantly performed by women. Acknowledging the importance of this type of work and women's voices (McNamara 2009) will highlight the important environmental, social, and economic contribution of unpaid foodwork as a legitimate pedagogical tool in the development of a more inclusive and sustainable food system.

THE GLOBAL ISSUE OF FOOD WASTE

Within our complex and corporatized food regime (McMichael 2009) lies the paradox of food shortages and food insecurity amidst staggering food surplus and waste. An estimated 30–50 % of food is wasted annually (Gustavsson et al. 2011; IMG 2013), while approximately one billion people are malnourished (Naylor 2011). Cloke (2013) identifies this particular food regime as a system that profits from being wasteful. In the "food waste regime" framework that Gille (2012) developed, she argued that waste constitutes a social relationship, and within this social relationship, it is important to highlight the issue of risk and unequal power relations. Such unequal power relations mean that within the modern industrial food system, those with more power can shield themselves from risk while increasing another's exposure to risk (Gille 2012). An example of this would be a large agroindustry's ability to produce surplus food which shields itself from the risk of lower profit, while increasing the risk of smaller-scale farmers as they are unable to compete from a pricing standpoint. This unequal exposure to risk according to Gille is a "key source and result of power" (2012, 31). Those who are unable to shield themselves from this risk (i.e., from the effect of dumping surplus food), such as peasants and small farmers, are negatively impacted as food dumping/food aid destroys the price of their domestic product (OXFAM 2005). It follows that the import of cheap surplus food from one country can result in the wastage of domestic food in another country. This particular circumstance results in economic, environmental, and social losses (Gille 2012).

Food waste research has significantly grown as it is generally agreed that the amount of food wasted and lost globally has major ecological, economic, and moral implications (Kummu et al. 2012). Food losses and waste impact scarce natural resources such as freshwater, cropland, and fertilizers. Currently, the agricultural sector is responsible for 70 % of global freshwater withdrawal (Kummu et al. 2012), and it is unfathomable to think that close to a half of the food produced using scarce water does not even get eaten. Not only does preventing food from being wasted reduce the natural resources required to grow food, it also reduces greenhouse gas emissions approximately eight times more than diverting the food waste from the landfill to anaerobic digestion (Quested et al. 2013). International calls from scholars, policy makers, and even religious figures such as Pope Francis (McKenna 2013) have raised the importance of reducing and preventing food waste (Evans et al. 2013; FAO 2012; IMG 2013). In academia, it is generally agreed that households are the largest generators of food waste (Gooch et al. 2014; WRAP 2011). Consequently, research on household food waste has grown (Evans et al. 2013; Ganglbauer et al. 2013; Williams et al. 2012). Interestingly, this research has mainly focused on food waste generated by consumers in the Global North (Gooch et al. 2014; Evans et al. 2013) and has generally neglected household food waste in the Global South. A literature review of food waste studies confirms this gap as it is argued that people in developing countries in general practice a "Buy Today Eat Today" food culture so they waste less (Parfitt et al. 2010). While a few studies have briefly addressed food waste in developing countries (Yates and Gutberlet 2011), the majority of studies focus primarily on issues of agricultural loss caused by improper storage facilities or modern farming infrastructure (Oelofse and Nahman 2013). In the limited research that examines food waste in developing countries, there seems to be a generalized assumption that people in developing countries waste less food because they are "too poor to waste" (IMG 2013).

It is estimated by the United Nations (2014) that 66 % of the world's population is projected to be urban by 2050, with the most rapid growth estimated to occur in Asia and in Africa. It is further projected that the number of middle-class consumers will grow to 5 billion people by 2030, with a large majority of the growth to occur in Asia (Kharas 2010). A literature review of food waste research conducted by Parfitt et al. (2010) found that the diversification of diet and urbanization are correlated to an increase in the generation of food waste at the later stages of the food supply chain. These middle-class and affluent populations are increasingly mimicking the consumption patterns of rich countries (Godfray et al.

2010). The growth of urban population in developing countries and the need to feed this growing population often entail the extension of modern corporate food supply chains requiring integrated infrastructures such as roads, transportation, and storage networks all of which can lead to the generation of more food waste along the chain (Parfitt et al. 2010). Considering that many cities in developing countries have weak waste collection infrastructures (Meidiana and Gamse 2011), a high generation of organic waste (Oberlin and Szántó 2011), and lower-income people who are saddled with the disproportionate burden of living amidst this waste, the issue of food waste in developing countries requires urgent attention. One way of addressing this issue is through unpaid foodwork.

Unpaid Foodwork

Brady, Gingras, and Power argue that unpaid work in the form of foodwork (i.e., producing, preparing, procuring, serving, and cleaning) in the home can represent "a potential source of power, resistance, and creativity" (2012, 123). However, scholarly literature has mainly focused on broader concepts such as "housework" or domestic work as well as "paid and unpaid work" (Bakker 1998; Bianchi et al. 2000; Bittman et al. 2003; Eichler and Albanese 2007) while neglecting the potential environmental contributions of food-related unpaid work. In addition, while research on food waste is growing rapidly (Evans et al. 2013; Ganglbauer et al. 2013; Williams et al. 2012), there is a lack of research on the role of alternative knowledge such as folktales/storytelling, traditional knowledge, and intergenerational learning as tools for knowledge transmission to prevent and reduce household food waste in developing countries. Policy and educational awareness initiatives such as the "Love Food Hate Waste" (www.lovefoodhatewaste.com) campaign in the UK are formally addressing the issue of food waste in the public sphere. However, it is useful to consider that learning about environmental issues can also be transmitted through different methods of knowledge transmission and "informal learning" such as folktales, storytelling, riddling, and many others (Houston 2013; Jirata 2012), especially in the domestic sphere. For example, Houston argues that environmental justice storytelling "provides a framework for understanding multiple realities of environmental problems that are not necessarily discernible through policy or scientific practice" (2013, 419). Alternative learning through informal unpaid learning can also offer culturally sensitive learning tailored to specific needs of the family or culture.

Moreover, storytelling and folklore represent a gendered, non-positivist discourse, which has for millennia been carried by women across culture, time, and space (McNamara 2009). The devaluation of such alternative forms of education by women through the positivist discourse is tied to the distancing of food and the viewing of food as a commodity (i.e., commodity fetishism) (Coles and Crang 2010) rather than as an important source of building social and environmental relations.

According to Blackburn, "there is a fundamental theoretical error in describing women's domestic work as 'unpaid'; it is the error of applying market concepts to non-market work" (1999, 1). While this chapter employs the terminology of "unpaid foodwork" in describing some of the alternative methods of learning in the household, this chapter acknowledges the limitations and problems of using this term. In this chapter, the term "unpaid foodwork" refers to work that occurs in the domestic economy rather than in the capitalist market economy (Blackburn 1999). Under the dominant "market" ideology, domestic household work or foodwork can easily be overlooked. As Blackburn argues, the consequence of this ideological perspective is "an undervaluing of much of the work done by women" (1999, 13).

Learning, Food Knowledge, and Food Literacy

To understand the environmental potential of food literacy in the household, it is beneficial to look at the historical transition on food provisioning practices as well as the meaning of food prior to the industrialization of the food system. In the classic waste anthology *Waste and Want*, Strasser points to the historical transition wherein food preparation moved from "home to factory, from production to consumption, from handcraft to purchasing" (1999, 28). For example, in an 1835 edition of *The American Frugal Housewife*, the issue of food waste hierarchy was addressed, urging women:

> look frequently to the pails—the slop pails, which held pig feed—"to see that nothing is thrown to the pigs which should have been in the grease pot"—where fats were saved for cooking and soapmaking. "Look to the grease-pot, and see that nothing is there which might have served to nourish your own family, or a poorer one" (Strasser 1999, 6).

The importance of food literacy is based on the notion that with more knowledge, one has the skills to potentially waste less. As Strasser argues, "people in different social categories—rich and poor, old and young, women and men—sort trash differently in part because they have learned different skills" (1999, 10). These food skills are key because they enable less food waste by transforming leftovers or surplus food into a new meal and by wasting less food in the process of cooking. An example of this would be making meals out of things that are commonly thrown out—broccoli stalks, offal, potato peels, and so on. Due to industrialization and the mass production of food products, "expert knowledge of material became irrelevant; leftovers and scraps that they once might have valued became trash instead" (Strasser 1999, 14).

The issue of food waste in Indonesia parallels this trend toward modernization and industrialization, increasing significantly with rapid urbanization and the rise of the middle-income group. Studies have documented that there are a growing number of middle- to upper-income groups in Asia including lower-income Asian countries with highly consumptive and Westernized lifestyles (Hobson 2004; Leichenko and Solecki 2005; Goodman and Robinson 2013; Arai 2001). Consequently, concerns over food waste have largely become invisible with rising incomes, full employment, and the regime of excess/surplus food. In this food regime, farmers are directed to produce the maximum amount of food without considering the distribution and the potential market for their foodstuffs (Evans et al. 2012). Unpaid foodwork as an alternative learning tool has the potential to reconnect the moral, environmental, and economic concerns associated with the acts of wasting food.

LEARNING AND GENDER-BASED UNPAID FOODWORK

In her work on Embu women's food production and traditional knowledge in Kenya, Wane (2003) found that women learn foodwork at a very early age, with girls observing their mothers during play. The example of learning from observing the mothers in the Embu women was also corroborated by interview respondents in Indonesia. In one of the low-income households, Rosida (the names of those interviewed in this study have been changed to preserve anonymity) explained to me how her daughters learned to cook:

> I never really officially taught them how to cook, but when I cook they observe me and they ask me questions, "so do you do it like this ma?" So I explain, this, this and this, so when she got married, she already knew how to cook and what she needs. I never really taught both my daughters but

they just watched me and she ask me questions like what is this for? So I let her know this is for this and we write it down so she won't forget (Rosida interview, July 3rd 2014).

Interestingly, Rosida emphasized twice in her interview that she "never really taught" her daughters how to cook. Despite providing them with explanations and answering their questions as they observed her cooking, Rosida did not view what she did as teaching. The natural way in which she actually taught her daughters reflects the essence of unpaid foodwork. In this case, the unpaid foodwork has the effect of providing food literacy for her daughters, and this "informal" learning is not based on a market relationship but on a social relationship. This type of work is also under-valued as even Rosida herself did not realize or value her own contributions to the food knowledge of her daughters.

When asked where Rosida herself learned to cook, she answered "I learned from my parents [mother]." This continuous line of learning from mothers to daughters can be disrupted in the case of the upper- and middle-class population. In my study, some of the factors that cause the disruption include the employment of domestic helpers who are responsible for cooking and the type of foods that are purchased (frozen, processed foods such as chicken nuggets). Tuti is one of my upper-income household participants and a full-time professional. She works in the capital city and commutes from Bogor on a daily basis. She recently transitioned to a new domestic helper and is trying to train her to cook. When I asked if she likes to cook, she responded: "I don't really enjoy cooking, I force myself to enjoy it, I do it when it's a necessity ...." I also asked her if she learned how to cook and if so, from where? Tuti responded that while she learned a few basic things from her mother, she mostly learned from recipe books that she purchased. It is not surprising that there is a difference in the methods of learning about food literacy from Tuti and Rosida based on their class and income.

In one case, Sinta (who is from an upper-income household) has a son who knows how to cook. However, his cooking knowledge is derived from his studies abroad at a chef school, and not from unpaid work/parental observation. It is worth noting that the upper-income households have more ability to access formal learning and that food literacy is usually gained from paid resources, cooking books in the case of Tuti, and chef school in the case of Sinta's son. In fact, Sinta admits that her son's experimentation with making new foods has led to food wasting. In one example, she remembered purchasing a kilogram of eggs and only having one left at the end of the day. Sinta also found out that her son attempted to make ravioli, but it turned out very tough. Therefore, her household's ability to take more risk (e.g., in the experimentations of making food) results in the creation of more food waste. Sinta also prefers to use new oil to cook her food for health purposes, so the leftover cooking oil is given to her domestic helper.

Learning and Faith/Spiritual-Based Unpaid Foodwork

While the section above has addressed unpaid foodwork and learning from the perspective of gender, another type of unpaid foodwork employed by the households in my study relates to moral or ethical foodwork. In the interviews, the Muslim respondents in my study use the term "Mubazir" to relate to the sinful act of being wasteful, and this term is found in the Holy Quran. *Mubazir* in general means "wasteful"/"extravagant." For example, when I asked Suci who is a lower-income respondent if food gets wasted in her household, she said that, "It happens, but I have a chicken, so instead of being mubazir [unused/wasted] I give it to the animal" (Suci Interview, 2014). When considering the food waste hierarchy (Stuart 2009), feeding animals is on the third level of the hierarchy of food waste prevention, just after "at source reduction" and feeding the hungry (but before composting and landfilling/incineration). Therefore, through applying the Quranic injunction of avoiding Mubazir, households have made their faith one of the learning tools that has influenced them to prevent and reduce food waste.

In terms of the potential impact of the moral unpaid foodwork, Indah, one of the upper-income respondents, quoted the following verse of the Holy Quran to display her moral stance on wasting food:

> And give thou to the kinsman his due, and to the poor and the wayfarer, and squander not *thy wealth* extravagantly. (Holy Quran, Chapter 3: 27)

This verse embodies the philosophy that Indah abides by when it comes to provisioning food for her family. Indah (upper-income) is a retiree and leads a senior Quranic reading group for ladies in her community. She is the only household in my study who practices composting. She is also very knowledgeable about environmental issues and waste, which she partially credits to her experience living abroad where recycling is made easy. Indah is an example of a respondent who is highly aware and knowledgeable about food waste prevention and reduction. She actively composts and grows a lot of her own vegetables with the help of her son who is learning about hydroponics and aquaponics (especially organic catfish rearing). Her entire home is an example of a **closed-loop food system**. A closed-loop food system is a system of resource recycling (Carney 2012), which means that whatever food she does not consume gets composted or fed to the fish. She then uses the compost to grow vegetables in her backyard, and she consumes both the fish and vegetables and the cycle repeats. Our current industrial food system is a linear chain and not a closed-loop system, so food waste has been for the most part going in the landfill. This is also true in the case of Bogor, Indonesia, where food waste consists of 69 % of the total solid waste collected by the municipality (Municipality of Bogor 2011). However, food waste was not always landfilled. Modern industrial waste has arguably catalyzed the Bogor waste crisis. As one of my upper-income respondents, Sarah, recounted when I asked her about the transformation in the type of household waste and how it is managed:

> Before, until the 1980s, you can pretty much dig and put the food waste in a hole. Yes dig a hole and you put the waste in, so there is not a lot of waste outside. But what becomes problematic now is the packaging. Before, there were only a small amount of plastic and tin can waste (Sarah, Interview, July 5th 2014).

Joko also corroborated practices of food waste management prior to modern retail and reliance on municipal waste infrastructure:

> There was no plastic when we used to throw waste before, so food waste and yard waste goes to one hole, and another hole is kept open to prepare for when the other hole is full. We then dig the other hole again because it's basically compost (Joko, Interview, July 6th 2014).

Unlike my other respondents who were no longer composting or separating food waste, Indah was the only one who has been able to continue to compost due to her commitment to the environment. In a tour of her backyard, she showed me her makeshift compost bin made of bricks and covered with a metal covering. She also had three fish ponds, one of which is an aquaponic system where she feeds some of the food scraps (especially coffee grinds) to her fish, and a medium-sized hydroponic operation. With this small operation, she is able to employ an individual to manage the operation, creating a job opportunity for the community. Her son sells the catfish as a side business marketed as organic, some of them already marinated, cleaned, and ready to fry. In a tour of her kitchen, I noticed scraps of soybean skin. She told me that she just made soymilk from scratch and will cook the soybean skin as a filling for an omelet for added protein. In our interview, she tells me about living more sustainably and the importance of reducing waste. She credits her increasing awareness to her son who is learning about growing organic vegetables. In this case, unpaid foodwork works both ways intergenerationally, as Indah applies her Islamic learning of not being wasteful to her household, while her son who is trained in hydroponics and aquaponics applies his expertise to create a closed-loop system in her house. A quote by Fatimah, one of my respondents, concludes this section perfectly, "Do not forsake what has been provided from the Almighty. Everything is from the Almighty."

Learning and Cultural-Based Unpaid Foodwork

To begin the discussion of learning and cultural-based unpaid food-work, I will return to the Javanese tale of the Crying Rice. According to Janowski and Kerlogue, rice "is associated with women and the female principle throughout insular Austronesian and mainland Southeast Asian groups" (2007, 9). From an Indonesian context, rice is deeply essential to Indonesia's identity and is the main food staple in Java. Rice is so essential that for several of my respondents, the "Tale of the Crying Rice" was often recounted to their children as a caution to not waste food. Fatima is one of my upper-income respondents, and Bibi is her domestic helper who has worked with her for several decades. When I asked whether there are cultural injunctions against wasting food, Fatima said that she sometimes uses the tale of the Crying Rice to encourage her grandson to finish his food: "Please clean up your place, if not it [the rice] will cry." During our interview, Bibi then arrived and when she entered the living room, Fatima asked her about the Crying Rice story. According to Bibi, the story started a long time ago during the rice-harvesting season. The myth was that a stalk of rice was left behind during harvest, and when the farmer went out, she heard a crying sound. As she walked to find the source, she realized it was the rice. This folktale serves as a traditional reminder of the Javanese connection to agriculture and rice. As Janowski and Kerlogue (2007) wrote, "Although both women and men are involved in cultivating rice, women are almost always the main decision makers in rice-growing and they tend to be responsible for the religious and ritual aspects of rice-growing" (10). While this story is predominantly told to small children, the folktale serves as a pedagogical reminder of the moral, economic, social, and environmental impact of wasting food.

CONCLUSION

While formal campaigns and public policy to reduce food waste in various countries such as France and the UK have garnered global attention, this chapter has demonstrated a more quiet and alternative approach to reduce and prevent food waste through unpaid foodwork. Unpaid foodwork has contributed to food and food systems education through intergenerational observation, traditional knowledge, faith-based learning, and folktales/storytelling in Indonesian households. Using the case study of households in Bogor, Indonesia, it was found that respondents who were participating in unpaid foodwork did not realize the contribution that they were making to food literacy and the furthering of food knowledge and skills. From the case study and the literature, the passing on of food knowledge resulted in, among other things, the knowledge of how to store food, how to preserve food, how to make food by using products that require an added level of competence in producing, and how to minimize food waste.

As 66 % of the world is estimated to become urban by 2050 (United Nations 2014), and the supermarket penetration will continue to grow (Neilson and Pritchard 2007), it is imperative that scholars take into consideration the impacts of urbanization and the modernization of the food system on people's relationship with food. As Strasser (1999) has demonstrated, the industrialization of food is correlated to increased consumption and a decrease in food knowledge/literacy. With time scarcity and long commutes becoming the norm in Bogor, Indonesia, there is increasingly less time for households to develop a meaningful connection to food, which means that general food literacy will continue to decline. This trend can be halted and potentially reversed by acknowledging the role of women and alternative/traditional knowledge in creating a more sustainable food system.

This chapter also demonstrates the role of faith narratives in creating a moral framework that brings wastefulness into the realm of morality. Indigenous spirituality and the principle of seven generations are good examples of such teachings whereby relationships between humans and the environment are interlinked (Lavallee and Poole 2010). Similarly, it is no coincidence that my Muslim respondents stated that their faith motivates them to not be extravagant and wasteful. Finally, Java's strong agrarian ties have given birth to a folktale that has tied the Javanese identity to food. By doing so, it then also ties the identity of the individual to the land and to the growers of that food. While the "Tale of the Crying Rice" does not have to be taken literally, the issue of food waste is morally preposterous when considering that we have more than enough food to feed 10.5 billion people. This is indeed a reason to shed tears as land, water, labor, and life get lost when food gets wasted at the current global rate. The various types of unpaid foodwork performed in the household serve as a useful pedagogical tool to reconnect the missing link between food, land, and people, and develop a more sustainable food system.

Works Cited

Arai, K. (2001). Only yesterday in Jakarta: Property boom and consumptive trends in the late new order metropolitan city. 東南アジア研究, 38(4), 481–511.

Bakker, I. (1998). *Unpaid work and macroeconomics: New discussions, new tools for action*. Ottawa: Status of Women Canada.

Bianchi, S. M., Milkie, M. A., Sayer, C. L., & Robinson, J. P. (2000). Is anyone doing the housework? Trends in the gender division of household labor. *Social Forces, 79*(1), 191–228.

Bittman, M., England, P., Sayer, L., Folbre, N., & Matheson, G. (2003). When does gender trump money? Bargaining and time in household work. *American Journal of Sociology, 109*(1), 186–214.

Blackburn, R. M. (1999). Is housework unpaid work. *International Journal of Sociology and Social Policy, 19*(7/8), 1–20.

Brady, J., Gingras, J., & Power, E. (2012). Still hungry: A feminist perspective on food, foodwork, the body, and food studies. In M. Koç, J. Sumner, & A. Winson (Eds.), *Critical perspectives in food studies* (pp. 122–135). Toronto: Oxford University Press.

Carney, M. (2012). "Food security" and "food sovereignty": What frameworks are best suited for social equity in food systems? *Journal of Agriculture, Food Systems, and Community Development, 2*(2), 71–87. Retrieved from http://search.proquest.com/docview/1016735888?accountid=14771.

Cloke, J. (2013). Empires of waste and the food security meme. *Geography Compass, 7*(9), 622–636.

Coles, B. F., & Crang, P. (2010). Placing alternative consumption: Commodity fetishism in Borough Fine Foods Market, London. In T. Lewis & E. Potter

(Eds.), *Ethical consumption: A critical introduction* (pp. 87–102). London: Routledge (15).

Delormier, T., Frohlich, K. L., & Potvin, L. (2009). Food and eating as social practice—Understanding eating patterns as social phenomena and implications for public health. *Sociology of Health & Illness, 31*(2), 215–228. doi:10.1111/j.1467-9566.2008.01128.x.

Duffy, M. (2007). Doing the dirty work. *Gender & Society, 21*(3), 313–336. doi:10.1177/0891243207300764.

Eichler, M., & Albanese, P. (2007). What is household work? A critique of assumptions underlying empirical studies of housework and an alternative approach. *The Canadian Journal of Sociology, 32*(2), 227–258.

Evans, D., Campbell, H., & Murcott, A. (2012). A brief pre-history of food waste and the social sciences. *The Sociological Review, 60*(S2), 5–26.

Evans, D., Campbell, H., & Murcott, A. (2013). *Waste matters: New perspectives on food and society.* London: John Wiley & Sons.

FAO. (2012). *The role of producer organizations in reducing food loss and waste.* Retrieved from http://www.fao.org/docrep/016/ap409e/ap409e.pdf

Ganglbauer, E., Fitzpatrick, G., & Comber, R. (2013). Negotiating food waste: Using a practice lens to inform design. *ACM Transactions on Computer-Human Interaction, 20*(2), 11:1–11:25. doi:10.1145/2463579.2463582.

Gille, Z. (2012). From risk to waste: Global food waste regimes. *The Sociological Review, 60*(S2), 27–46.

Godfray, C. Beddington, J. R., Crute, I. R., Haddad, L., Lawrence, D., Muir, J., et al. (2010). Food security: The challenge of feeding 9 billion people. *Science, 327*(5967), 812–818. Retrieved from http://www.sciencemag.org/content/327/5967/812.full

Gooch, M., & Felfel, A. (2014). *$27 billion revisited: The cost of Canada's annual food waste.* Value Chain Management International. Retrieved from http://vcm-international.com/wp-content/uploads/2014/12/Food-Waste-in-Canada-27-Billion-Revisited-Dec-10-2014.pdf

Goodman, D. S. G., & Robinson, R. (2013). *The new rich in Asia: Mobile phones, McDonald's and middle class revolution.* London: Routledge.

Gustavsson, J., Cederberg, C., Sonesson, U., van Otterdijk, R., & Meybeck, A. (2011). *Global food losses and food waste: Extent, causes and prevention.* Study conducted for the International Congress SAVE FOOD! At Interpack 2011, Düsseldorf, Germany. Rome: Food and Agriculture Organization of the United Nations.

Hobson, K. (2004). Researching 'sustainable consumption' in Asia-Pacific Cities. *Asia Pacific Viewpoint, 45*(2), 279–288.

Houston, D. (2013). Environmental justice storytelling: Angels and isotopes at Yucca Mountain, Nevada. *Antipode, 45*(2), 417–435.

IMG (British Institute of Mechanical Engineers). (2013). *Global food waste not, want not*. Retrieved from http://www.imeche.org/knowledge/themes/environment/global-food

Janowski, M., & Kerlogue, F. (Eds.). (2007). *Kinship and food in Southeast Asia*. Copenhagen: NIAS Press.

Jirata, T. J. (2012). Learning through play: An ethnographic study of children's riddling in Ethiopia. *Africa: The Journal of the International African Institute, 82*(2), 272–286.

Kharas, H. (2010). *The emerging middle class in developing countries*. http://www.oecd.org/social/poverty/44457738.pdf

Kummu, M., de Moel, H., Porkka, M., Siebert, S., Varis, O., & Ward, P. J. (2012). Lost of food, wasted resources: Global food supply chain losses and their impacts on freshwater, cropland, and fertiliser use. *Science of the Total Environment, 438*(1), 477–489.

Kusenbach, M. (2003). Street phenomenology: The go-along as ethnographic research tool. *Ethnography, 4*(3), 455–485. doi:10.1177/146613810343007.

Lavallee, L. F., & Poole, J. M. (2010). Beyond recovery: Colonization, health and healing for indigenous people in Canada. *International Journal of Mental Health and Addiction, 8*(2), 271–281.

Leichenko, R. M., & Solecki, W. D. (2005). Exporting the American dream: The globalization of suburban consumption landscapes. *Regional Studies, 39*, 241–253.

McKenna, J. (2013). Pope Francis says wasting food is like stealing from the poor. *The Telegraph*. Retrieved July 12, 2015, from http://www.telegraph.co.uk/news/worldnews/the-pope/10101375/Pope-Francis-says-wasting-food-is-like-stealing-from-the-poor.html

McMichael, P. (2009). A food regime genealogy. *The Journal of Peasant Studies, 36*(1), 139–169.

McNamara, P. (2009). Feminist ethnography: Storytelling that makes a difference. *Qualitative Social Work, 8*(2), 161–177.

Meidiana, C., & Gamse, T. (2010). Development of waste management practices in Indonesia. *European Journal of Scientific Research, 40*(2), 199–210.

Municipality of Bogor. (2011). *Layanan Kebersihan*. Retrieved February 9, 2014, from http://www.kotabogor.go.id/index.php?option=com_content&task=view&id=3316&Itemid=771&limit=1&limitstart=9

Murcott, A. (1995). Social influences on food choice and dietary change: A sociological attitude. *Proceedings of the Nutrition Society, 54*, 729–735.

Naylor, R. L. (2011). Expanding the boundaries of agricultural development. *Food Security, 3*, 233–251.

Neilson, J., & Pritchard, B. (2007). The final frontier? The global roll-out of the retail revolution in India. In D. Burch & G. Lawrence (Eds.), *Supermarkets* and *agri-food supply chains: Transformations in the production and consumption of foods*. Cheltenham/Northampton: Edward Elgar Publishing Ltd.

Oberlin, S., & Szántó, G. (2011). Community level composting in a developing country: Case study of KIWODET, Tanzania. *Waste Management and Research, 29*(10), 1071–1077.

Oelofse, S. H. H., & Nahman, A. (2013). Estimating the magnitude of food waste generated in South Africa. *Waste Management and Research, 31*(1), 80–86.

OXFAM. (2005). *Food aid or hidden dumping* (Oxfam briefing paper No. 71). Retrieved from https://www.oxfam.org/sites/www.oxfam.org/files/bp71_food_aid.pdf

Parfitt, J., Barthel, M., & Macnaughton, S. (2010). Food waste within food supply chains: Quantification and potential for change to 2050. *Philosophical Transactions of the Royal Society, B: Biological Sciences, 365*(1554), 3065–3081. doi:10.1098/rstb.2010.0126.

Quested, T. E., Marsh, E., Stunell, D., & Parry, A. D. (2013). Spaghetti soup: The complex world of food waste behaviours. *Resources, Conservation and Recycling.* doi:10.1016/j.resconrec.2013.04.011.

Shove, E., & Pantzar, M. (2005). Consumers, producers and practices understanding the invention and reinvention of Nordic walking. *Journal of Consumer Culture, 5*(1), 43–64. doi:10.1177/1469540505049846.

Strasser, S. (1999). *Waste and want: A social history of trash*. New York: Henry Holt & Company.

Stuart, T. (2009). *Waste: Uncovering the global food scandal*. New York: Norton & Company.

Teng, P., & Trethewie, S. (2012). *Tackling urban and rural food wastage in Southeast Asia: Issues and interventions* (Policy brief No. 17). Singapore: RSIS Centre for Non-Traditional Security (NTS) Studies.

United Nations. (2014). http://esa.un.org/unpd/wup/Highlights/WUP2014-Highlights.pdf

Wane, N. (2003). Embu women: Food production and traditional knowledge. *Resources for Feminist Research, 30*(1–2), 137.

Williams, H., Wikström, F., Otterbring, T., Löfgren, M., & Gustafsson, A. (2012). Reasons for household food waste with special attention to packaging. *Journal of Cleaner Production, 24*, 141–148.

WRAP. (2011). *New estimates for household food and drink waste in the UK.* Retrieved from http://www.wrap.org.uk/content/new-estimates-household-food-and-drink-waste-uk

Yates, J. S., & Gutberlet, J. (2011). Reclaiming and recirculating urban natures: Integrated organic waste management in Diadema, Brazil. *Environment and Planning A, 43*(9), 2109–2124.

CHAPTER 3

Learning, Food, and Sustainability in Health Care Settings

Donna Appavoo

INTRODUCTION

Food systems and health systems are interdependent. In the biomedical tradition, however, strategies that focused on the development of these systems evolved in isolation from one another. Many non-communicable diseases such as **type 2 diabetes** and obesity have an etiology that is strongly linked to food systems. These diseases are taking an ever-increasing toll on health and health systems globally, and in North America. In response, some in health professional organizations propose learning to adopt a more integrated approach to improve food system characteristics.

In Canada, health care food environments such as hospital kitchens, cafeterias, and retail food outlets maintain a focus on the nutrient content and safety of the foods served. Central in the development of food and nutrition policy for hospitals and medical clinics are the presiding guidelines for biological markers such as blood sugar levels, body mass index (BMI), and daily energy requirements (measured in Kilojoules of calories). Similarly, the educational tools used by health professionals are based on these same criteria. This perspective is currently the dominant food ideology in contemporary society, with significant implications for food production, provisioning, consumption, and human health. An emerging

D. Appavoo (✉)
Chang School, Ryerson University, Toronto, ON, Canada

© The Author(s) 2016
J. Sumner (ed.), *Learning, Food, and Sustainability*,
DOI 10.1057/978-1-137-53904-5_3

alternative narrative to this focus on the nutrient constituency of foods is one of prioritizing community food security, underpinned by the promotion of local sustainable food systems (DOC 2007), consistent with an **ecohealth approach**.

This chapter will examine the historical development of the nutrient-focused ideology in nutrition education and the more recent focus on foodways that value locality and community. It will use a case study of rural diabetes nutrition educators to investigate the implications of re-conceptualizing food and nutrition education. In this case study, there is evidence that nutrient-oriented food and nutrition policy continues to be the predominant influence shaping contemporary nutrition pedagogy, although other influences were found, including the role of local sustainable food and sense of community. In the emerging alternative narrative of nutrition education, the role of food as it is related to the everyday experiences of local sustainable food and sense of community are important themes supporting both food system and health system change.

Nutrition Education in Health Care

Within the biomedical approach to health care, food is valued primarily as a source of nutrients. In the health care setting, the dietitian is the health professional most closely aligned with food knowledge and food work. The history of dietetics as a profession, and nutrition as a distinct scientific discipline, parallels the institution of western medical practice (Liquori 2001). Dietetics is founded on the philosophy that optimal nutrition is essential for the health and well-being of every person. Based on the science of human nutritional care, the practice of dietetics involves the application of empirical knowledge about nutrition in relation to specific health outcomes (Cannon 2005). This section provides an overview of the evolution of the nutrition profession and pedagogical approaches in health care settings between 1900 and the present day.

Between 1900 and 1930, in the early years of the profession of dietetics in North America, the role was primarily one of fulfilling clinical prescriptions issued by medical doctors who dominated the biomedical hierarchy (Kennedy 2008). These prescriptions were directed at specific health conditions related to particular disease states, such as the relationship between adequate intake of Vitamin C and the prevention of scurvy. The 1920s discovery of insulin therapy in the management of diabetes by the Nobel prize-winning work of Frederick Banting and Charles Best underpinned a key role for dietitians (CDA 2015). Complementing this discovery was the development of the expertise of dietitians who helped patients understand the importance of regulating the intake of macronutrients (proteins, carbohydrates, and fats) as an integral component in the successful management of their disease. Enhancing the knowledge and skills of individual patients to enable them to follow prescribed diet plans that detailed the patterns of timing and quantity of these nutrients was the primary objective of the nutrition education encounter.

The next defining era of nutrition practice and education corresponds with the food provisioning constraints brought on by the two world wars and related economic depression in the first half of the twentieth century. Public health nutrition emerged at this time as many nations began to link the importance of a well-nourished population with one that was better able to service national interests including the health of "factory workers and foot soldiers to increase national advantage" (Cannon 2005, p. 702). Agriculture policy emphasized food production quantity to meet these demands (MacRae 2012). National nutrition education campaigns developed in consultation with nutrition professionals focused on ensuring food abundance, complementary to policies that encouraged the rise of the productionist-oriented agro-industrial food system. The publication and wide distribution of government-sponsored national food guidelines constituted one such strategy.

In the early years of the twenty-first century, a number of critical analyses of these prescriptive nutrient-focused approaches arose from the physical and social sciences as well as other communities of interest. Reductionist approaches to valuing food primarily in terms of its elemental nutrient components rather viewing it as part of a nested interdependent system began to come under scrutiny. This over-reliance on nutrient-based analysis, dubbed "**nutritionism**" (Scrinis 2008), facilitates market commodification of food systems that privileges corporations and their control over food value chains. Central to such an ideology, the presiding guidelines for a "nutricentric" person's life are biological markers such as blood sugar levels, glycemic index (GI), BMI, and daily energy requirements (measured in Kilojoules of calories) (Scrinis 2008). In contrast, "cultural eaters" (Dixon 2009) prioritize alternative foodways that place a high value on locality, history, and cultural identity (McMichael 2005; Pettoello-Mantovani 2005). The "re-localized" shift in food production and procurement that is integral to these alternative food systems raises wider debates about the risks of exclusionary politics that simple binaries such as "local" and "corporate," "industrial," and "organic" may play in the unintended marginalization of groups at risk of food insecurity (Born and Purcell 2006; Marsden and Franklin 2013). Transitions that prioritize the livelihoods of producers, the food security of consumers, and the environmental sustainability of modes of production have the potential to play a significant role in the building of sustainable and place-based transitions.

One response to these kinds of analyses is a call for an expansion in the role of (professional) health practitioners to adopt an ecohealth approach. In other words, their jobs would be expanded to include relationship building in the community and advocacy work with respect to food security concerns (Arya 2007) and issues of food system sustainability (Harvie et al. 2009; Wilkins 2009; Worsley et al. 2014). This approach would move food learning beyond the development of a specific set of knowledge and skills relating to nutrients to one more concerned with the capacity of the broader community to support healthy food choices. As a relatively new and integrative strategy for thinking about health, the ecohealth approach presents challenges to health practitioners, planners, and researchers trained and acculturated in the more deterministic biomedical model, as well as patients who are accustomed to attending to health care concerns within this paradigm (Rapport et al. 2001). Institutionalized and established ideologies and "accepted" cultural practices will require a shift in training and the allocation of additional resources. Thus, awareness and acknowledgment of these conventional epistemological perspectives constitute a first step toward the successful adoption of new health-promoting practices.

At the time of this review, several professional bodies responsible for representing and setting operational standards for North American health care professionals had published position statements available on their websites supportive of an ecohealth approach. These include the American Medical Association (2009), the American Dietetic Association (2007), and the Dietitians of Canada (DOC) (2007). As an example, the organization that represents nutrition professionals in Canada, the DOC published a position statement in 2007 that advocated for a comprehensive approach to nutritional health care assessed at the community level and suggested that

> Community food security exists when all community residents obtain a safe, personally acceptable, nutritious diet through a *sustainable food system* that maximizes healthy choices, community self-reliance and equal access for everyone. (DOC 2007, p. 1 emphasis added)

This statement urges dietitians to advocate individually and through participation in coalitions for the development and implementation of policies and programs that support community food security. As a component of these actions, support for local food systems is recommended. "Promoting local food production and consumption is one strategy to move toward a more sustainable food system" (DOC 2007, p. 5). This attention to food systems capacity at the community scale represents a significant shift from the traditional mandate for health professionals to provide the individual patient with the food skills and knowledge to effectively manage their disease, particularly those working in hospital settings.

DIABETES NUTRITION EDUCATION

An increase in the prevalence of type 2 diabetes in Ontario is on pace with the trend occurring at the global scale (Booth et al. 2012). In response, the Ministry of Health and Long-Term Care launched the Ontario Diabetes Strategy (ODS) program in 2008, with a goal of increasing the quantity of provincially funded diabetes education personnel. Despite the linkage between healthy eating and diabetes prevention and management, policy related to community food security is not addressed in the ODS implementation strategies and evaluation. Ninety-seven percent of this funding is directed to service delivery for people with diabetes, with the remaining three percent directed to prevention strategies (McCarter 2012). The primary outcome of this funding is an increase in the total number of diabetes education staff, in some cases doubling the complement. There is also an increase in the number and configuration of health services organizations involved. Originally, hospital-based diabetes education centers were the only organizations delivering education, with supportive resources available from the County Public Health Departments and the Canadian Diabetes Association.[1] Pursuant to the ODS, diabetes education was also made available within collaborative care settings. In Ontario, these are community health centers and family health teams that offer access to a range of health professionals such as physicians, nurses, dietitians, social workers, and pharmacists working together in a patient-centered care model. The parameters set out by the Ministry of Health and Long-Term Care to measure the outcome of such education are the frequency of patient visits to diabetes health services and biomedical indicators of individual patient blood sugar control. These measures are useful in that they enable health providers to have a picture of disease management for patients accessing the health care system, and program administrators to have a profile of the population with diabetes accessed. The limitation is that the measures do not give any indication to the health care team or to administrators about the nature of the constraints that individual patients in the community setting face in managing their disease. In the words of one program manager:

> So right now diabetes education is measured by the number of warm bodies going through the door. There's no quality of care measures included, whether it's quality of education, or quality of messaging, or quality of outcomes. And that is a huge gap [] you've got some really good leadership and really good educators who have a lot of experience and insight, but if they're not given the opportunity or power to be able to use that because of the rigidity of the structure and funding in measurement requirements, it's a wasted resource. It's a wasted opportunity.

Collaborative efforts, intrinsic to an ecohealth approach, including those promoting local food, are minimal between health care providers working under these different employers as each must prioritize fulfilling the mandate set out for them under the auspices of their current employment arrangement and the provincial reporting requirements. It is unclear who has the authority to resolve these overlapping mandates, particularly since the level of inter-agency collaboration is community specific. The collaborative efforts that are being undertaken reflect initiatives on the part of community-level workers rather than organizational support from provincial management structures.

Against this backdrop of changes to diabetes nutrition education resources, I examined how diabetes nutrition educators working in rural communities in southwestern Ontario describe their education strategies (Appavoo 2014). Not unexpectedly, the sites most often referred to with reference to education were clinical care settings such as medical clinics, community health centers, and hospitals. The primary education formats involved didactic individual and group sessions with the goal of improving knowledge and skills related to diabetes food management.

During patient encounters, the diabetes nutrition educators in the study covered concepts that were consistent with those established as important by the Canadian Diabetes Association (CDA 2013) and set out in the required knowledge and skills to be certified as a Diabetes Educator in Canada (CDECB 2012). It is important to note that the certification specifics relate to individual encounters; the elements of the definition of community food security are not included. This means that the knowledge and skills to make food choices that translate into "healthy blood sugars" are key. In accordance with this, the educators spent time with patients in the clinic setting collecting a comprehensive history of food habits, preferences, skills, and food access. They also detailed patterns of activity and medication regimes and concurrent health concerns. Together, the educator, patient, and the family members responsible for food preparation designed food plans that took all of these factors into consideration. In designing food plans, lists of appropriate foods were reviewed in consultation with resources based on Canada's Food Guide, and food labels with nutrient evaluations were a topic of scrutiny. Plastic and pictorial representations of foods were used to illustrate food portion sizes. Real food was absent.

The public space in the health services site outside of the clinic room was less structured than the clinic room. Patients chose from the information rather than being specifically directed to it. All waiting areas in the health services facilities had a selection of pedagogical resources: popular press magazines and pamphlets sponsored by various commodity marketing boards (e.g. Ontario Milk marketing board), non-government health organizations (e.g. Heart and Stroke Foundation), and pharmaceutical companies (e.g. Eli Lily). Any locally developed information resources such as promotion of the **Good Food Box** as well as maps of local food retail outlets were also often available. There were no specific policies regarding the availability of educational materials based on source of the materials. Messages such as those that may be found in popular press magazines might not be consistent with those offered in the formal diabetes educator—patient meetings. As a result, they could very well detract from the messages of the health services encounter. Similarly, promotion of local sustainable food choices can be reinforced in this setting. Thus, policies about the sources and content of information in this less formal space should not be neglected given that it is the space that the patient moves through prior to, and after, the formalized education encounter.

The study also revealed issues in the area of food procurement. In the health sector institutions involved with food provisioning as well as education (hospitals and long-term care facilities), food procurement is not interlinked with local food production. In addition, the role that local agricultural production plays in local food availability is an evolving one. In this particular rural area of southwestern Ontario, agriculture and food production is a key economic driver. Thirty-three percent of the provincial agricultural land is located in this region. The predominant economic development model is agro-industrial agriculture, with local produce traveling out of communities for processing and distribution (Smithers and Johnson 2004). Key challenges identified in sourcing local products for food service for local health care institutions include finding local suppliers who can meet the institution's requirements in terms of volume, consistency, ease of ordering and delivery, and product types (Hammel 2012). The lack of processing for locally produced foods is a particular challenge, because local processing capacity continues to decline in the area, attributed largely to provincial policies around food inspection (Carter-Whitney 2009). The management structure of food services is also a barrier to local food procurement. Currently, the operation and management of food services across all hospitals in the area is outsourced to private food service companies as a response to budget constraints. Food made "from scratch" or "on-site" food preparation has been replaced by "thermos," flash-frozen food meals produced in facilities far removed from the one in which they are served. The institutions now lack the infrastructure and human resources to work with less processed and potentially more variable and seasonal local products. The downsized kitchen facilities and staffing also result in fewer options for volunteers, visitors, and staff who must remain on site for their meals. In view of the importance of small hospitals in contributing to the social and health fabric of rural communities, and in many cases as a site of formalized "food education," it is unfortunate that "local sustainable food" is not yet a priority. "Overall, there is a disconnect between the institutions, the broader community and the local food and agricultural sector" (Hammel 2012, p. 4). The patient as "learner" in the health care setting is not oblivious to this dissonance as identified by one educator:

> About a year ago we did displays about eat local [at the hospital]. That totally backfired because in a hospital with food contracted out, a patient picked that up.

Leaving "real food" out of the clinical education encounter and prioritizing pre-cooked and packaged food sourcing for health care facilities jeopardizes the opportunity for a health care setting to be a place of food learning in two important ways. Firstly, the development of a relationship based on credibility is compromised by these food-sourcing practices. Secondly, the opportunity for experiential learning, connecting patients with "real food" is missed. What remains is the "hidden curriculum" (Callenbach 2005, p. 42) that is unspoken, but nevertheless transmitted: processed foods.

Within the formal sites of learning described by educators in the study, the explicit curriculum as set out in diabetes education guidelines is one of promoting food choices that can best support the health of the individual patient. However, the hidden curriculum delivered within these health care settings is one in which processed, packaged, and specifically quantified food items are most valued. Acknowledgment of the importance of the social dimension of food is obscured by a lack of attention to it in the formal reporting and education requirements.

Opening the Door to an Alternative Nutrition Education

The social dimension of food, in particular issues of food security, generated an interest in "local sustainable food" among nutrition educators in the study. These local sustainable food options provide a platform for re-positioning "food" and "food experiences" in the workplace and community.

"Locating" Local Sustainable Food

Although it was not a part of the standardized package of resources and training, all the health providers interviewed did describe actions supportive of local food systems. Concern about economic access to food was the most significant motivation for increasing patients' awareness of local food options. Respondents evidenced their remarks on this by referencing national and local data on diabetes prevalence among low-income populations, and personal experiences in diabetes care such as this one:

> One of the things we know about diabetes is that there's a disproportionate number of people who are really struggling economically who have diabetes and sometimes it's a decision: are you going to get your medication or your food? Or are you going to eat or have a roof over your head?

These comments about food security were not directly in support or in opposition to promotion of local food within diabetes nutrition education. Food security was the most significant concern, using adjectives such as "profound" and "huge." Underlining its importance, these food security comments were made in the first part of the narrative in response to the interview question about local sustainable food, prefacing and qualifying any other remarks. There was a lack of consensus as to whether enhanced access to local food served as a proximate and tenable strategy in addressing these challenges. For example, it was noted that local food is not necessarily the most affordable source of fruits and vegetables available to patients:

> The balance has to be cost for people. We haven't quite got that worked out—how to produce something locally for less cost than flying it from China.

Regardless of whether or not they were convinced of the utility of local community food initiatives in enhancing the food security of patients, educators provided information about local food programs and activities considered by them to be relevant to the patient, such as the availability of fruits and vegetables from local farmers' markets in the area. Several also reported their own participation in actions that would serve to improve local food accessibility such as participating in the implementation of Good Food Box programs, advocating for enhanced food supplement money for persons with diabetes, participating in the development of local food charters, and personal patronage of local food retail opportunities. This finding, that the primary motivating factor for health care practitioners to promote local food initiatives is almost invariably linked to concerns about economic access to healthy foods, is consistent with that reported by Mount et al. (2013) in their examination of support for community food projects in other areas of Ontario.

Despite the absence of "local sustainable food" in the priorities for diabetes education in clinical settings, the diabetes nutrition educators did reveal important ways that, conceptually and practically, it is being incorporated into their work life and daily experiences. These educators supported local sustainable food systems in their communities in ways consistent with the importance placed on the value of community food security by the DOC (DOC 2007). Their efforts included those in the clinic setting, such as increasing awareness of local food resources through distribution of available information to patients and documenting food access constraints in the patient's clinical records. They also included efforts outside of the clinic setting: personal patronage of local food opportunities, planning and implementation of community-based educational opportunities for knowledge, and skill building around local food preparation such as cooking workshops involving local food and advocacy for policy and infrastructure that would facilitate local food access.

Educators acknowledged in their comments and reported community activities that the attributes of local sustainable mapped closely to the elements of the DOC framework for community food security—food access, community self-reliance, and healthy, culturally acceptable food choices. It is important to recognize in food policy development, implementation and evaluation, that the nutrient profile of these local foods is not the foremost consideration in supporting these systems. At the community level, the priority is a food system that underpins the non-nutritive contributions that local food can make in a region, such as improved access to healthy food and community relations.

Cultivating a Sense of Community

Community relations around food issues are important in several ways. Not only can community-based action support local food systems, they also have an effect on the interactions between health care professionals and patients. All of the community interactions described by the educators involved meeting people in the community as they pursued their own personal food acquisition and recreation activities in places such as the grocery store, the farmers' market, and the community center. The informal conversations about food arose because of the educators' health care role, but occurred in a place in the community that was about "food" rather than "health care."

> You see people around and in the community a lot more than just when they are here to see you for a medical appointment. I don't have a problem with it. I know several times I have been at the grocery store and people have come up to me and said what kind of yogurt is better?[ ] I enjoy that. I find it rewarding and a sense of community.

This sense of community contributes to shaping the actions and interactions of health care professionals.

From an administrative perspective, additional community-based responsibilities added to the mandate of health care workers may not be welcomed (Rourke 2010). They may be construed as adding yet another task to the workday rather than enriching the experience of the educator in their role. That said, Kilpatrick et al. (2009) observed that rural health professionals in particular are ideally placed to influence community-level determinants of health given that the majority live within, or near, the communities they serve. These workers, described by Kilpatrick as "boundary crossers," understand the culture and language of community and health service domains, and typically have the trust of both. In this context, the "educator" and the "patient" each have their own distinct role in the clinical setting ascribed by the education guidelines and reporting requirements. But they also have a shared role in the community at large as they are both interacting with their environment as "eaters" and "shoppers" involved with the procurement, preparation, and consumption of food. This shared role is what sets the emerging alternative narrative of nutrition education apart from the more biomedical learning experiences in the clinical setting. The interactions in food environments outside of these institutional boundaries most closely resembled Kilpatrick et al.'s (2009) findings. Encounters in real food environments helped to blur the boundary and foster trust in the relationship. The diversity of formal interactions between patients and caregivers in educational settings was complemented by informal interactions in non-clinical community settings. The character of these encounters was described by one educator as follows:

> I was born and raised in a small town so I know how that is. I think that's why I ended up wanting to come back to a smaller community, because I like that. Not that I want to know everybody's business. It is just that comfort of a smaller community; people know each other and help each other out.

In terms of patient relations, there was consensus that opportunities for encounters between patients in non-clinical settings, such as the grocery store and the farmers' market, fostered trust in the client/provider relationship. It also fosters a relationship in which patients can (re)configure their position not only in the food system setting, but also in the health care setting.

In addition to enhancing the patients' experience, this sense of community, created through diverse interactions and interconnections, also enhanced the experience of the diabetes nutrition educators in pursuing their role in health professional work. This finding aligns with other analyses of capacity in rural health services, that a key factor associated with health professional retention is personal and professional satisfaction and recognition in the community (Habjan et al. 2012). This connection, or as interviewees refer to it "sense of community," is consistent with the concept of "sense of place," described by Doreen Massey (in Cresswell 2004) as a "product of interconnecting flows—of routes rather than roots" (p. 13). This is an important finding because it supports relations of care in the community. With a strong sense of community, health service providers are more likely to maintain a variety of connections in the community both personally and professionally. In turn, maintaining these connections underpins the contribution of their skills and resources toward a healthy and vibrant community.

Diabetes nutrition educators in the study also referred to their "roots" in a community, their familiarity, and affinity for rural lifestyles and connections as the rationale for maintaining their role in a rural setting and engaging with local food systems promotion.

> In my [patient] assessment we talk about hobbies and gardening [...] and you know I will ask because my roots are rural. And I grew up with a garden so I don't know any better. My roots.

Future possibilities for local sustainable food systems and health systems are "rooted" in a familiarity with the culture and past and present experiences of community.

RECOMMENDATIONS FOR DEVELOPING AN ALTERNATIVE APPROACH TO NUTRITION EDUCATION

The role of the diabetes nutrition educator is influenced by several interacting factors that include training, workplace, community, and policy. All of these factors can open up opportunities for an alternative approach to nutrition education that includes local sustainable food and community food security. Professionals from different professional backgrounds— dietitians, nurses, pharmacists and health educators, social workers, and physicians—all participate in diabetes nutrition education. Training has a bearing on education in two ways: training curricula and educator qualifications. To facilitate the diabetes nutrition educators' ability to incorporate local sustainable food in education experiences, diabetes educator training standards that include knowledge of community food security and skills to take action on the elements of community food security are required. A review of training and standards for attainment of certification as a diabetes nutrition educator revealed no requirement for community food security knowledge nor the skills to promote it (CDECB 2012). Additionally, there were no consistent requirements, and uneven support, for the qualifications required to deliver diabetes education in the case study area.

Guidelines for incorporating practical and theoretical information about local sustainable food systems and community food security into nutrition training for professionals are now available (ADA 2010; Harmon et al. 2011). Recommended learning experiences are those that include systems-oriented problem solving, community engagement, and collaborative work with other stakeholders to "bridge the gaps between food system policy and practice" (Harmon et al. 2011, p. 8). Incorporating these strategies into training and certification programs for professionals involved in nutrition education will help to prepare future educators to incorporate local sustainable food system considerations into their practice. Although there are exemplars of Canadian programs that have community engagement as a training priority for health professionals, such as the Northern Ontario School of Medicine (Strasser et al. 2009), these approaches are not standard. Adoption of these strategies as customary will require updates to professional certification standards. For the current workforce, participation in continuing education that develops these skills is contingent upon both financial and logistical support from employers.

Within the workplace, current reporting requirements also influence diabetes nutrition educators. These requirements focus on providing the knowledge and skills to patients to make food choices in quantities that translate into "healthy blood sugars." The everyday lived experience of food access is secondary. Food security data collected by educators is not currently collated and communicated in a standardized way among care team members and as a component of the more centralized reporting requirements. This absence is not a reflection of a lack of efficient strategies to collect such data. For example, in examining the relationships between women's mental health and food insufficiency, Heflin et al. (2005) reports the use of a single item measure of household food insufficiency. With this indicator, eligible patients could be readily connected with community food programs that are well situated to foster local food connections. Further, this data could be integrated with community capacity indicators, such as volunteer contributions to local food programs, and costs. Linking patients with appropriate community resources can be an important contribution to enhancing community food environments on the part of the health service provider.

In view of the importance of small hospitals in contributing to the social and health fabric of rural communities, and in many cases providing a site of formalized "food education" experiences, it is unfortunate that "local sustainable food" is not yet a priority for these workplaces. In addition, the workplace confusion generated by overlapping mandates among health services organizations and the shifting base of support for citizen community service organizations is troubling. The rapid changes leave staff and community members anxious about what might come next and thus tentative about engaging in new initiatives. Will the unexpected increases in diabetic nutrition education resources currently experienced be followed by a shift in provincial priorities that will leave fledging initiatives in the lurch without the financial or institutional support to carry on?

The rural health professional's interactions both in their place of work and in the community at large provide fertile ground for multi-sectoral community-based action linking health and food systems that exemplify an ecohealth approach. In the experience of the individual service providers in the study, the basis for their actions in support of local sustainable food was their sense of community. Sense of community in this context was described as generated both from contemporary experiences of everyday interactions with the people and places of their rural community and place of work, and from "rootedness" or a personal history of life and work experiences in similar landscapes. That said, research participants noted that the development of supportive food policy would facilitate further action to position local sustainable food as an integral part of the broader socio-economic base of the rural community. From the perspective of this research, food policies, such as the **Ontario Local Food Act,**[2] that provide an environment supportive of local sustainable food procurement by public sector institutions are essential. Local policy-makers in the area are taking some tentative steps. For example, some community food initiatives are now using newly developed local food charters as a rationale for incorporating support for local sustainable food in community-based programs such as the Good Food Box. Although these initiatives are as yet vastly overwhelmed by the firmly entrenched agro-food industry and the biomedical approach to health, they open the door to an alternative nutrition education.

CONCLUSION

Food systems and health systems are clearly interconnected, and nutrition education has a primary role to play in uncovering and supporting the many facets of this interconnection. The emerging alternative narrative in nutrition education, based in an ecohealth approach, offers the most promising avenue for addressing complex inter-systemic issues such as diabetes. Nutrition educators who adopt this approach by understanding the importance of local sustainable food and developing their sense of community are in an effective position to promote change in both the food system and the health system.

NOTES

1. The Canadian Diabetes Association is a non-government organization that supports programming for people with diabetes and the health professionals who work with them. As part of their mandate, they publish education materials and clinical practice guidelines for use in health care settings.
2. The Ontario Local Food Act sets local food procurement benchmarks for public sector organizations such as hospitals and schools. This Act was in the process of being passed through parliament at the time the interviews took place.

REFERENCES

ADA. (2007). Position of the American Dietetic Association: Food and nutrition professionals can implement practices to conserve natural resources and support ecological sustainability. *Journal of the American Dietetic Association, 107,* 1033–1043.

ADA. (2010). *Healthy land, healthy food and healthy eaters: Dietitians cultivating sustainable food systems.* American Dietetic Association. http://old.eatright.org/cps/rde/xchg/ada/hs.xsl/education_22069_#NU_HTML.htm

AMA. (2009). *Resolution 405, A-08 sustainable food.* Chicago: American Medical Association. Action of the AMA House of Delegates Annual Meeting 2009.

Appavoo, D. (2014). *Recognizing the role of gender and food security in type 2 diabetes nutrition education in rural southwestern Ontario* (Unpublished PhD dissertation). Waterloo: University of Waterloo.

Arya, N. (2007). Applications of science-based decision-making: Medicine, environment and international affairs. In G. R. Burthold (Ed.), *Psychology of decision making* (pp. 1–7). Hauppauge: Nova.

Booth, G., Polsky, J., Gozdyra, G., Cauch-Dudek, K., Kiran, T., Shah, B., et al. (2012). *Regional measures of diabetes burden in Ontario.* Toronto: St Michael's Hospital and the Institute for Clinical Evaluative Sciences.

Born, B., & Purcell, M. (2006). Avoiding the local trap: Scale and food systems in planning research. *Journal of Planning Education and Research, 26,* 195–207.

Callenbach, E. (2005). The power of words. In M. K. Stone & Z. Barlow (Eds.), *Ecological literacy: Educating our children for a sustainable world*. San Francisco: Sierra Club Books.

Cannon, G. (2005). The rise and fall of dietetics and of nutrition science, 4000 BCE–2000 CE. *Public Health Nutrition, 8*(6A), 701–705.

Carter-Whitney, M. (2009). *Bringing local food home: Legal, regulatory and institutional barriers to local food*. Toronto: Canadian Institute for Environmental Law and Policy.

CDA. (2013). *Clinical practice guidelines*. Toronto: Canadian Diabetes Association. http://guidelines.diabetes.ca/.

CDA. (2015). *History of diabetes*. Toronto: Canadian Diabetes Association. http://www.diabetes.ca/about-diabetes/history-of-diabetes.

CDECB. (2012). *Canadian diabetes educator eligibility criteria*. Toronto: Canadian Diabetes Educator Certification Board. http://www.cdecb.ca/.

Cresswell, T. (2004). *Place: A short introduction*. Oxford: Wiley-Blackwell.

Dixon, J. (2009). From the imperial to the empty calorie: How nutrition relations underpin food regime transitions. *Agriculture and Human Values, 26*, 321–333.

DOC. (2007). *Community food security: Position of dietitians of Canada*. Toronto: Dietitians of Canada.

Habjan, S., Kortes-Miller, K., Kelley, M., Sullivan, H., & Pisco, L. (2012). Building capacity in rural health services: The effect of continuing education. In J. Kulig & A. Williams (Eds.), *Health in Rural Canada* (pp. 118–136). Vancouver: UBC Press.

Hammel, K. (2012). *Grey Bruce broader public sector institutional local food project*. Owen Sound: Grey-Bruce Health Unit.

Harmon, A., Lapp, J., Blair, D., & Hauk-Lawson, A. (2011). Teaching food system sustainability in dietetic programs: Need, conceptualization, and practical approaches. *Journal of Hunger and Environmental Nutrition, 6*, 114–124.

Harvie, J., Mikkelsen, L., & Shak, L. (2009). A new health care prevention agenda: Sustainable food procurement and agricultural policy. *Journal of Hunger and Environmental Nutrition, 4*, 409–429.

Heflin, C., Siefert, K., & Williams, D. (2005). Food insufficiency and women's mental health: Findings from a 3-year panel of welfare recipients. *Social Science and Medicine, 61*(9), 1971–1982.

Kennedy, E. (2008). Nutrition policy in the U.S.: 50 years in review. *Asia Pacific Journal of Clinical Nutrition, 17*(S1), 340–342.

Kilpatrick, S., Cheers, B., Gilles, M., & Taylor, J. (2009). Boundary crossers, communities, and health: Exploring the role of rural health professionals. *Health and Place, 15*, 284–290.

Liquori, T. (2001). Food matters: Changing dimensions of science and practice in the nutrition profession. *Journal of Nutrition Education and Behaviour, 33*, 234–246.

MacRae, T. (2012). Food policy for the 21st century. In M. Koc, J. Sumner, & A. Winson (Eds.), *Critical perspectives in food studies*. Toronto: Oxford University Press.

Marsden, T., & Franklin, A. (2013). Replacing neoliberalism: Theoretical implications of the rise of local food movements. *Local Environment, 18*(5), 636–641.

McCarter, J. (2012). *2012 annual report of the office of the Auditor General of Ontario* (p. 457). Toronto: Office of the Auditor General of Ontario.

McMichael, A. (2005). Integrating nutrition with ecology: Balancing the health of humans and biosphere. *Public Health Nutrition, 8*(6A), 706–715.

Mount, P., Hazneb, S., Holmes, S., Fraser, E., Winson, A., Knezevic, I., et al. (2013). Barriers to the local food movement: Ontario's community food projects and the capacity for convergence. *Local Environment, 18*(5), 592–605.

Pettoello-Mantovani, M. (2005). The social and environmental dimensions of nutrition science. *Public Health Nutrition, 8*(6A), 749–752.

Rapport, D., Howard, J., Lannigan, R., Anjema, C., & McCauley, W. (2001). Strange bed fellows: Ecosystem health in the medical curriculum. *Ecosystem Health, 7*(3), 155–163.

Rourke, J. (2010). WHO recommendations to improve retention of rural and remote health workers—Important for all countries. *Rural and Remote Health, 10*, 1654. http://www.rrh.org.au.

Scrinis, G. (2008). On the ideology of nutritionism. *Gastronomica: The Journal of Food and Culture, 8*(4), 39–48.

Smithers, J., & Johnson, P. (2004). The dynamics of family farming in North Huron County, Ontario. Part I. Development trajectories. *The Canadian Geographer, 48*(2), 191–208.

Strasser, R., Lanphear, J., McReady, W., Topps, M., Hunt, D., & Matte, M. (2009). Canada's new medical school: The Northern Ontario School of Medicine: Social accountability through distributed community engaged learning. *Academic Medicine, 84*(10), 1459–1464.

Wilkins, J. (2009). Civic dietetics: Opportunities for integrating civic agriculture concepts into dietetic practice. *Agriculture and Human Values, 26*, 57–66.

Worsley, A., Droulez, V., Ridley, S., & Wang, W. (2014). Dietitians' interests in primary food production: Opportunities for greater involvement in the promotion of environmental sustainability. *Journal of Hunger & Environmental Nutrition, 9*, 64–80.

PART II

Learning, Food, and Sustainability in the School

CHAPTER 4

Learning, Food, and Sustainability in the School Curriculum

Pamela A. Koch

INTRODUCTION

We all need to eat food regularly in order to survive. Yet, our **global food system** runs on a bottom line of corporate profits and a frank disregard for health, **ecological sustainability, social justice**, and equity. One way to move toward a food system that keeps us—and the planet—healthy is for all citizens to become more food literate. Imagine a world where how our food system works is common knowledge, instead of only in the hands of corporate executives. Imagine a world where everyone has the ability and desire to make **"good food"**[1] choices and knows at least a bit about how to grow and cook food. Imagine a world where "green-washing" and food packages with false and confusing health claims are a thing of the past. In this world, people would know which foods are healthy, ecologically sustainable, and socially just. This is the future we need to survive as a species. It is imperative that learning about food becomes integrated throughout our educational system so today's children become tomorrow's adults equipped with the critical knowledge and analytical skills they need to make challenging decisions about food. We will need to determine how to produce food as climate change increases, and how to create a

P.A. Koch (✉)
Program in Nutrition, Teachers College, Columbia University,
New York, NY, USA

J. Sumner (ed.), *Learning, Food, and Sustainability*,
DOI 10.1057/978-1-137-53904-5_4

safety net so all people are food secure and can eat a diet that promotes health, instead of a diet linked to high medical costs and greenhouse gases. These issues are only expected to worsen over the coming decades, especially since we are not taking any real actions to solve these problems now (Neff et al. 2011).

Concerns about what children learn about food are not new. In 1932, Mary Swartz Rose wrote "Teaching Nutrition to Boys and Girls" (Rose 1932), and the 1959 book, "Promising Practices in Nutrition Education in the Elementary School", discusses why it is important for children to learn about food, highlighting a third grade class that was studying, "where does food come from?" and "how does food grow?", "[a]s the boys and girls learned about foods, food sources, and how foods are grown they became more concerned about their eating habits" (Jacobson et al. 1959). In 1973, Borgstrom proclaimed, "Education has failed to convey to most Westerners, and in particular to each American, an awareness of [their] dependence on distant prairie soils, dairy farms, feed lots and rangelands. This large-scale feeding from many thousands of miles away contributed dramatically to the Western world's losing touch with ecological reality. In fact, it is a key factor of the present crisis. Technology has not changed in one iota man's basic dependence on soil, water, and food" (Borgstrom 1973). A year later, writing about the energy crisis, Blake wrote that we would need to do with less—less food and less goods. He felt the way to achieve this was through education. "Education about our universe, our planet...[and a]bout resources and food. About how much ENERGY is needed to boil a kettle; to make the kettle; to make a glass bottle to hold milk or a tin to hold food; to make a tractor; to cultivate the land, sow crops, harvest and dry them; to process food, market and distribute it, cook it or freeze it. How much ENERGY is needed to raise and distribute water which is the first and most important food for all life; including the mass microbial population of the soil" (Blake 1974). These are the kind of big connections that could inspire people to think differently about food and make different choices. This kind of thinking led to many broad, forward-thinking curricula about food, the food system, and connections to ecological sustainability and social justice (Katz and Goodwin 1976; Goodwin and Pollen 1974).

However, in 1980, Gussow reminded us that the industrialization of food was dehumanizing us. "The production and preparation of food used to be the activities about which much of human life was focused. We have moved away from that. That we no longer understand how food is grown, what it takes to grow it, or how dependent we are on the skills of farmers bodes ill for our future plenty. That we no longer understand the importance of breaking bread together may bode equally ill for our future ability to live together" (Gussow 1980). This combination of broad, change-oriented thinking and grave concerns about the industrialization of the food system continues into the twenty-first century.

Content and Experiences Appropriate for Food Education

Thinking about any field in education, the first thought that comes to mind is "what knowledge do we want to teach?" Yet, for education about food, knowledge alone is not enough (Contento 2015). The ultimate goal of nutrition education is to move students toward eating patterns that promote personal health, social justice, and ecological sustainability of the planet. As stated above, food that fits into this kind of eating pattern has been termed "good food" (Tagtow and Hinkle 2008), and throughout the rest of this chapter, eating a diet made up of mostly good foods is referred to as a **"good food diet."**

Our current food supply is brimming with foods that are **highly processed**, unhealthful, high carbon footprint, and heavily advertised. Given this food environment, eating a good food diet is a tall order. Thus, nutrition education has to be cleverly and carefully designed to be effective.

Contento's definition of **nutrition education** is "any combination of educational strategies, accompanied by environmental supports, designed to facilitate voluntary adoption of food choices and other food- and nutrition-related behaviors conducive to health and well-being…[and] delivered through multiple venues and involves activities at the individual, community, and policy levels" (Contento 2015). She also outlines three components for effective nutrition education:

1. *Enhance Motivation:* get students personally excited about WHY to eat a good food diet. This can be done by making students aware of the challenges of our current food system, getting them angry at the system, teaching them health benefits of good foods, and providing experiences growing, cooking, and eating good food.
2. *Facilitate Ability:* provide students with the knowledge and skills they need for HOW TO eat a good food diet. This could be specific

factual knowledge (such as the proper serving size of vegetables is about the size of your fist) or skills on how to read the ingredient on the list on food packages to determine the amount of "real food" in the product.

3. *Create Supports:* enable students to feel supported in WHERE, WHEN, and WITH WHOM to eat good food. This can include building good food diet social networks, teaching skills to navigate through the environment to find good food, and advocating for change so communities have more good food and less unhealthful food.

In addition to these three components, what is crucially important to move students toward a good food diet is education that is **"behaviorally focused"** (Contento 2015). That is, we need to break down a "good food diet" into small, clearly understood, manageable pieces. These pieces are the behaviors (e.g., make half your plate fruits and vegetables, drink more tap water, eat more locally produced foods, replace processed snacks such as chips and candy with fruit, eat smaller portions of meat). In a lesson, focus on one behavior and make the activities and content of the lesson broad and exciting. For example, a lesson with fourth graders on the behavior "replace processed snacks such as chips and candy with fruit" can *enhance motivation* by discussing that fruit gives our body what it needs to think clearly and be physically active; tasting fruits that were grown locally; and examining the large carbon footprint associated with producing, packaging, and transporting chips and candy. Then, the lesson can *facilitate ability* by pointing out places on a map to buy fruit close to the school and discussing how to put fruit in reusable plastic containers to prevent squishing in backpacks. Finally, the lesson can *create supports* by having students make up short "raps" about why fruit is a great snack.

As another example, a lesson for high school students on "drink tap water" could include learning about the history and process of their local food shed and investigating how bottled water companies have negatively impacted the water supply in the communities where they obtain their water.

In short, instead of thinking about the topic when teaching about food, think "what's the behavior?" and exciting activities that will motivate student to engage in that behavior.

There are also different approaches appropriate for different ages so food and learning can be sequential and comprehensive. The next sections discuss three age groups: lower elementary, upper elementary and middle school, and high school.

Lower Elementary Students

For younger students (about kindergarten through third grade), hands-on experiences including gardening, cooking, and tastings are exciting and open the mind and the palate. For this age group, what is key is "good experiences with good food." Additionally, get families involved. Students feel supported when what they learn in school is modeled at home. Also, students learn about food through school meals, with many students eating at least one meal a day, and sometimes up to three meals a day at school. What is served, how mealtime is treated, and the atmosphere in the cafeteria all teach students about eating and values about food. School meals are an important part of food and learning in school, particularly for younger students. The program Veggication (Bai et al. 2014) is an excellent example of a program that takes this approach.

Upper Elementary and Middle School Students

As students get a bit older, in addition to those "good experiences with good food," they are also ready to begin grappling with understanding our complex food system. This may include comparing and contrasting their experiences with food in the garden, cooking classroom, or school cafeteria to food in their day-to-day lives. Often there are stark differences. By facing this, head-on students begin to understand our complex food system and realize how much the system[2] dictates their choices. They can also explore the tactics that are used in marketing food and how these influence our views about food, our food choices, and our health. They can become empowered to navigate through the system to seek out—and demand—choices that will help them care for their health and the health of the planet. One curriculum that combines studying food systems with learning about health in thoughtful, exciting ways is the Linking Food and the Environment (LiFE) curriculum series with modules on *Growing Food* (Koch et al. 2007), *Farm to Table & Beyond* (Koch et al. 2008), and *Choice, Control, & Change* (Koch et al. 2010).

High School Students

As students move into their teenage years, three additional kinds of experiences can be layered onto previous learning: (1) Learn about the nutritional content of food and how the vitamins, antioxidants, and phytochemicals in fresh, whole, plant foods promote health and how the sugar, fat, and salt added to processed food impair our health; (2) examine food policies and become advocates for change; and (3) participate in programs where they educate younger students. Three excellent curricula for high school are Farm to School Youth Leadership Curriculum (Institute for Agriculture and Trade Policy 2014), Teaching the Food System (Johns Hopkins Center for a Livable Future 2010), and Food Fight (2015).

THE BEHAVIOR CHANGE PROCESS FOR SCHOOL-BASED NUTRITION EDUCATION

Much has been debated about the appropriate outcomes for nutrition and food-based education (Contento 2015) due to a wide range of programming and differing views on what kinds of information can change behavior. Regardless, there is a basic flow for the change process, which is depicted in the simplified logic model in Fig. 4.1. Programming is conducted to change toward a healthier food environment in the school, which could lead to changes in students' values, knowledge, and skills about food [short-term] which could lead to changes in eating behaviors [medium-term], which could lead changes in health status and direction

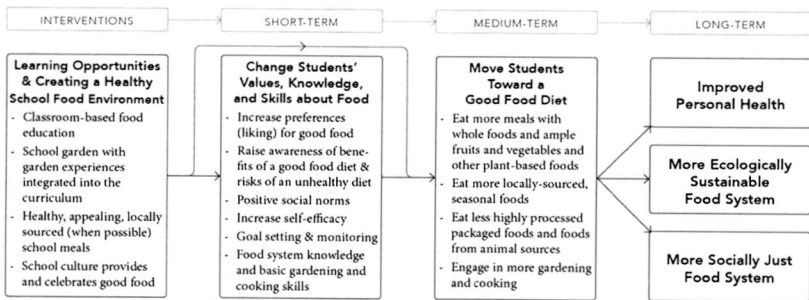

INTERVENTIONS	SHORT-TERM	MEDIUM-TERM	LONG-TERM
Learning Opportunities & Creating a Healthy School Food Environment - Classroom-based food education - School garden with garden experiences integrated into the curriculum - Healthy, appealing, locally sourced (when possible) school meals - School culture provides and celebrates good food	**Change Students' Values, Knowledge, and Skills about Food** - Increase preferences (liking) for good food - Raise awareness of benefits of a good food diet & risks of an unhealthy diet - Positive social norms - Increase self-efficacy - Goal setting & monitoring - Food system knowledge and basic gardening and cooking skills	**Move Students Toward a Good Food Diet** - Eat more meals with whole foods and ample fruits and vegetables and other plant-based foods - Eat more locally-sourced, seasonal foods - Eat less highly processed packaged foods and foods from animal sources - Engage in more gardening and cooking	**Improved Personal Health** **More Ecologically Sustainable Food System** **More Socially Just Food System**

Fig. 4.1 The change process for nutrition and food-based education in schools

of the food system [long-term]. There are some programs, such as Smarter Lunchroom (2014), that change the food environment (e.g., location of the salad bar, placing fruit in baskets) that are expected to directly change behavior. The dashed line that connects environment (first box) directly to behavior (third box) represents this type of program.

Interventions: Create a Healthy School Food Environment

As childhood obesity has risen over the past several decades, there has been a steady increase in school-based food and nutrition education programs, as well as evaluation studies of the impacts of these interventions. While various interventions have seen positive changes, there is not yet a clear understanding of what types of interventions lead to what types of impacts. Most in the field believe that more comprehensive programming is needed to obtain and sustain true impacts, particularly long-term health outcomes (Gross 2013).

Farm to School is an example of a program that takes a comprehensive approach, with three core elements: education, school gardens, and procurement. These are the same as the first three bullets in the interventions box in Fig. 4.1, and when they are implemented together, there can be a change in culture, the final bullet. The grassroots National Farm to School Network (NFSN) in the USA has grown tremendously over the past few decades (http://www.farmtoschool.org/). Farm to School is also now a Program of the United States Department of Agriculture (USDA) (http://www.fns.usda.gov/farmtoschool/farm-school), and the NFSN and USDA Farm to School Program work closely together. This combination has the potential to join together policy change with programming for a transformation in how students view and experience food in school. Some published studies have shown positive impacts of Farm to School programs on students' consumption of vegetables as well as students' knowledge and attitudes (Bontrager 2014; Moss et al. 2013).

Due to the grassroots and local nature of Farm to School, there is no set programming for the three core elements. Many have investigated and recommended ways to more systematically structure Farm to School programming and connect it to the psychosocial theories that guide academic research on school-based nutrition education interventions (Berlin et al. 2013; Roche et al. 2012; Radcliffe 2012; Joshi and Radcliffe 2012).

To evaluate Farm to School Programs, the NFSN developed an evaluation guide, *Evaluation for Transformation: A Cross-Sectoral Evaluation*

Framework for Farm to School (Joshi et al. 2014). This guide outlines the potential outcomes that can be achieved by Farm to School and offers common language, guidelines, and metrics that can be used across programs and their respective evaluations.

Given the comprehensive nature of Farm to School, combined with many schools having multiple food-related programs implemented simultaneously, we need a way to measure the overall healthfulness of the school food environment. FoodCorps (www.foodcorps.org) is a national AmeriCorps program that pairs service members with service sites that work with schools. FoodCorps is developing the FoodCorps Healthy School Progress Report, which has indicators based on what the literature has shown to be effective at increasing fruit and vegetable consumption in students.

Short-Term Behavior Change: Change Students' Values, Knowledge, and Skills about Food

As depicted in Fig. 4.1, we expect short-term changes within students. Early school-based nutrition education interventions followed a theory model that was often not consciously chosen, but implicitly followed, called the Knowledge-Attitudes-Behavior model. This posits that changes in knowledge (typically factual knowledge) will lead to changes in attitudes which will lead to changes in behavior (Contento 2015). Yet, this model is not effective at changing behaviors. Hence, the field has increasingly moved toward **psychosocial theories** that contain "determinants" (i.e., the values, types of knowledge and skills that happen in individuals as they change behaviors) for both the development of interventions and outcome measure tools. Most of these theories follow what is described above as Contento's first two components of nutrition education, with one set of determinants that enhance motivation through addressing personal meanings and value toward good food and another set that facilitate the ability to change through addressing knowledge and skills (Contento 2015).

One of the most widely used psychosocial theories in school-based nutrition education interventions is social cognitive theory. When social cognitive theory is applied to Farm to School, three determinants have been found to lead to the most behavior change: (1) decrease fear of trying new foods (**neophobia**); (2) increase perception that it is socially desirable and acceptable to eat vegetables and fruits (social norms); and (3) increase confidence in abilities to eat fruits and vegetables (**self-efficacy**). This study also found that students respond very well to having "food system knowledge" as the base of the education. As a result, Berlin et al. (2013) called for more systematic inclusion of determinants of social cognitive theory into Farm to School programs.

There have been some analyses that have examined how determinants from multiple psychosocial theories change students' fruit and vegetable consumption (DiNoia and Byrd-Bredbenner 2014; Diep et al. 2014). Diep et al. (2014) called for more research specifically to understand the practical- and experience-based procedures that can complement theory to make interventions effective at changing behavior.

Overall, based on what is known in the literature, the theory-based determinants that are most appropriate for nutrition education to have the greatest likelihood of changing behavior are:

- *Increased preferences (liking) for good food:* how much students like a certain food is associated with how much they eat that food, and overall decreased neophobia particularly of vegetables has been linked with increased consumption.
- *Enhanced awareness of benefits of a good food diet and risks of unhealthy diet:* when students believe they will obtain benefits that they value from eating healthy food and there are risks they want to avoid associated with unhealthy food, they will change their eating; what is most important is to make the benefits and risks personally meaningful to the students.
- *Positive social norms:* when students believe that other students as well as adults value eating a good food diet and make a good food diet part of their lives, they are more likely to do the same.
- *Increased self-efficacy:* when students have increased confidence in their ability to make good food choices, they make these choices more often, and this goes hand in hand with their belief that they can overcome barriers to make change.
- *Goal setting and monitoring:* when students set personal goals (that are clear, small enough to be achievable and big enough to make a difference) and monitor their progress, they are more likely to move toward a good food diet; in the nutrition education, literature goal setting and monitoring are called "self-regulation skills."
- *Food system knowledge and basic gardening and cooking skills:* when students understand our food system and learn skills to critically ana-

lyze this system, these can change the way they eat; also having confidence in gardening and cooking makes it more likely students will do these practices in the future.

Medium-Term Behavior Change: Move Students toward a Good Food Diet

The purpose of framing interventions and their evaluations around theory-based psychosocial determinants is to make interventions more effective at changing behavior and sustaining that behavior change. Yet, choosing the appropriate behaviors, measuring behavior change, and understanding the process of behavior change present many challenges. A review of the methodologies and their pros and cons is outside of the purpose of this chapter, but below is a broader discussion of what behaviors are appropriate as well as an example on how to better understand the process of change that goes on within students. The "Move Students Toward a Good Food Diet" box on Fig. 4.1 provides examples of appropriate behaviors.

To choose the right behaviors for a particular group, you need to know what you want to accomplish, understand your audience, and review the evidence from the research literature. Also, the behaviors need to be broad enough to be meaningful while specific enough to be clear and measurable. The following two examples illustrate the process of choosing behavior for two school curricula.

1. *Choice, Control & Change* (Koch et al. 2010) is a 19-lesson, middle-school science curriculum with the goal of helping students adopt behaviors that would help prevent obesity. Based on what is known about middle-school-aged students, they are gaining independence and spend increasingly more time with friends, want to make choices on their own, and are often rebellious. Thus, the curriculum chose behaviors the students could take control of on their own, and the literature indicated would help to promote "energy balance" and reduce risk of obesity. The behaviors chosen were:

   - Eat more fruits and vegetables—aim for at least four cups a day.
   - Drink more water—aim for 64 ounces a day.
   - Walk more, including stairs—aim for at least 10,000 steps a day.

- Drink fewer sweetened beverages—aim for no more than eight ounces a day.
- Eat less frequently at fast-food places—aim for no more than three times a week.
- Eat fewer processed snacks—aim for no more than one small or medium each day.

These were chosen as behaviors that students are often making for themselves. The activities that motivated the students around each behavior had the students analyze their environment and study marketing strategies to get them angry at the system, instead of feeling guilt over their choices, so they would want to make change. The behaviors were measured through a food frequency questionnaire called EatWalk Survey and showed positive change (Contento et al. 2010). Interviews with students indicated that their experiences with the curriculum helped them to recognize a tension between the foods that were available in their neighborhood and what they wanted to eat to take care of themselves, and then they strived to overcome barriers, made specific plans for how they could make behavior changes, and then developed personal agency where they felt they could continue their positive changes.

2. The *Food Day School Curriculum* (Koch and Contento 2011) includes five lessons to teach around Food Day, October 24. Food Day has a broad agenda to get people to "eat real," meaning to eat whole foods produced through a sustainable just food system. The creative challenge of crafting behaviors for this short curriculum was to capture the spirit of the Food Day message with behaviors that were concrete, understandable, and actionable. The behaviors chosen were:

- Eat Real—eat more whole foods from plants and animals and fewer overly processed foods.
- Mostly Plants—make three-quarters of your plate whole foods from plants.
- Not Too Much—eat fewer overly processed foods with excessive sugar and fat.
- Navigate the Environment—navigate through the environment to "Eat Real," "Mostly Plants," and "Not Too Much."
- Be an Advocate—create and implement plans that will make positive changes to the food environment in your community.

The first three behaviors are the actions related to food, based on the book by Michael Pollan, *In Defense of Food* (2008), while the last two behaviors develop skills to help students move toward these behaviors. They learn about where to find more whole, plant-based food options in their environment and how they can "navigate through" to seek these foods out. With the final behavior, they learn that they can be agents of change by working to make changes in their community through starting gardens, or making more real food options available in stores.

To enable those who educate school children about food to become better at creatively choosing appropriate behaviors and lesson activities around those behaviors that successfully move students toward a good food diet, we also need to understand how students synthesize what they learn about food into their experiences in their daily lives. Burgermaster (2015) did in-depth photo solicitation interviews with 18 students who were part of the Food, Health & Choices trial, a fifth grade curriculum and wellness policy intervention that had very similar behaviors to the *Choice, Control & Change* curriculum described above. The behaviors were divided into "Choose More" (fruits and vegetables and physical activity) and "Choose Less" (sweetened beverages, processed packaged snacks, fast food, and screen time). Burgermaster investigated the behavior change process and found that students could be divided into four groups.

First were students who were activated (4 of the 18) by what they learned in the intervention. These students discussed how they were motivated by the curriculum and fully adopted at least four of the six behaviors during the intervention. Alex, one activated student said, "But then I stop and think; I take a step back, I take a deep breath and say, 'Ok, Alex. What is a better benefit, the apple, the cake or the Doritos?' And then I say, 'Of course the apple. It tastes sweet, it tastes good and it gives me the carbohydrates, it gives me the sugar, it gives me the energy I need'."

Next were students who were inspired (7 of the 18). These students also discussed their motivation, but this was always mixed with discussions of barriers that kept them from enacting the behaviors. Most of their barriers came from what was readily available in their neighborhoods, or even in their homes. For these students, the barriers were so challenging that they kept them from changing their behaviors. These "inspired" students teach us a very important message. It is important to combine efforts to make neighborhoods more healthful by "making the healthy choices the easy choices" with the "food and learning" that takes place in schools. This quote by Precious shows how what is available in the neighborhood influences what students eat, "...I like fruits, but like in the morning, I don't, that's not what I want to eat in the morning. I'd rather eat candy to make myself hype... So usually I just buy candy."

The third group consisted of students who were reinforced (5 of the 18)—they were already practicing some healthy behavior, and the curriculum affirmed the reason why this is important. Ezequiel, one of the boys in this group, pondered why making healthy choices was so hard for other students: "Maybe their parents are not paying attention to them and their kids they take, they are like sneaking into the kitchen and take stuff and without looking at the nutrition facts. If I sneak in the kitchen I will take something that is healthy like an orange."

The final two students were indifferent. They would only practice healthy behavior if they were made to by their families, and the intervention was not able to change this attitude, as demonstrated by Jasmine, "When I go to the restaurant with my mother and my sister and when it's time to order they tell me not to pick the fast food, they tell me to pick healthy stuff and when sometimes I pick the fast food, they always say no she doesn't want that, she wants this and they pick the healthy things."

School-based programs related to food, whether in the school garden, in the classroom, or part of school meals, can be more effective when there are carefully chosen and clearly communicated behaviors, and when we pay attention to the process students go through to change their behavior and help students to work through the challenges they encounter, particularly living in neighborhoods where unhealthy food is abundant and healthy food is hard to come by. Additionally, the home is a powerful force that influences children's eating behaviors, and thus it is important to communicate behavioral nutrition messages to families and also encourage students to tell their families about what they are learning (Contento 2015; Gross 2013).

Long-Term Behavior Change: Health, Ecological Sustainability, and Social Justice

The ultimate purpose of teaching about food is the larger, longer-lasting outcomes. The first involves students' health and the importance of reducing obesity and other chronic diseases in children. This can increase their quality of life as well as save health care costs and create a healthy economy (Whitehouse Task Force on Childhood Obesity 2010). Second, the more a good food diet is adopted, the more people will make food choices that are ecologically sustainable, reducing the carbon footprint from food. And third, the more they will become aware of social justice issues and believe in fair wages and good working conditions for those who work all along the food chain. Combining school-based education about food with creating more healthful home environments and neighborhoods affords us the best opportunities to achieve these long-term goals.

Integrating Food-Based Education into the Curriculum

Over the past two decades, one of the most significant changes to education systems has been a move toward all education being framed around educational standards that outline what content students should be learning across various academic subjects. In the USA, the 1994 reauthorization of the Elementary and Secondary Education Act mandated that all public education in the USA follows rigorous content standards and that student assessments follow these standards (IOM (Institute of Medicine) 2013) (page 14). Other countries made similar moves toward standards-based education as well.

This has meant that almost all education that happens during school hours must address these standards. Because food is something that students interact with daily in their lives, it can provide the content for the real-life application of standards across subject areas. As an example, after students learn to add and subtract fractions in math class, experiences in the garden and/or cooking classes can provide students with real-life experience with fractions. Food can be the content for Language Arts standards to read and critically evaluate non-fiction works. Students can read works about food and the food system. Many middle-school-aged students are reading Michael Pollan's *Omnivore's Dilemma Young Reader's Edition* (2009) in English class. Additionally, students can learn about food in science units on the topics ranging from plants to ecology.

When food is incorporated into the school curriculum, those who are creating the programs and writing the curriculum need to make an important choice about if it is a **"supplemental curriculum"** or a **"replacement unit."** If the program is supplemental, it is not as crucial to follow standards per se and can—and should—be connected to many different academic subjects. The *Food Day School Curriculum* discussed above is an example of a supplemental curriculum. To create a curriculum that is a replacement unit, it must squarely fit into one core academic subject and must teach to the standards of the unit it is replacing. In this way, those making curricular decisions will have confidence to pull out their current unit and replace it with the food-related unit. The *Choice Control & Change* curriculum discussed above was developed as a science unit to replace a unit where students learned about "dynamic equilibrium of the human organism." This unit was about achieving balance in the body's system, and *Choice, Control & Change* was about achieving energy balance. Another example of an excellent food education curriculum that fits squarely into one academic subject is *Math in the Garden* (White et al. 2006).

Both supplemental curriculum and replacement units have important places in the school curriculum. A report on food and nutrition programs being introduced into New York City schools (Porter et al. 2014) found that most of the programs that were being implemented were supplemental, and the schools were enthusiastic about making these programs part of the school curriculum and school culture (Porter et al. submitted). Also of note was that about 5 of the 20 programs being offered had in their mission to implement their program specifically in high-needs schools, that is schools in low-income neighborhoods that typically have poorer outcomes, and it was only because of those targeted programs that high-needs schools were getting the same level of programming as schools in middle-class neighborhoods.

POLICIES AND PRACTICES TO INCREASE FOOD-BASED EDUCATION

In the USA, there has been discussion of the pros and cons of having educational standards for nutrition and food-based education, with a conference dedicated to this in March, 2013 (IOM (Institute of Medicine) 2013). The pros are that it would make this subject mandated—and tested—in schools, thus dedicating classroom time to this issue. The cons are that mandated subjects take on a different meaning and then what is covered is often dictated by large textbook publishers instead of from a place of passion and local relevance, as is the case with so many of the current programs. In addition to formal, national policy, many localities are inspiring food-based education, such as Grow to Learn, the school garden network, and support system encouraging active school gardens in New York City (http://www.growtolearn.org/) and California's "A Children's Garden of Standards" (California Department of Education 2011).

Policies can also impact the school food environment. For example, in the USA, it has been mandated that schools that are part of the USDA National School Lunch Program have wellness policies. While it has been hard to get these policies fully implemented (Longley and Sneed 2009), mandated wellness policies along with a general trend toward more food-based programming in schools have inspired many schools to develop activity wellness committees.

Additionally, when states have Farm to School program laws or laws related to locally grown, the availability of fruits and vegetables in the school lunch program seems to increase (Nicholson et al. 2014). While this is a complicated relationship to understand, and there have not been studies to link availability with consumption, it is a promising trend that can show how policies can work to create a healthy food environment in schools.

Conclusion

The future that we are actively working toward is one where we meet three important goals. First, students have education about food throughout their schooling that gets them involved in cooking and excited about eating real, wholesome food. Second, schools have meal programs that serve healthy food, sourced locally when possible, and reduce stigma that school meals are only for poor children. And third, schools have gardens and students' experiences in the garden are entwined in their core curriculum. Taken together, these goals teach students to value food, value the natural environment and all people, and value health. As mentioned in the introduction, we need today's children to become tomorrow's adults who will be able to make critical decisions about how to produce food and what policies we need around food. With food and learning integrated into the school curriculum, this is possible.

Notes

1. Good food is defined as food that is healthy, green, fair, and accessible/affordable.
2. This makes the education take on a broader "system-blame" approach which can build the power, excitement, and awareness needed to change and is more effective than education that either directly or indirectly takes an individualistic "victim-blame" approach that makes it appear that choices

are our free will, which can make people feel guilty about their own actions, mask the power and influence of the food system, and often stifle change.

REFERENCES

Bai, Y., Suriano, L., & Wunderlich, S. M. (2014). Veggiecation: A novel approach to improve vegetable consumption among school-aged children. *Journal of Nutrition Education and Behavior*, *46*, 320–321. doi: http://dx.doi.org/10.1016/j.jneb.2013.12.004 also see http://www.veggiecation.com/

Berlin, L., Norris, K., Kolodinsky, J., & Nelson, A. (2013). The role of social cognitive theory in farm-to-school-related activities: Implications for child nutrition. *Journal of School Health, 83*, 589–595. doi:10.1111/josh.12069.

Blake, T. M. (1974, April). *What magic wand?* Soil Association, Reprinted in Gussow, J. D. (1978). *The feeding web* (p. 279). Palo Alto: Bull Publishing Company.

Bontrager, Y. (2014). Farm to elementary school programming increases access to fruits and vegetables and increases their consumption among those with low intake. *Journal of Nutrition Education and Behavior, 46*, 341–349. doi:10.1016/j.jneb.2014.04.297.

Borgstrom, G. (1973). *The food and people dilemma*. Bemont: Wadsworth Publishing Company. Reprinted in Gussow, J. D. (1978). *The feeding web* (p. 64). Palo Alto: Bull Publishing Company.

Burgermaster, M. (2015). *Food, health & choices implementation and context: The case for a comprehensive approach to process evaluation in school-based childhood obesity prevention trials*. Doctoral dissertation, Teachers College Columbia University.

California standards: California Department of Education. (2011). Nutrition education resource guide for California schools: Kindergarten through grade twelve, http://www.cde.ca.gov/ls/nu/he/nerg.asp. Accessed 28 June 2015.

Contento, I. R. (2015). *Nutrition education: Linking research, theory and practice* (3rd ed.). Burlington: Jones and Bartlett.

Contento, I. R., Koch, P. A., Lee, H., & Calabrese-Barton, A. (2010). Adolescents demonstrate improvement in obesity risk behaviors after completion of Choice, Control & Change (C3), a curriculum addressing personal agency and autonomous motivation. *Journal of the American Dietetic Association, 110*, 1830–1839.

Diep, C. S., Chen, T. A., Davies, V. F., Baranowski, J. C., & Baranowski, T. (2014). Influence of behavioral theory on fruit and vegetable intervention effectiveness among children: A meta-analysis. *Journal of Nutrition Education and Behavior, 46*, 506–546.

DiNoia, J., & Byrd-Bredbenner, C. (2014). Determinants of fruit and vegetable intake in low-income children and adolescents. *Nutrition Reviews, 72*(9), 575–590.

Food Fight. (2015). *Food fight in the classroom.* http://foodfight.org/our-work/foodfight-in-the-classroom/. Accessed 28 June 2015.

Goodwin, M. T., & Pollen, G. (1974). *Creative food experiences for children.* Washington, DC: Center for Science in the Public Interest.

Gross, R. (2013). School-based obesity prevention programs: A meta-analysis of randomized controlled trials. *Obesity, 21*(12), 2422–2428.

Gussow, J. (1980). What corporations have done to our food. *Business and Society Review, #85,* 19–21, p. 21.

Institute for Agriculture and Trade Policy. (2014). *Farm to school youth leadership curriculum.* http://www.iatp.org/issue/farm-to-school. Accessed 28 June 2015.

IOM (Institute of Medicine). (2013). *Nutrition education in the K-12 curriculum: The role of national standards: Workshop summary.* Washington, DC: The National Academies Press.

Jacobson, W. J., Boyd, F. L., & Hill, M. M. (1959). *Promising practices in nutrition education in the elementary schools* (p. 8). New York: Bureau of Publications, Teachers College Columbia University.

Johns Hopkins Center for a Livable Future. (2010). *Teaching the food system.* http://www.jhsph.edu/research/centers-and-institutes/teaching-the-food-system/. Accessed 28 June 2015.

Joshi, A., & Radcliffe, M. M. (2012). Causal pathways linking farm to school to childhood obesity prevention. *Childhood Obesity, 8*(4), 305–314.

Joshi, A., Henderson, T., Ratcliffe, M. M., & Feenstra, G. (2014). *Evaluation for transformation: A cross-sectoral evaluation framework for farm to school.* National Farm to School Network. http://www.farmtoschool.org/resources-main/evaluation-framework

Katz, D., & Goodwin, M. T. (1976). *Food: Where nutrition politics & culture meet.* Washington, DC: Center for Science in the Public Interest.

Koch, P. A., & Contento, I. R. (2011). *Food day school curriculum.* Washington, DC: Food Day, Center for Science in the Public Interest.

Koch, P. A., Calabrese-Barton, A., & Contento, I. R. (2007). *Growing food: Linking food and the environment curriculum series.* South Burlington: National Gardening Association.

Koch, P. A., Calabrese-Barton, A., & Contento, I. R. (2008). *Farm to table & beyond: Linking food and the environment curriculum series.* South Burlington: National Gardening Association.

Koch, P. A., Contento, I. R., & Calabrese-Barton, A. (2010). *Choice, control & change: Linking food and the environment curriculum series.* South Burlington: National Gardening Association.

Longley, C. H., & Sneed, J. (2009). Effects of federal legislation on wellness policy formation in school districts in the United States. *Journal of the American Dietetic Association, 109,* 95–101. doi:10.1016/j.jada.2008.10.011.

Moss, A., Smith, S., Null, D., Long Roth, S., & Tragoudas, U. (2013). Farm to school and nutrition education: Positively affecting elementary school-aged children's nutrition knowledge and consumption behavior. *Childhood Obesity, 9,* 51–56. doi:10.1089/chi.2012.0056.

Neff, R. A., Parker, C. L., Kirschenmann, F. L., Tinch, J., & Lawrence, R. S. (2011). Peak oil, food systems, and public health. *American Journal of Public Health, 101,* 1587–1597. doi:10.2105/AJPH.2011.300123.

Nicholson, L., Turner, L., Schneider, L., Chirqui, J., & Chaloupka, F. (2014). State farm-to-school laws influence the availability of fruits and vegetables in school lunches at US public elementary schools. *Journal of School Health, 84,* 310–316.

Pollan, M. (2008). *In defense of food: An Eater's manifesto.* New York: The Penguin Press.

Pollan, M. (2009). *Young readers edition the omnivore's dilemma: The secrets behind what you eat.* New York: Dial Books.

Porter, K. J., Koch, P. A., Peralta, R., & Contento, I. R. (2014, March). *Expanding nutrition education programs in New York City elementary schools. Understanding practice to inform policy.* Laurie M. Tisch Center for Food, Education & Policy, Program in Nutrition at Teachers College, Columbia University.

Porter, K. J., Koch, P., & Contento, I. R. (under review). Nutrition education in elementary schools: How and why schools initiate, implement, and institutionalize nutrition education programs from outside organizations. *Journal of School Health.*

Radcliffe, M. M. (2012). A sample theory-based logic model to improve program development, implementation, and sustainability of farm to school programs. *Childhood Obesity, 8*(4), 315–322.

Roche, E., Conner, D., Kolodinsky, J. M., Buckwalter, E., Berlin, L., & Powers, A. (2012). Social cognitive theory as a framework for considering farm to school programming. *Childhood Obesity, 8*(4), 357–363.

Rose, M. S. (1932). *Teaching nutrition to boys and girls.* New York: The McMillian Company.

Smarter Lunchroom Self Assessment. (2014). *Food & brand lab.* The Cornell Center for Behavioral Economics in Child Nutrition Program.

Tagtow, A., & Hinkle, A. (2008). *A vision for "good food" for public health: Linking sustainable food systems to healthy people & healthy communities.* American Public Health Association. http://www.apha.org/NR/rdonlyres/85D628FE-2C5A-486E-8B2D-F47336613708/10825/AVisionforGoodFoodforPublicHealthAPHATagtowHinkleO.pdf

White, J. M., Barret, K. D., Kopp, J., Manoux, C., & Johnson, K. (2006). *McCullough Y math in the garden: Hands-on activities that bring math to life.* Burlington: National Gardening Association.

Whitehouse Task Force on Childhood Obesity. (2010, May). Solving the problem of childhood obesity in a generation. Report to the President.

CHAPTER 5

Developing a Learning Garden on a Mid-Western Land Grant University

Christopher D. Murakami

Introduction

I remember standing in front of the crowd of preschoolers, parents, and other leaders at the Mid-Western Land Grant University (MWLGU) while nervously delivering a speech that told the story of how our Learning Garden (LG) developed and what I learned from the process. In my best sport coat, a remarkable find at a thrift store, I took the microphone and read from the notes on my smart phone, standing next to the Dean for the College of Environmental and Human Sciences, the Department Co-Chair for Family Studies, the Director of the United States Department of Agriculture - Agricultural Research Services (USDA-ARS) division, and the donors who put forth the $50,000 contribution to build the major phase of the LG:

> First, I'd like to say thank you to [the Dean and other administrators] for showing your support today and over the past several years and for seeing the potential in our shared vision of this outdoor classroom that supports teaching, research, and outreach to promote healthy human development in [the state] and throughout our country. (May 1, 2014—Chris, Garden Dedication Speech)

C.D. Murakami (✉)
Assessment Resource Center, University of Missouri, Columbia, MO, USA

© The Author(s) 2016
J. Sumner (ed.), *Learning, Food, and Sustainability*,
DOI 10.1057/978-1-137-53904-5_5

I was quick to acknowledge these administrators and the benefactors graciously, though it was one of only a few times that I interacted with them directly throughout a nearly four-year planning and community development effort. I was anxious while writing and delivering this speech, not because I was speaking in front of a large audience, but because I knew I was expected to tell a celebratory story of interdisciplinary collaboration and the campus community dedication to supporting healthy development and leave out some of the details and frustrations experienced along the way while leading a group of students and campus leaders and navigating the structures and culture of this large state institution to establish the LG.

To be clear, there was a remarkable achievement to celebrate that day and obviously the need to acknowledge the contributions of the many different partners involved in the LG project. On May 1, 2014, the last and most capital-intensive phase of the LG officially opened. It is a collaboration between the Early Childhood Education Center (ECEC) that is part of the Family Studies Department in the College of Environmental and Human Sciences and a division of the USDA-ARS that oversees a People's Garden project on campus. The garden program engages children ages 1.5 to 5 years old in regular and developmentally appropriate garden experiences and supports pre-service early childhood teachers as they learn to engage young children in food and garden-based learning. The LG is dedicated to helping children develop a healthy relationship with food, nature, and the community. The produce from the garden is used to supplement or replace meals prepared for the 70 children in the education center, and extra produce is shared with families or donated to local food pantries. For example, during the 2014 growing season, more than 2000 pounds of fresh produce was donated to hunger relief agencies from this collection of neighboring gardens. While pursuing my PhD in Science Education, I led this interdisciplinary group of stakeholders on campus over a four-year period to create the garden.

As I write this autoethnographic account of developing the LG on a MWLGU, I am faced with a similar tension of how to tell competing and multidimensional stories about the decisions that were made during the dozens of planning meetings and phases of the project. During the garden opening and dedication, I assumed my role at the institution to deliver a congratulatory and triumphant speech to congenially honor the dedication of the many collaborators on the project. However, in this chapter, I work to deconstruct the celebratory narratives embedded in the process of creating this and other LG programs using a theoretical lens of **Political Ecology of Education**. Further, I elaborate upon the "managing healthy soils ecosystems" model for garden education by critically examining program decisions embedded in the practice of "balancing fertility" or generating support for LG programming (Murakami & Gillich, In Review). This chapter focuses on answering two interdependent research questions: (1) What were the challenges presented to the garden developers as they tried to access space on the MWLGU? (2) What key decisions were made during the program development process and who or what influenced those decisions?

Answering these two questions through a reflexive and narrative account is meant to help current and aspiring garden and food educators better understand the practice of making institutional progress toward **Good Food Education**. Examining my participation in the development of the LG program on the MWLGU brings to light issues embedded in restructuring and reimagining the way people learn about and through experiences with food and agriculture. Other authors in this book and across the good food education movement represent active resistance and social change toward a similar goal of engaging learners throughout their lifespan in food and agriculture education to better understand how to manage human and natural resources in a way that increases equity, social justice, and ecological sustainability. This chapter describes the process of making this progress in a situated higher education context and uncovers some of the challenges and opportunities of pragmatic compromises. The hope is that sharing this story will allow readers to think about their own institutional contexts through new lenses and provide nuance and complexity to narratives around garden-based education.

In this chapter, I start by briefly describing the theoretical lens and methodological process for compiling, analyzing, and representing these narratives. Next, I present a concise description of the development process and identify key decisions that emphasize some of the institutional barriers encountered and explore how navigating these barriers led to the program, as it exists today, but also compromised some of the initial vision of primarily undergraduate student stakeholders for the program. These decisions are described in two thematic vignettes and supplemented using quotations from the narrative interviews with founding members of the LG program. These themes are inspired by the language of the collaborators and follow chronological order to help represent two key steps of the program development process: (1) Accessing Space—"Finding a place to touch campus" and (2) The Design—"The fence." To conclude, I reflect upon the tradeoffs that were made along the way and provide insights for those creating or reimagining LG and food education programs.

The Political Ecology of Developing a Learning Garden

Political Ecology (PE) is an approach to inquiry that aims to identify the influences of power in the construction and resolution of environmental issues (Robbins 2004). In this chapter, PE is used as a "hatchet and a seed" to help deconstruct dominant narratives associated with LG education and demonstrate the ways that local and global self-awareness can lead toward social justice and sustainability (Robbins 2004, p. 3). Adding a pedagogical perspective, the **Political Ecology of Education** "analyzes the role of public policies and economic incentives in shaping the content of sustainability education, environmental behaviors, and conceptions of the interrelationships between nature and society" (Meek 2014, p. 4). Using Political Ecology of Education helps the field of food education focus on ways that politics, culture, economics, and history are all at play in shaping learning environments and the ways that learners come to form relationships with food and human ecologies. Other scholars have used political ecology to study land access issues and to understand how rules are created to manage natural resources (Agrawal 2005). In this chapter, I focus on the process of developing a LG program through this lens of accessing space on a Land Grant University to create a program to help others learn to manage natural resources and build healthy relationships with food. Key decisions made throughout phases of the project are critically examined from multiple perspectives to understand issues of power and make the unwritten rules for accessing this land more transparent.

In a forthcoming book chapter, Murakami and Gillich present a model to describe the practices of urban agriculture educators. One key dimension of this model is the work of "Balancing Fertility" or generating engagement and aggregating and allocating resources to help enhance the productivity or effectiveness of an educational program. Political ecologists examine issues of gaining access to land, and in this chapter, I explore the ways that this access might bring along compromise that impacts the overall "fertility" of a LG program. I also consider the tradeoffs that are made in the educational program in response to broader issues of power that might increase access to land resources but compromise engagement or participation. For example, Fusco and Barton (2001) argue that the process of establishing a community garden for urban youth helped learners increase ownership and agency because of their central involvement and control over the direction of the project. In the context of this project, however, many of the core garden organizers arguably lost ownership as the program became more institutionalized. The Political Ecology of Education helps focus on the decisions that were made by core organizers in the project to "balance fertility" for the LG project by gaining access to land and think critically about potential sources and sinks of program fertility.

One source of fertility for LG programs is a growing body of research that helps empirically justify the creation of garden programs in a variety of educational contexts. Garden education is supported through empirical literature that suggests benefits associated with affective, behavioral, and cognitive dimensions of science, health, and environmental learning (Blair 2009). These narratives, or storylines, in garden education research represent enhanced interest in developing LG environments that create healthier relationships with food and nature in school or informal settings. This growing movement is supported by numerous studies that explore the impact of learning experiences in gardens and a variety of outcomes for children. For example, experiences in gardening help increase children's willingness to try and abilities to identify vegetables (McAleese and Rankin 2007; Morris and Zidenberg-Cherr 2002). Further, school gardens have been associated with improving children's environmental attitudes as well as performance on standardized tests in science (Klemmer et al. 2005). Brown and Williams (2011) provided a framework for describing the learning that happens in these school gardens and uses the lived experiences of teachers, principals, and administrators to describe why they value LGs. However, their volume does not sufficiently describe the challenges of developing LG programs. This chapter shares some of the stories of resistance and change encountered while developing a LG at a Land Grant University.

The confluence of narratives in the research provides useful tools for leaders who are hoping to advocate for the development of LGs. However, there has been limited empirical focus on the political, economic, and cultural barriers that constrain garden education program development. Further, researchers have not yet problematized prioritizing certain garden education research narratives over others. For example, although there are many reasons to advocate for building gardens, is it problematic for a program to focus on one (e.g. improved nutrition behaviors) to take advantage of cultural and social willingness to address contemporary issues like childhood overweight and obesity? In this chapter, I share some of the narratives that were used to overcome the barriers to create the garden program and consider some of the tradeoffs and messiness associated with wielding these narratives to help bolster LG programs.

CRITICAL ETHNOGRAPHIC METHODS

In this paper, critical ethnographic methods (Barton et al. 2003; Flores 2007; Maanen 1988) are used to understand power structures, narratives, and the many diverse perspectives of stakeholders involved in this local context. Other participants directly involved in the design aspects of the LG were recruited to share their experiences in narrative interviews that elicited their motivations, experiences, barriers, and accomplishments. These interviews were audio recorded, transcribed, and open coded for themes. The findings were later confirmed with the collaborators (Tracy 2010). To answer the research questions, narrative inquiry was used to elicit stories from participants and construct narrative vignettes to represent my findings. This approach allowed me to generate rich, authentic accounts of other participants involved in the LG development process and also provided flexibility to share in-depth descriptions and commentary on key decisions. I act as the narrator to weave together these stories and consider issues of power that were encountered. Meeting minutes from planning sessions that spanned a nearly four-year period (October 2010–May 2015), group artifacts like sketches/logic models, and email correspondence with founding members were used to help document and validate key details of the program development. Each of the vignettes was written to include the most powerful selections from the narrative interviews that focused on the interrelated issues of accessing land and making decisions during the LG creation. Drafts of the manuscript were shared with the four participants to confirm details, and follow-up questions were asked to justify critical aspects of the analysis.

KEY COLLABORATORS

Table 5.1 provides an overview of the research participants who represent a subset of the core team during the time period under study. Research participants were assigned pseudonyms to help preserve identities as much as

Table 5.1 Participant name and brief description of campus affiliation

Participant name	Campus affiliation
Jamie	Undergraduate student, major: education, Office of Campus Sustainability Staff
David	Director of Office of Campus Sustainability
Michelle	Undergraduate student, major: sustainable agriculture, minor: women's studies, Elected officer of environmental student organization
Jeff	Volunteer coordinator for Office of Campus Student Involvement
Chris	Author, Doctoral Student, major: Science Education, Graduate Teaching Assistant—Early Childhood Education Center

possible. These collaborators ranged from undergraduate students to program directors on campus. People who were considered part of the core team of program developers were recruited to participate in the interviews for this research project. Other collaborators consented to be recorded during planning meetings but were not interviewed. Throughout the narratives in the findings, other players are described using only a generic title that indicates their rank and role on campus.

LAND GRANT UNIVERSITY CONTEXT

Land Grant Universities are important sites for initiating larger scale changes in the food system. Land Grant Universities were created through a series of legislative acts (Morrill Acts of 1862 and 1890, Hatch Act of 1887, and Smith-Lever Act of 1914) in the nineteenth and early twentieth centuries to help increase access to higher education for the common citizen and support training in the manual and liberal arts (Campbell 1995). Today, there are Land Grant Universities in each state that have a common mission for rigorous teaching, advanced research, and community outreach or extension. Land Grant Universities are well positioned to have widespread impact on regional natural resource management. Learning how to make progressive changes in these contexts presents a special but important challenge.

Especially in Mid-Western US contexts, Land Grant Universities are often dominated by large commodity groups that have a vision of sustainability and change in the food system that is often in contrast to movements in food education, agroecology, and food sovereignty. However, at this particular institution, like many other research-intensive universities, there is a widespread movement to support interdisciplinary participation to help support initiatives like a LG that naturally spans work across colleges of education, health sciences, and agriculture. Recently, this MWLGU was recognized for its efforts in sustainability initiatives regarding plans to reduce campus carbon emissions as well as increases in curricular focus on sustainability in required and elective courses. The Office of Campus Sustainability was created in 2009 to help prioritize and support these initiatives. In the fall of 2010, after dreaming up the idea to create a community garden on campus, I found the Office of Campus Sustainability, knocked on their door, and starting compiling a team to figure out how to gain access to land. The finding sections present stories about the two key phases of the project from this institutional context and span the time period from October 10, 2010, to May 1, 2014.

FINDINGS

Themal Vignette #1: "Finding a Place to Touch Campus"

As with any garden, an important first phase of the LG program development was finding a space. Before the winter of 2010, Jamie explained that she and many other employees and students who worked in the Office of Campus Sustainability had dreamed about a vegetable garden on campus among the broader landscape that was meticulously managed as part of the Campus Botanic Garden (CBG). The campus likely rebranded its landscape management to position it as a CBG to help garner support from alumni and the community to help make the landscape a beautiful place to observe a variety of horticultural plantings and themed garden areas. When Jamie first asked the Director of the CBG about getting a vegetable garden established on campus that students could manage, she recalled that "of course he just blew me off and I expected that, so, 'well it's never going to happen.' That was my impression" (Jamie, interview 3/1/2012). From the beginning, with the help of David, we all knew that the Director of the CBG was a key gatekeeper for accessing land, but we were unsure the best way to avoid being ignored. In this early phase, in the fall of 2010, the group of mostly student organizers kept coming back to this idea that the Botanic Garden team was convinced that a garden managed by students would become a "weed patch." It was unclear whether or not that was based on previous experiences of the landscape division working with undergraduate students who are notoriously absent during the summer growing season in the region.

In her interview, Michelle talked about being frustrated that the intended relationship between students and the physical landscape of campus was more about observation rather than active participation in land management. "We look at the pretty flowers but nobody eats from it. Students, to my knowledge, students don't care for it. I certainly never cared for it" (Michelle, Interview, 3/15/2012). She expanded on this idea and argued that this was one of the most powerful reasons for creating a garden on campus that undergraduate students can help manage. "Campus is this arbitrary place that nobody wants to be connected to. I think that the garden could really help like literally bring people to campus. Like, have people touch campus." For Michelle, a campus environmental and women's rights activist, her involvement in the garden was motivated by this desire to "touch campus" and deconstruct the architecture and landscape features that elevate the power of an institution but disconnect people from developing a sense of place. This narrative of developing a sense of place on what Michelle described as an otherwise sterile campus was extremely powerful for me, and motivated my own teaching and research interests in science education to focus on the promise of food and garden-based education to drive multidimensional environmental learning.

However, this idea of taking a piece of the Land Grant University back to connect with on an environmental level was perhaps too much of an activist position that, as a group, we decided would not help encourage the long-term persistence of our garden program. We soon realized the extent to which land was at a premium in central campus, but also knew that we needed to build broader support for the project with faculty members and colleges, outside of volunteer or student organizations, to circumnavigate the perceived hesitation of administrators to let students "dig into" the expansive lawns and picturesque courtyards. Guerrilla gardening was often joked about, and like many other garden enthusiasts, we started seeing every open green space as the possible location for our amorphous community garden.

During a holiday party for the Division of Operations, which included staff in the Office of Campus Sustainability and the CBG, the Director of the Botanic Garden pulled Jamie aside, and said that he needed to talk to her about getting this garden started on campus, because some important people on campus heard about it and wanted to help get it started. An email was sent out to the loosely affiliated group of students and staff interested in the garden project and eventually the Director for Fundraising and Development for the College of Environmental and Human Sciences along with the Director of the ECEC and the Nutrition Department Chair were part of a meeting in March of 2011. We finally had some faculty and broader institutional support for the garden program. Building this partnership, however, shifted the narrative of our group from getting a space for undergraduates to "touch campus" to establishing a LG to engage young children in gardening activities and creating a center for research and teacher training that could help teachers and researchers address pressing issues like childhood overweight and obesity.

During the interviews with the participants, it became clear that the decision to include these partners from early childhood education was critical to gaining buy-in from gatekeepers like the Director of the Botanic Garden, but also meant that undergraduate students and representatives from the office of student sustainability or volunteer organizations were going to have a lesser role in actively managing the garden. Jeff recalls what this decision meant for the direction of the garden project:

> Having the, umm, the colleges get interested in it was good, and having money and development people and stuff. But I think that there's a danger there too, because all of a sudden this first garden got hijacked, basically, by the ECEC. Which, I'm okay with that because this means this thing is going to happen and we're going to have something to look at and be proud of and the next one is going to be easier to do and will be more open to people just coming and growing things. (David, Interview, 3/9/2012)

This selection from David's interview struck me because it was the first time that I realized the decision to partner with nutrition and early childhood education meant that some of the original garden coordinators like Jeff, Jamie, David, and Michelle were going to have a diminished role in the garden program. In contrast, as a PhD student in education, I was just able to shift some of my interests to pursue early childhood education and was eventually able to negotiate a research assistantship to help develop the garden program. The main story of justifying the garden changed from creating a place for undergraduate students to garden, to developing a robust research and teaching program that could help generate curriculum and interventions to address issues like childhood obesity. In the process, though, we were able to get pledges of $5000 from the nutrition department to initiate the design process and garnered support from the senior development officer for a college who joined our team to help find an appropriate donor to support the project.

The Director of the CBG and representatives from our organizing group started looking for spots on the main campus. While it is not feasible to describe each of the six spots that were proposed and then eliminated, it is worthwhile to share one example that represents the nature of the challenge of accessing space. Jeff, a volunteer organizer for sustainability efforts on campus, summarized that this work was challenging because in many spaces, "someone else sees [a location] as like, this is where our hall plans to expand in twenty years. Or, umm, you know, or just, not even having a plan, but kind of being like, *this is our territory*" (Jeff, Interview, 3/16/15). Jeff was referring to one site that was on the south side of the main library that was in an ideal, high-profile location, close enough for the children in the ECEC to access. While the landscape department thought this space might have been appropriate, the director of the library got wind of these plans and went to an Associate Chancellor who swiftly squashed the idea without much justification or explanation. I was told through email from Jeff, "just so you know, the library site is out, we'll talk about it at our meeting on Friday." Other sites were negated because long-term plans included possible expansion, or the possibility of drifting biocides that get sprayed on nearby air conditioning units, or possible legacy radioactive contaminants in the area.

On June 8, 2011, we finally got clearance from all of the appropriate power holders on campus to start planning and proposing a garden on a small piece of land, surrounded by a parking lot and two aging greenhouses. This space would eventually become home to the MWLGU LG. To finally get approval on a space took about six months. During this time, the group of what was first passionate students, turned into an effort supported by two different departments as well as buy-in from the main gatekeeper to land. Gaining access to this land and building these partnerships came along with a shifting purpose and vision for the garden program. What started as dreams of a garden where any student on campus could learn to practice managing soil resources to connect with good food, turned into visions of a garden that would support a research and teaching program to scaffold nutrition education. While these visions are not necessarily mutually exclusive, it is noteworthy that the latter narrative was easier to use to gain access to land to potentially garner support for future community garden projects. Michelle, a leader in environmental groups on campus, reflected in her interview that during this time, "people were kind of confused because they thought it was going to be this undergrad garden, but I was able to explain it to them that sometimes things happen like this. It's actually a really good thing." (Michelle, Interview, March 15, 2012). On the one hand, it makes sense in the cultural context of a Land Grant University for space to be dedicated to reaching these missions of teaching, research, and outreach, but noteworthy that doing so in this case minimized an emphasis on supporting empowerment and environmental stewardship that did not fall within the bounds of an institutional department. It would have been possible for core organizers to reject this partnership, but the offer of financial and institutional support seemed to address a significant barrier that we were facing—in short, not being taken seriously. We all examined research and rhetoric around community gardens to start crafting the most compelling narrative that reflected interested stakeholders on campus. The result was a project that proposed to create a space for young children to connect with food and nature—an easy project to sell to potential donors or granting agencies. Next, we needed to create the design for the project, which eventually opened up new challenges and institutional barriers.

Themal Vignette #2: "The Fence"

The design phase of the LG took place from roughly June of 2011 to November of 2013, when ground was broken on the final phase of the garden. Once gaining official approval to access the space on campus in 2011, we focused primarily on engaging stakeholders from the CBG as well as the Director of the ECEC. Jennifer, a graduate student in agriculture education with experience in landscape design, offered her design services to the group and first developed a series of concept sketches as well drafts of designs that were to scale and included specifications for plants and themed sections of the garden. Jennifer, a single mother and full-time student, drew on her experience of managing a similar campus garden to craft beautiful sketches that unified and inspired the organizers. Jeff recalled that these sketches helped make the garden program "come alive." Throughout this design process, there were regularly competing ideas about what the garden should look like that became more complicated as the landscape services representatives and administrators conveyed some of the institutional concerns about the design. These meetings were extremely arduous and left many organizers like Michelle frustrated:

So, I'm used to working with a group of students and then having someone OK it – instead of actually working with adults. It's just like, I just remember that I would be really, really frustrated in meetings because people nit picked on things. Especially the design, we spent a lot of time with the design. *The fence.* The fence specifically. Someone wanted this fence, but it was like "Oh well we should do this fence." I wanted to bring in the sustainable aspect of it, like why are we buying a new fence? Can't we make a fence? (Michelle Interview, March 15, 2012)

During the interview, I reminded Michelle that there were different fences proposed from different parties involved. She and another undergraduate student were in support of and involved in building a fence out of old tires, clay and straw, and a rammed earth wall that could have engaged a large number of students to "touch campus" and kick off the construction of the LG program. She recalled:

OK yeah [...] I thought that it was a great idea. There are so many tires, you could pull them out of the river. Just literally trash. And you could make a really legitimate barrier with them. It's done at parks, it's done at people's farms. I've seen it before. It's not this fabricated wall fantasy.

Over a period of several meetings, spanning roughly a month that included independent research by several different committee members to evaluate the cost, aesthetics, and integrity of the fence, they presented their findings, which the group deliberated. Ideas like Michelle's were swiftly dismissed because of the liability of a fence like that built by volunteers as well as concerns that the Architectural Review committee and the Campus Review Committee might have an issue with this type of rammed earth fence.

Eventually, the campus facilities representative suggested we use a four-foot-tall chain-link fence with a black powder coating in our design. It is the same fencing that surrounds a nearby garden plot operated by the USDA. It is supposed to have a lifespan of 30 years and withstand a car if some "crazy driver" runs into the fence (the reason we needed the fence was to protect children from possibly wandering into traffic near the garden location). The fence, which would have to be professionally installed, would cost over $5000—our entire budget at that point. It was explained that the Architecture Review Committee would be much more likely to approve our plans for the garden if we went with this fencing design. The black chain-link fence made it onto the final plan but was only 10% of the $50,000 proposed price. A ridiculous quote for what was initially meant to be a rather simple garden. In this committee, most of the decisions were made by consensus, but that did not mean that everyone always agreed. Consensus was forced because we knew the progress depended upon willingness to agree with the administrative perspectives. To some extent, many of the organizers resolved that their input was not really going to be valued greatly because it was more the role of the university administrators to determine what would be permissible. Doing so, however, drastically increased the proposed cost for the garden design and in the process also consumed the $5000 we had at the time to cover the costs for having the campus landscape architect develop an executable plan.

Focusing on this issue of a fence uncovers some of the tension between institutional power holders and the student organizers who hold drastically different operational definitions for concepts like sustainability. In the eyes of the administrators, they were hoping to create a design that would be robust enough to withstand the rigors of the review committees that needed to approve construction or other large-scale changes on campus, minimize liability risk, and create something that would physically last for many years, regardless of the upfront costs. From a student perspective, sustainability meant using available resources and encouraging community engagement in the garden construction process. This definition also included being mindful of soil management practices, the life cycle of products that would be used in the construction, and other dimensions of environmental responsibility.

There were many other examples of these dilemmas in the design process that were all essentially resolved by yielding authority and expertise to representatives from the Botanic Garden and landscape services. However, they were quick to make sure that they would not be in charge of the regular maintenance of the garden once it was built. In order to make progress, however, we had to work within the rules of the institution.

This is of course understandable given the roles and responsibilities that campus administrators have on a large institution of higher education. A $50,000 price tag might seem like a lot for creating a garden, but it is relatively small in terms of the millions of dollars that are used in regular ongoing campus renovations. When we were given the final costs for building the LG, it seemed as if it was a strategic way for the university to either generate revenue from the project or keep it from progressing. At the same time, the design process also generated a stunning plan for what our garden could look like and included aspects that would help make the garden accessible for learners with varying abilities. This garden, when built, would become a nearly permanent installation in a central location and provide a foundation for teaching and research that had the potential to impact the region and country.

In the midst of this design process, I started looking to build relationships with the "neighbors" near the physical location of the future garden. I was knocking on doors in the nearest building and happened to meet the Director of the USDA-ARS that managed a neighboring garden plot. It was winter then, and during the previous year, part of the plot was used for growing corn varieties as part of the lab's research, and the other section was being used for the People's Garden Project that was launched to celebrate the 150th anniversary of the USDA (once called the People's Department when founded by Abraham Lincoln in 1862). The Director of the USDA-ARS division was excited about the opportunity to partner with the ECEC, and in the spring of 2012, we started engaging children in the regular garden experiences that would eventually expand into the final phase of the garden in 2014. Additionally, I inquired about a small space outside of one of the greenhouses in that area of campus that seemed to be abandoned and underutilized. I received a Campus Ecology Fellowship from the National Wildlife Federation in 2011 to support the creation of a community garden on campus. Because the timeline for the project had been significantly delayed, I had unspent grant money that I was able to use to build two small raised beds and initiated programming on May 30, 2012, in this unclaimed space. Instead of asking for an opinion regarding the type of fence to put around this small garden, I opted instead to fashion a barrier out of woven wire rabbit fencing. This raggedy fence still stands today (though it has been run over by a garbage truck on numerous occasions), and landscape services or the ominous architectural review committee have not issued any formal complaints.

Our programming began in 2012 and we finally had a design for the final version of our LG. We relied on the development officer in the college to use the beautiful renderings and an artfully crafted prospectus to find a suitable benefactor. In March 2013, we received official confirmation that a pledge of $50,000 was made to begin construction on the LG that was finally finished in November of 2013.

REFLECTIONS

On that crisp day in May when I was addressing the crowd of supporters, I wanted to proclaim that this project was an act of social resistance and evidence of a new wave of food activists that were taking back Land Grant

Universities from commodity groups and corporate interests to engage in the morally justifiable but contextually radical act of growing one's own food. Throughout the development process, however, I learned that those types of arguments in this Mid-Western context were not going to help me make progress toward the proximal goal of getting access to space on campus or longer-term goals of changing the way that people throughout their lifespan learn to responsibly manage natural resources. Making a statement like that could have lost key support for the project from people unwilling to align with activist narratives or identities because it might compromise the future integrity of a program. Throughout the process, I learned, for better or worse, to silence the more provocative statements or positions and instead lead with unifying messages of "interdisciplinary collaboration" and emphasized the beauty and strength of the garden design and infrastructure that can last for years. However, I could not help but think about my other collaborators who showed up to Friday morning meetings not because they were compelled to change children's nutrition behaviors and prevent childhood obesity by gardening, but because they thought their university should be more open to undergraduate students building a space on campus that did not look "conventional" or because, "there's certain things you can't learn in the classroom."

When I finally got an email about the plans for starting the construction of the garden in the fall of 2013, I was surprised that the first step for creating the garden was to apply several doses of glyphosate, the active ingredient in Roundup, to get rid of the Bermuda grass that was growing in the area. I offered to coordinate a group of students and parents from the ECEC to remove the grass using a forked hoe, the only way I have found to effectively remove this noxious weed that is resistant to otherwise systemic herbicides like glyphosate. This request was denied, and the first step in building what was supposed to be an alternative and sustainably managed community garden on the campus was, of course, spraying RoundUp. Like many other times throughout the design process, I thought about being dogmatic about my dedication to agroecological practices that emphasize community connection to agriculture. But in the end, and every other time, I decided to yield to the institutional power holders to ensure the project would continue, even if it meant compromising some of the initial values that brought together the community organizers.

CONCLUDING THOUGHTS

The purpose of this chapter was to explore the process for accessing space to create a LG program on a MWLGU and also examine some of the implications of the key decisions that were made along the way, paying particular attention to powerful narratives and navigating institutional barriers. These two vignettes present the key phases of accessing space and designing the garden that both included decisions to elevate narratives supporting garden education as an intervention in childhood overweight and obesity, and also silenced alternative perspectives for sharing ownership of public land to support sustainable land resource practices. These decisions were easy to justify in the context of the project, but later reflection raised a counter narrative of student leaders feeling as if power holders on campus were interested in disconnecting students from the direct management of land resources and also creating financial barriers to land management that were difficult to navigate. The unwritten rules for managing space on Land Grant Universities seem to be that management needs to present limited liability, align with teaching/research missions, and also have the potential to generate revenue. While these rules are understandable in this and other institutional contexts, it systematically precludes other alternative uses of public land to support emancipatory food learning. Latching on to dominant narratives around overweight and obesity prevention was again understandable to justify the creation of this and other gardens, but most garden and food educators would agree that those benefits are slippery at best, and we should be intentional about searching for new ways to document, describe, or quantify the benefit of LGs that help expand the purposes of food education beyond nutrition interventions. Now that the MWLGU LG program has been created, I am looking forward to supporting this type of expansive research and teaching that can help provide stronger and more nuanced arguments for supporting widespread learning through food.

REFERENCES

Agrawal, A. (2005). *Environmentality: Technologies of government and the making of subjects*. Durham: Duke University Press.

Barton, A. C., Ermer, J. L., Burkett, T. A., & Osborne, M. D. (2003). *Teaching science for social justice*. New York: Teachers College Press.

Blair, D. (2009). The child in the garden: an evaluative review of the benefits of school gardening. *Journal of Environmental Education, 40*(2), 15–38.

Campbell, J. R. (1995). *Reclaiming a lost heritage: Land-grant and other higher education initiatives for the twenty-first century.* Ames: Iowa State University Press.

Flores, M. T. (2007). Navigating contradictory communities of practice in learning to teach for social justice. *Anthropology & Education Quarterly, 38*(4), 380–402.

Fusco, D., & Barton, A. C. (2001). Representing student achievements in science. *Journal of Research in Science Teaching, 38*(3), 337–354.

Klemmer, C. D., Waliczek, T. M., & Zajicek, J. M. (2005). Growing minds: The effect of a school gardening program on the science achievement of elementary students. *HortTechnology, 15*(3), 448–452.

Maanen, J. V. (1988). *Tales of the field: On writing ethnography.* Chicago: The University of Chicago Press.

McAleese, J. D. & Rankin, L. L. (2007). Garden-based nutrition education affects fruit and vegetable consumption in sixth grade adolescents. *Journal of the American Dietetic Association, 107*(4), 662–665.

Meek, D. (2014). Sustainability education: What's politics got to do with it? *Journal of Sustainability Education, 7.* http://www.jsedimensions.org/wordpress/content/sustainability-education-whats-politics-got-to-do-with-it_2014_12/

Morris, J., & Zidenberg-Cherr, S. (2002). Garden-enhanced nutrition curriculum improves fourth-grade school children's knowledge of nutrition and preferences for some vegetables. *Journal of the American Dietetic Association, 102*(24), 91–93.

Robbins, P. (2004). *Political ecology.* Malden: Blackwell.

Tracy, S. J. (2010). Qualitative quality: Eight "big-tent" criteria for excellent qualitative research. *Qualitative Inquiry, 16*(10), 837–851.

CHAPTER 6

Food Education: From Normative Models to Promoting Agency

Kristiina Janhonen, Johanna Mäkelä, and Päivi Palojoki

INTRODUCTION

This chapter focuses on developing **food education**. Its starting point is the complexity of modern lives and the importance of acknowledging students as active agents in their educational experiences. The text is divided into three sections; each offers a distinct viewpoint on the background and potential of developing food education: *the shifting focus of food education, promoting agency through food sense,* and *creating collaborative food education in Finland.* The article leans on the multidisciplinary expertise of the authors in the fields of education, home economics pedagogy, and sociology of food; the first two explore teaching and learning about food and eating and the third one emphasizes food as a part of culture and identity. Finnish food education is presented in the article as a case for taking students' **agency** and **participation** as premises for educating about food and eating. In addition to the promotion of personal well-being and health, food education is seen as a medium for understanding the complexities of the world and supporting sustainable lifestyles embedded in everyday **practices**. According to Gad and Jensen (2014), the concept of practices is complex and can refer to either location or action. In this article,

K. Janhonen (✉) • J. Mäkelä • P. Palojoki
Department of Teacher Education, University of Helsinki, Helsinki, Uusimaa, Finland

© The Author(s) 2016
J. Sumner (ed.), *Learning, Food, and Sustainability,*
DOI 10.1057/978-1-137-53904-5_6

practices are understood as a combination of the two: as daily activities that take place in the specific context of the school. In reference to food education, practical learning activities are defined as those that include a basic element of touch, taste, preparation, or acquisition of food items.

The Shifting Focus of Food Education

Food education is often defined as education providing knowledge and skills about healthy and nutritionally balanced eating. Accordingly, food education was originally seen as a part of nutrition education, referring to the use of food items as tools for teaching about nutritionally relevant issues (Gussow and Contento 1984; Contento 2011). However, due to broader societal changes, these initial aims have changed considerably during the course of the past century. For example, in Scandinavia and elsewhere (Brembeck 2013; Hirdman 1983; Rautavirta 2010), the turn of the twentieth century was marked by an emphasis on prevention of nutritional deficiencies, care of the poor, and education of women to cope with their everyday life (1890–1930) (Janhonen et al. 2015). This period was followed by a focus on promoting a versatile diet (1940–1950), which related to food shortages and re-construction work after the World War II. The quantification of food requirements from the twentieth century onwards, and the increase in knowledge of the nutritional status of the population, also played an important role in the early stages of organizing such institutional meals as school lunches (Rautavirta 2010; Smith 2013). In the following decades (1960–1990), the challenges connected to lack of food were replaced with those related to abundance and wider opportunities for food choices (Ibid.). As the contexts and circumstances within which food choices are made have changed, so have the focal points of public health promotion and food education. Within home economics education in the Nordic countries, for example, food education was originally focused on food as nutrition; this focus shifted from the 1990s onward to an interdisciplinary approach to food that acknowledges cultural and social perspectives and challenges pedagogical applications that are distant and abstract from the perspective of the everyday lives of the students (Höijer 2013 referring, e.g., to Benn 1996 and Palojoki 1997).

In contemporary Western societies, food is not only nourishment, but also a medium of self-expression and fulfilment. Today, food as a source of enjoyment and construction of self-image is available to almost all social groups, and is therefore an important part of people's lifestyles. At present, food and health-related information is amply available and food education has become a part of official institutions, such as schools and health facilities (Brembeck 2013). Furthermore, a growing number of professionals from different fields are interested in influencing themes around food and eating (Sumner 2013). These professionals include educators, researchers, leaders from non-governmental organizations (NGOs), and corporate actors, who might not always agree upon the most important values and aims that drive food educational initiatives. Nevertheless, it has become evident that the mere distribution of information or simple restriction of freedom of choice is not enough for effective food education and changing food habits (Contento 2011). Increasingly, food education is also used to refer to education with broader aims, such as those promoting sustainable food choices, a deepened understanding of wider food systems, and skills related to cooking, traditions, and culinary culture (Janhonen et al. 2015; Kimura 2011).

Within the broader field of education, definitions of teaching and learning can roughly be said to have moved from a focus on behaviourism to social constructivism (Hager 2012). Educational researchers have further suggested that the nature of learning has changed altogether, promoting an understanding of learning as dynamic and as taking place beyond formal schooling (Bransford et al. 2000; Park 2011; Kuusikorpi 2014). Concurrently, traditional participatory models that emphasize the integration of children into the adult community have not succeeded in producing meaningful content for children, apart from young children that are to a high degree dependent on adults (Brougère 2012). Furthermore, studies promoting young people's food literacy have rarely been successful (Brooks and Begley 2014). Consequently, instead of relying on deterministic or behaviouristic models, modern education has shifted the emphasis to pupils' perspectives (Cook-Sather 2002) and adopted pedagogical approaches that promote the agency and genuine participation of students. According to Arnold and Clarke (2014), this increasing interest in students' agency in education is a part of a debate about the relevance of education, the disengagement of students, and a shift towards defining learning as a complex social activity. In comparison to participation work done in non-governmental agencies or community work, however, emphasizing young people's participation is a relatively new approach in schools (Cross 2011; Pekkarinen and Vehkalahti 2012; Spencer and Doull 2015).

The use of the specific term food education has increased considerably in research publications since the late 1990s (Janhonen et al. 2015). Nevertheless, the field of food education is far from unified: Sub-areas such as sensory food education, sustainability education, and health education can presently be identified; each respective sub-field has its own specialized interests and conceptual orientations (Ibid.). In recent years, especially themes related to sustainability have gained the attention of researchers and practitioners, providing supplementary perspectives to health- and nutrition-driven initiatives. Acknowledging sustainability as a part of food education has also been seen by some researchers as an opportunity for examining food-related learning in a broader context (Morgan and Sonnino 2008). However, even though serving fresh and locally produced food is generally considered to be important, cost efficiency often takes precedence in practice. Morgan and Sonnino (2008) have suggested that acknowledging more openly the normative backgrounds of sustainability approaches, as well as designing applications that consider contextual priorities, could help in overcoming these practical challenges. All in all, discussion around sustainability is increasing and public procurement of school food has become a significant theme at the forefront of these debates.

Promoting Agency Through Food Sense

An examination of the field of food education reveals an abundance of concepts and related definitions, as well as an overall transition from individually oriented guidance to broader approaches (Janhonen et al. 2015). Based on the conceptual richness, clearer definitions in relation to food education and food-related learning are needed to enable more effective collaboration between practitioners (Cross 2011). Furthermore, critical examination of the conceptual base of food education is necessary in order to secure coherence between the aims and practical pedagogical applications in teaching about food and eating in schools. Table 6.1 summarizes the current content areas and aims for learning in the order of historical shifts in the aims of food education.

From the rise of nutrition science during the eighteenth and nineteenth centuries (Falk and Gronow 1985; Jackson 2013) and a focus in the early twentieth century on preventing and curing diseases and educating people about health-related issues (Rautavirta 2010), food education of the twenty-first century is marked by a tendency to emphasize sen-

Table 6.1 Content areas and aims for learning of food education

Field of education	Food education
Broad content areas	Nutrition
	Health
	Sustainability
	Senses and experiences
Aims of learning	Health literacy
	Food literacy
	Health senses
	Food senses

sory, experiential, and child-centred forms of learning (e.g., Koistinen and Ruhanen 2009). Furthermore, understanding sustainability as an inevitable part of its content areas is a contemporary concern (Risku-Norja et al. 2012; Åbacka 2008). The aim of wide-ranging food education, as called for in this article, is to acknowledge each of the presented content areas as comprehensively as possible. The aims for learning outcomes within food education are presented in the table in the form of four concepts, which are also listed in the order of their historical appearance in academic literature. Below, an overview of these concepts is provided, along with justifications for our suggestion of promoting students' agency in food education through the concept of **food sense**.

During the past decade, the term **food literacy** has gained attention within the area of food education. However, a fuller understanding of the term requires an examination of the concepts **health literacy** and **health sense**, which are closely related to the conceptual background of food literacy. In the field of health education, health promotion, and public health, the concept of health literacy refers to people's ability to obtain, interpret, and use health-related information, as well as to interpret their own and other's health condition (e.g., Nutbeam 2009; Ormshaw et al. 2013; Paakkari and Paakkari 2012). Acquiring health literacy has also been seen as empowerment (Kilgour et al. 2015; Speros 2005), as a skill that helps in meeting the complex demands of modern society (Sørensen et al. 2012), and as an important element in achieving productive citizenship, personal life quality, and individual and social well-being (Marks 2012). Even though broader definitions of the concept include the importance of the surrounding community in shaping health behaviour, the community-related aspect is mostly seen as a source of (positive) social pressure and emotional support (Ojajärvi 2015).

The concept health sense, on the other hand, was developed by Finnish youth researchers (Hoikkala et al. 2005; Puuronen 2006) as a critique towards the concept of health literacy and its excess emphasis on the individual and the individual's knowledge of health (Ojajärvi 2015). According to Ojajärvi's (2015) definition, health sense includes the everyday routines and habits that are a part of health-related activities in different situations. The concept further acknowledges the idea that health decisions are made as a part of the broader cultural and community surroundings and as a result of social processes (Ibid.). Importantly, health decisions are not always made solely from the perspective of the health benefits of actions. In other words, the definition of health sense enables the examination of the perspectives of those adolescents that are not interested in health or healthiness. The concept further aims to grasp a solid connection to young people's lives and a broader and more sensitive approach to health behaviour.

The term food literacy builds upon much research done to investigate the relationship between food knowledge and food choices (Vaitkeviciute et al. 2015). In comparison to the concepts of health literacy and health sense, food literacy typically refers to a stronger emphasis on food preparation and other practical food-related skills (Brooks and Begley 2014; Pendergast and Dewhurst 2012). Researchers using the term often also acknowledge the challenges of motivating young people to act in accordance with nutritional guidelines and bring forth the need for approaches that include an examination of personal and environmental factors on the background of declining nutrition knowledge and choosing unhealthy options (Brooks and Begley 2014). In a similar vein, Vidgen and Galleos (2014) define food literacy as associated with the everyday practicalities of healthy eating and as a way to promote resilience. However, the authors (Vidgen and Galleos 2014) emphasize that the term currently lacks a common definition among research publications. In addition, even though the concept broadly defined includes food knowledge, skills, and behaviours, studies using the term typically use food knowledge as a proxy for food literacy, resulting in a quite narrow focus (Vaitkeviciute et al. 2015).

Therefore, it is not surprising that the concept of food literacy has also received a critique among scholars, who claim the term to support food education as an exercise of mastering superficial information and not taking sufficient notice of the social, cultural, economic, and environmental factors related to desired health behaviours. Kimura (2011), for instance, refers to a 'food literacy approach' as a framework that 'posits individual knowledge and skills as sole reasons for inappropriate food choices, dietary behaviors, and culinary practices'. She (Ibid.) sees food literacy as a highly individualistic and apolitical term that also enables the privatization and gendered pressures of food education. To conclude, though food literacy seems to have succeeded in reaching a more practice-bound definition of adolescents' food choices, it is still quite closely connected with the conceptual backgrounds of health literacy and the individual and knowledge-based approach of much health and nutrition research. Therefore, a broader conceptual base for food education than the ones offered by current interpretations of food literacy is needed.

If the target is to promote adolescents' agency within food education, the aims for learning outcomes should include not only the individual's pre-determined knowledge (on nutrition or health), but also the ability to critically evaluate differing situations, and to flexibly act in accordance with changing demands. The former includes the capability to conceive food choices as a part of wider social and cultural contexts and the potential of challenging surrounding circumstances. In our previous work (Janhonen et al. 2015), we have suggested the concept of food sense as a learning outcome for food education reaching for these goals. The definition of food sense embraces an understanding of cultural and social meanings that relate to food and eating as local and global systems, as well as the opportunity of potentially acting against one's knowledge of a healthy and sustainable diet. From a pedagogical perspective, however, the overall aim of food education is to support the learners' desires and courage to take food-related knowledge as a part of their own food choices. Thus, the notion of food sense aims to promote students' agency and empowerment, as well as joy and pleasure attached to food. Importantly, knowledge in relation to food sense refers not only to the ability to make nutritionally balanced choices, but also to the ability to understand the complexities of the surrounding world; such distinctions support healthy and sustainable eating. Leaning on Mäkelä and Niva's (2015) definition of sustainable culinary culture, we suggest that sustainability as a part of food sense means examining food-related processes and choices as collective rather than merely individual activities.

The concept of food sense as defined above could be used as a starting point for developing context-specific and participatory food education in schools, as well as for implementing curricula and plans for action. The definition calls for approaches that acknowledge adolescents' perspectives in a more flexible and open manner, accept varying definitions of healthy and sustainable eating, and are attached to students' everyday practices and experiences in a viable manner. From a teacher's point of view, promoting students' agency and moving beyond normative models for food education means detachment from the notion of the educator as the traditional 'authorized knower' (de Laine 2001). This denotes moving towards a dialogic and collaborative relationship with students, where teachers and students can learn together and from one another in a constructivist way (Venäläinen 2010).

CREATING COLLABORATIVE FOOD EDUCATION IN FINLAND

In Finland, health education, home economics education, and school lunch provision are all considered to be a part of food education in schools. Food- and health-related themes are also taught in other school subjects, such as physical education and chemistry. In the Finnish National curriculum that will go into effect in 2016 (POPS 2014), food education will be one of the broad subject areas for teaching, which is why developing specific aims and operation models for schools is especially important and topical at the moment. Although there is still much potential for improvement, the Finnish format for food education already provides specific opportunities for executing collaborative food education in schools, such as school meals, cooperation between school subjects, and organization of student councils.

The connections between school food and young people's health are widely recognized (e.g., Raulio et al. 2010; Sahota et al. 2013; Elinder et al. 2014), therefore, the significance of developing the quality and organization of **school meals** is well supported. However, at present, there is remarkable variation among countries as to how serving and developing school meals are approached.[1] From an educational perspective, school meals can be seen either as simple eating events or understood in a more elaborated form of food education, as in this article, as contexts of learning about and experiencing food and different tastes, and as opportunities for contesting prevailing power relations. It is our argument that defining school meals narrowly as opportunities for nourishment leaves much of their pedagogical potential unused. Understanding the school meal situation as a versatile opportunity for food education means including children and adolescents more actively as partners in designing and developing school meals (Benn and Carlsson 2014; Risku-Norja et al. 2012). Evidence from prior studies suggests that comprehensive agendas that take into consideration both pupils and the staff members are key in conveying health-related messages (e.g., Kilgour et al. 2015).

In Finland, the provision of tax-paid hot school meals has been a part of health promotion in schools for over 60 years (FNBE 2008, 2012). The meals must meet nutritional guidelines and provide one-third of the students' daily energy intake. In recent years, much attention has been paid to the role and significance of the school catering staff. For example, the school catering staff's nutrition awareness and modern tracking systems have helped Finnish schools to offer lunches that are in line with national nutrition recommendations. Lintukangas (2009) has further stated that the presence and guidance of the school catering staff during school meals can help in building a trusting relationship with the adolescents. From adolescents' perspective, members of the school catering staff could also be a source of support and safety (Ibid.). However, this requires investing in educating school catering staff as food educational professionals, as well as making their roles more visible as a part of the broader school community. Nevertheless, the school catering staff has the potential to work as significant partners in developing food education on a school-wide level (Lintukangas and Palojoki 2015).

In addition, cooperation between different school subjects could be developed and strengthened for collaborative food education in schools. As an example, cooperation between home economics education and chemistry could prove to be fruitful and function as a platform for sustainable food education. This cooperation could help in illustrating for the students the link between food preparation and meal construction, and the chemical characteristics of food items and nutrients. In addition, school subjects that have not traditionally participated in food-related teaching, such as language instruction and art, could also provide creative and innovative ways for executing food education (Janhonen et al. 2016). As does all cooperation, this requires careful planning to ensure that the applications are genuinely engaging for the pupils and meet the broader educational aims. For example, Juntunen (2012) has suggested that providing activating and experiential learning opportunities is crucial in promoting a personally meaningful relationship to themes related to sustainability. In terms of participatory school lunch development and sustainable food education, students' active participation could mean including pupils in measuring the amounts of food waste produced in the school and analysing both its sources and broader impacts during class activities.

In recent years, initiatives for approaching food education on the level of the school community have increased in the Finnish context. This has resulted in a growing interest in school food councils, which are presently being established in many Finnish schools. School food councils can at their best strengthen collaboration between different actors in the school and engage young people in developing matters that affect them with respect to school food organization. However, it is important to note that school councils can also be differentiating and adult-led forms of activity engaging only a limited group of pupils; therefore, they may not measure up to their promise of democratic and genuine participation (Bjerke 2011; Rabello de Castro 2011). On an operational level, studies show that even though young people are often 'involved' in many ways in school-based projects and that their opinions are being heard as members of youth parliaments or scrutiny committees, their opportunities to influence are rarely visibly connected with immediate decisions about service design, delivery, and commissioning (Percy-Smith 2012; Rönnlund 2014). Furthermore, the decision points are often defined in relation to quite conventional norms and maintain the prevailing circumstances, rather than promote genuine change (Valentine 2011). These are important aspects to consider when designing and developing school meal councils with students in Finland and elsewhere. To give specific examples, students within school meal councils are typically involved with decorating the school's dining room, voting for a special meal to be served once a month, or informing their fellow students about upcoming events, but they could also be more broadly included in decisions about the organization and content of school meals. The aims of school meal councils are rarely initiated by students themselves; therefore, active participation may be lower. Nevertheless, if carefully planned, school food councils bear the potential to work as an effective part of participatory food education in schools.

In sum, school meals, cooperation between school subjects and school food councils, offer promising prospects for enhancing collaborative food education in schools. In addition to experiences from school meal development, studies from other contexts offer useful insights to consider when designing participatory food educational initiatives on the level of the school community. For example, Pantea's (2012) study of young people as volunteers concluded that adolescents were more inclined to engage when they were provided with clear instructions and their rights and responsibilities were clearly itemized. When they had a sense of project ownership, an opportunity to influence decision-making, and were afforded tasks including choice and flexibility. On the contrary, adolescents presented disengagement when there was role ambiguity, an excess of or confusion with rules, when adult authority was implemented without clear justifications or the overall atmosphere was perceived as unfriendly (Ibid.). Importantly, as Bjerke (2011) brings forth, pupils do not necessarily ask for total control over decision-making, but primarily wish to be treated with dignity and respect and to have an opportunity to express opinions. Nevertheless, joint responsibility and inclusion of all actors in schools requires a re-evaluation of aims and roles, which might demand re-organization of the formal structures and habitual practices of the school community.

CONCLUSION

Today, children and young people are increasingly seen as active agents and their agency is seen as an important concept in defining their rights and participation within educational practice (Backman et al. 2012; Bjerke 2011; Valentine 2011). Nonetheless, developmentalism as a theoretical stance still remains an influential approach in studying child–adult relationships (Rabello de Castro 2011). There is also a growing trend for seeing participation as an individual quality or a competence (Arnesen et al. 2010; Rönnlund 2014), and, in spite of good intentions, paternalistic and welfare approaches are often based on a premise that promotes integration to community and aims towards the child learning the norms and values transmitted by the broader culture (Aaltonen 2013; Stoecklin 2012). This poses a serious challenge to food education that aims to promote students' participation and agency, as well as collaboration between actors. Without approaches that take distance from top-down and adult-centred priorities, young people inevitably remain as actors with quite limited agency (Stoecklin 2012). Designing new models for action is especially important within Finnish food education now that participatory initiatives in schools are increasing and the importance of food education is being more broadly acknowledged in such official documents as the National Curriculum (Halinen 2015; POPS 2014). In addition, rigorous attempts to clarify the aims and core concepts of food education are crucial in order to support collaboration between different practitioners and promote long-lasting effects in schools.

Conceptualizing children and young people as active and reflexive agents requires acknowledgement of their ability to make real choices, also within the world of formal education (Redmond 2010). In participation work, this means genuinely including young people as partners in reaching a shared decision (Bjerke 2011), and potentially revising institutional aims (Rabello de Castro 2011). Valentine (2011) emphasizes that our understanding of children's agency should not be restricted to requirements for them to act as adults. Fleming (2012), on the other hand, calls for new ways for working in partnership with young people in schools and moving beyond young people 'having a say' to constructing meaningful dialogue. In this article, we suggest the concept of food sense as a potential platform for discussion and as a tool for specifying school level curriculums for food education. The presentation of the term food sense has further aimed at taking distance from the individual and knowledge-based focus that has been critiqued in reference to the concept food literacy. Our definition of food sense acknowledges the cultural, social, and societal dimensions of eating, the context- and practice-bound aspects of food choices, as well as the notion of sustainability according to its broad definition. In sum, the core idea of food sense is to be able to make sense of complex and wide-reaching subject areas that take root in everyday practices, as well as to understand the relations of one's own choices to community and structural surroundings. These skills are seen as ways to support healthy and sustainable eating in changing everyday situations.

The present article has provided examples of how food education is being currently executed in Finland, and aimed at offering insights for teachers working in schools beyond the Finnish context. It is evident that much work still needs to be done, in Finland and elsewhere, in order for food education to be acknowledged as a common responsibility and executed coherently throughout the school community. Promoting collaborative approaches within food education means re-evaluating the role(s) of adults and acknowledging also the educational potential of the school catering staff (Lintukangas 2009). From a teacher's perspective, changing the positions of the adult requires encountering pupils in a reflexive and interpretive manner, instead of adopting the traditional expert role. Importantly, meaningful dialogue connected with young people's everyday lives can offer educational professionals opportunities to see their own experiences in novel ways, and provide young people with spaces for developing their understanding of how their actions affect others and how other people's values and priorities might not always be in line with theirs

(Percy-Smith 2012). Finally, it is important to support the professionalism of teachers working within food education, such as home economics teachers, in order to successfully promote students' critical thinking and understanding of the consequences of individual choices (Håkansson 2015).

The overall aim of food education is to support people's health and well-being, as well as lifelong learning about food and eating. However, the means through which this aim is being pursued varies considerably. The historical backgrounds of food education lie in teaching citizens about nutrition and health, preventing nutritional deficiencies, and helping the poor. Today, food education is increasingly understood to include themes that relate to practical skill development, sustainability, and students' agency. These new trends and shifts in focus require re-evaluation in reference to the conceptual base, aims, and operation models of food education in schools. Promoting collaborative food education that acknowledges pupils' agency and participation means being open to different kinds of interpretations of healthy eating and valuing the experiences of those who are to be educated.

NOTES

1. More information about school food policies in different countries through The European Commission's Joint Research Centre's newsletter: https://ec.europa.eu/jrc/en/news/healthy-school-food-expo-milano-2015.

REFERENCES

Aaltonen, S. (2013). 'Trying to push things through': Forms and bounds of agency in transitions of school-age young people. *Journal of Youth Studies, 16*, 375–390.

Åbacka, G. (2008). *Att lära för livet hemma och i skolan: elevers uppfattningar av kost och hälsa, consumption och privat ekonomi samt hushåll och miljö* [To learn for life at home and at school: Students' perceptions of nutrition and health, consumption, as well as households and the environment]. Doctoral dissertation (monograph). University of Turku, Turku.

Arnesen, A.-L., Lahelma, E., Lundahl, L., & Öhrn, E. (2010). Agency in a changing educational context: Negotiations, collective actions, and resistance. *European Educational Research Journal, 9*, 159–163.

Arnold, J., & Clarke, J. (2014). What is 'Agency'? Perspectives in science education research. *International Journal of Science Education, 36,* 735–754.

Backman, Y., Alerby, E., Bergmark, U., Gardelli, Å., Hertting, K., Kostenius, C., & Öhrling, K. (2012). Learning within and beyond the classroom: Compulsory school students voicing their positive experiences of school. *Scandinavian Journal of Educational Research, 56,* 555–570.

Benn, J. (1996). *Kost i skolen – skolekost* [Food at school – School food]. Doctoral dissertation (monograph). Department of Biology, Geography and Home Economics, Köbenhavn: Danish School of Education.

Benn, J., & Carlsson, M. (2014). Learning through school meals? *Appetite, 78C,* 23–31.

Bjerke, H. (2011). 'It's the way they do it': Expressions of agency in child–adult relations at home and school. *Children and Society, 25,* 93–103.

Bransford, J., Brown, A., & Cocking, R. R. (Eds.). (2000). *How people learn— Brain, mind, experience, and school.* Washington, DC: National Academy Press.

Brembeck, H. (2013). The twenty-first-century "Food Consumer": The emergence of consumer science. In A. Murcott, W. Belasco, & P. Jackson (Eds.), *The handbook of food research* (pp. 293–308). USA & India: Bloomsbury.

Brooks, N., & Begley, A. (2014). Adolescent food literacy programmes: A review of the literature. *Nutrition & Dietetics, 71,* 158–171.

Brougère, G. (2012). Participation, learning and intercultural experience. In C. Baraldi & V. Ieverse (Eds.), *Participation, facilitation, and mediation: children and young people in their social contexts* (pp. 180–196). New York: Routledge.

Contento, I. (2011). *Nutrition education: Linking theory, research, and practice.* Sudbury: Jones and Bartlett Publishers.

Cook-Sather, A. (2002). Authorizing student perspectives: Towards trust, dialogue and change in education. *Educational Researcher, 31,* 3–14.

Cross, B. (2011). Becoming, being and having been: Practitioner perspectives on temporal stances and participation across children's services. *Children and Society, 25,* 26–36.

de Laine, M. (2001). *Fieldwork, participation, and practice: Ethics and dilemmas of qualitative research.* London: Sage.

Elinder, L. S., Heinemans, N., Zeebari, Z., & Patterson, E. (2014). Longitudinal changes in health behaviours and body weight among Swedish school children – Associations with age, gender and parental education – The SCIP school cohort. *BMC Public Health, 14,* 1503–1521.

Falk, P., & Gronow, J. (1985). Ravintotiede ja ruokahalun disiplinointi [Nutrition science and the disciplining of appetite]. *Tiede & Edistys, 1*(85), 47–53.

Fleming, J. (2012). Young people's participation—Where next? *Children and Society, 27,* 484–495.

FNBE (Finnish National Board of Education). (2008). School meals in Finland—Investment on learning. Available at: http://www.oph.fi/download/47657_school_meals_in_finland.pdf. Accessed 6 Aug 2014.

FNBE (Finnish National Board of Education). (2012). Finnish education in a nutshell. Education in Finland. Available at: http://www.oph.fi/download/146428_Finnish_Education_in_a_Nutshell.pdf. Accessed 7 Apr 2015.

Gad, C., & Jensen, C. B. (2014). The promises of practice. *The Sociological Review, 62*, 698–718.

Gussow, J. D., & Contento, I. (1984). Nutrition education in a changing world. A conceptualization and selective review. *World Review of Nutrition and Dietetics, 44*, 1–56.

Hager, P. (2012). Informal learning. In P. Jarvis & M. Watts (Eds.), *The Routledge international handbook of learning* (pp. 207–215). Great Britain, USA and Canada: Routledge.

Håkansson, A. (2015). Indoctrination or education? Intention of unqualified teachers to transfer consumption norms in home economics teaching. *International Journal of Consumer Studies, 39*, 682–691.

Halinen, I. (2015). What is going on in Finland? – Curriculum reform 2016. Available at: http://www.oph.fi/english/current_issues/101/0/what_is_going_on_in_finland_curriculum_reform_2016. Accessed 15 May 2015.

Hirdman, Y. (1983). *Magfrågan: mat som mål och medel: Stockholm 1870–1920* [The question of the stomach: Food as an aim and a tool]. Rabén & Sjögren: Tema nova.

Höijer, K. (2013). *Contested food. The construction of home and consumer studies as a cultural space*. Doctoral dissertation (articles). Digital Comprehensive Summaries of Uppsala Dissertations from the Faculty of Social Sciences 89.

Hoikkala, T., Hakkarainen, P., & Laine, S. (Eds.). (2005). *Beyond health literacy. Youth cultures, prevention and policy*. Helsinki: Finnish Youth Research Society and Stakes.

Jackson, P. (2013). Nutrition. In P. Jackson (Ed.), *Food words. Essays in culinary culture* (pp. 148–149). London/New York: Bloomsbury Academic.

Janhonen, K., Mäkelä, J., & Palojoki, P. (2015). *Peruskoulun ruokakasvatus ravintotiedosta ruokatajuun* [Secondary school food education from nutritional knowledge to food sense]. In H. Janhonen-Abruquah, & P. Palojoki (Eds.), *Creative and responsible home economics education*. University of Helsinki, Department of Teacher Education, in press.

Janhonen, K., Mäkelä, J., & Palojoki, P. (2016). Adolescents' school lunch practices as an educational resource. *Health Education, 116*, 292–309.

Juntunen, M. (2012). *Kestävä kehitys kemian opetuksessa: Lähestymistapana ympäristötietoisuutta edistävä tutkimuksellinen elinkaariajattelu* [Sustainable development in chemistry education: Research approach supporting life cycle-thinking and environmental awareness]. Licentiate thesis, University of Helsinki, Faculty of Science, Department of Chemistry.

Kilgour, L., Matthews, N., Christian, P., & Shire, J. (2015). Health literacy in schools: Prioritising health and well-being issues through the curriculum. *Sport, Education & Society, 20*, 485–500.

Kimura, A. (2011). Food education as food literacy: Privatized and gendered food knowledge in contemporary Japan. *Agriculture and Human Values, 28*, 465–482.

Koistinen, A., & Ruhanen, L. (Eds.). (2009). *Aistien avulla ruokamaailmaan. Sapere -menetelmä päivähoidon ravitsemus ja ruokakasvatuksen tukena* [Entering the world of food through the senses. The Sapere method as a support in daycare nutrition and food education]. Jyväskylän kaupungin sosiaali- ja terveyspalvelukeskuksen raportteja 1/2009. Helsinki: Sitra, Suomen itsenäisyyden juhlarahasto.

Kuusikorpi, M. (Ed.). (2014). *Perspectives from Finland – Towards new learning environments*. Finnish National Board of Education: Publications 2014:1. Tampere: Juvenes Print – Suomen Yliopistopaino Oy.

Lintukangas, S. (2009). *Kouluruokailuhenkilöstö matkalla kasvattajaksi* [School catering staff on the way to become educators]. Kotitalous- ja käsityötieteiden laitoksen julkaisuja 20. Doctoral thesis. Helsinki: Yliopistopaino.

Lintukangas, S., & Palojoki, P. (2015). School catering staff as food educators. In Hille Janhonen-Abruquah & Päivi Palojoki (Eds.), *Creative and responsible home economics education*. University of Helsinki, Department of Teacher Education, in press.

Mäkelä, J., & Niva, M. (2015). Citizens and sustainable culinary cultures. In A. Paloviita & M. Järvelä (Eds.), *Climate change adaptation and food supply chain management* (pp. 172–182). London: Routledge, Forthcoming.

Marks, R. (2012). *Health literacy and school-based health education*. Bingley: Emerald.

Morgan, K., & Sonnino, R. (Eds.). (2008). *The school food revolution: Public food and the challenge of sustainable development*. London: Earthscan.

Nutbeam, D. (2009). Defining and measuring health literacy: What can we learn from literacy studies? *International Journal of Public Health, 54*, 303–305.

Ojajärvi, A. (2015). *Terve sotilas! Etnografinen tutkimus varusmiesten terveysta-justa sosiaalisena ilmiönä* [Healthy soldier! Ethnographic study of servicemen's health sense as a social phenomenon]. Youth Research Network/ Finnish Youth Research Society, publications 163.

Ormshaw, M., Paakkari, L., & Kannas, L. (2013). Measuring child and adolescent health literacy: A systematic review of literature. *Health Education, 113*, 433–455.

Paakkari, L., & Paakkari, O. (2012). Health literacy as a learning outcome in schools. *Health Education, 112*, 133–152.

Palojoki, P. (1997). *The complexity of food-related Activities in a household context. Study of Finnish homemakers' food choices and nutrition knowledge.* Doctoral dissertation (monograhph). Research report 172. Department of Teachers Education, University of Helsinki, Helsinki.

Pantea, M.-C. (2012). Young volunteers' perspectives on their interactions with adults in position to facilitate their participation. In C. Baraldi & V. Ieverse (Eds.), *Participation, facilitation, and mediation: Children and young people in their social contexts* (pp. 161–179). New York: Routledge.

Park, J. Y. (2011). Design education online: Learning delivery and evaluation. *International Journal of Art and Design Education, 30*, 176–187.

Pekkarinen, E., & Vehkalahti, K. (2012). Johdanto: Instituutiot lapsuutta ja nuoruutta rakentamassa – lapset ja nuoret instituutioita uudistamassa [Introduction: Institutions constructing childhood and youth – children and young people rebuilding institutions]. In E. Pekkarinen, K. Vehkalahti & S. Myllyniemi (Eds.), *Lapset ja nuoret instituutioiden kehyksissä, Nuorten elinolot -vuosikirja 2012* (pp. 9–22.). Youth Research Network/ Finnish Youth Research Society, publications 131.

Pendergast, D., & Dewhurst, Y. (2012). Home economics and food literacy: An international investigation. *International Journal of Home Economics, 5*, 245–263.

Percy-Smith, B. (2012). Participation as mediation and social learning. Empowering children as actors in social contexts. In C. Baraldi & V. Ieverse (Eds.), *Participation, facilitation, and mediation: Children and young people in their social contexts* (pp. 12–29). New York: Routledge.

POPS. (2014). *Perusopetuksen opetussuunnitelman perusteet* [The basics of the national curriculum]. Available in Finnish at: http://www.oph.fi/download/163777_perusopetuksen_opetussuunnitelman_perusteet_2014.pdf

Puuronen, A. (2006). Mitä on terveys – tietoa, taitoa vai tajua? [What is health – Knowledge, skill or sense?]. In A. Puuronen (Ed.), *Terveystaju. Nuoret, politiikka ja käytäntö* (pp. 5–20). Finnish Youth Research Society: Youth Research Network/ Finnish Youth Research Society, publications 63.

Rabello de Castro, L. (2011). The 'good-enough society', the 'good-enough citizen' and the 'good-enough student': Where is children's participation agenda moving to in Brazil? *Childhood, 19*, 52–68.

Raulio, S., Roos, E., & Prättälä, R. (2010). School and workplace meals promote healthy food habits. *Public Health Nutrition, 13*, 987–992.

Rautavirta, K. (2010). *Petusta pitsaan – Ruokahuollon järjestelyt kriisiaikojen Suomessa* [From bark bread to pizza. Food and exeptional circumstances: Reactions of Finnish society to crises of food supply]. University of Helsinki, Faculty of Agriculture and Forestry, Department of Food and Environmental Sciences. Doctoral dissertation (monograph). Helsinki: Yliopistopaino.

Redmond, G. (2010). Children's agency and the welfare state: Policy priorities and contradictions in Australia and the UK. *Childhood, 17,* 470–484.

Risku-Norja, H., Jeronen, E., Kurppa, S., Mikkola, M., & Uitto, A. (Eds.). (2012). *Ruoka – Oppimisen edellytys ja opetuksen voimavara* [Food – The prerequisite of learning and asset of education]. Helsinki: University of Helsinki, Ruralia Institute, Publications 25.

Rönnlund, M., Anne-Lise, A., Lahelma, E., & Lisbeth, L. (2014). Democratic challenges: Students' active participation in everyday school life. In Ö. Elisabeth (Ed.), *Fair and competitive? Critical perspectives on contemporary Nordic schooling* (pp. 23–40). London: Tufnell Press.

Sahota, P., Woodward, J., Molinari, R., & Pike, J. (2013). Factors influencing take-up of free school meals in primary- and secondary-school children in England. *Public Health Nutrition, 17,* 1271–1279.

Smith, D. (2013). The politics of food and nutrition policies. In A. Murcott, W. Belasco, & P. Jackson (Eds.), *The handbook of food research* (pp. 398–409). USA and India: Bloomsbury.

Sørensen, K., Van den Broucke, S., Fullam, J., Doyle, G., Pelikan, J., Slonska, Z., & Brand, H. (2012). Health literacy and public health: A systematic review and integration of definitions and models. *BMC Public Health, 12,* 80.

Spencer, G., & Doull, M. (2015). Examining concepts of power and agency in research with young people. *Journal of Youth Studies, 18,* 900–913.

Speros, C. (2005). Health literacy: Concept analysis. *Journal of Advanced Nursing, 50,* 633–640.

Stoecklin, D. (2012). Theories of action in the field of child participation: In search of explicit frameworks. *Childhood, 20,* 443–457.

Sumner, J. (2013). Eating as if it really matteres: Teaching the pedagogy of food in the age of globalization. *Brock Education Journal – Special issue: The Impact of Globalization for Adult Education and Higher Education, 22,* 41–55.

Vaitkeviciute, R., Ball, L., & Harris, N. (2015). The relationship between food literacy and dietary intake in adolescents: A systematic review. *Public Health Nutrition, 18,* 649–658.

Valentine, K. (2011). Accounting for agency. *Children and Society, 25,* 347–358.

Venäläinen, S. (2010). *Interaction in the multicultural classroom: Towards culturally sensitive home economics education.* Doctoral dissertation (monograph). University of Helsinki, Faculty of Behavioural Sciences, Department of Teacher Education.

Vidgen, H., & Galleos, D. (2014). Defining food literacy and its components. *Appetite, 76,* 50–59.

PART III

Learning, Food, and Sustainability in Social Movements

Learning through Story as Political Praxis: The Role of Narratives in Community Food Work

Kim L. Niewolny and Phil D'Adamo-Damery

INTRODUCTION

As Melissa Orlie (2009) has noted, the "madness" of the industrial food system is increasingly difficult to deny. The manner in which this dominant system operates has resulted in socioeconomic and ecological excesses that cannot be sustained. For over three decades, there has been a groundswell of academic, policy, and community-based concern and activism around this social, economic, and ecological unsustainability. The academic literature, for instance, is replete with works theorizing and advocating approaches for building alternative food systems that stem from a range of disciplinary perspectives and methodological orientations (e.g., Allen 1993, 2004, 2010; Alkon and Agyeman 2011; Constance et al. 2014; Feenstra 2002; Goodman et al. 2014; Hendrickson and Heffernan 2002; Hinrichs 2003; Lang 2009; Kirschenmann and Falk 2010). The grassroots sector has been particularly accredited with the emergence of alternative food movements and networks in the Global North and Global South (Allen 2004). These movements embrace such expressions as local and regional food systems

K.L. Niewolny (✉) • P. D'Adamo-Damery
Department of Agricultural, Leadership and Community Education,
Virginia Tech, Blacksburg, VA, USA

© The Author(s) 2016
J. Sumner (ed.), *Learning, Food, and Sustainability*,
DOI 10.1057/978-1-137-53904-5_7

(Clancy and Ruhf 2010), community food work (Slocum 2007), community food security (Hamm and Bellows 2003), and food sovereignty (Patel 2009). Although social purposes, locations, and approaches vary, the work of movement actors can be seen as a massive effort to challenge and transform the pervasive and hegemonic gender-race-class politics of food access and availability (Julier 2015). The ways in which food movement sectors variably perform as a response to the wake of globalizing forces fueled by neoliberal conditions and policies is also worthy of note (Guthman 2008). These food movement discourses, and their sociohistorical roots, therefore, serve as a rich seedbed for social critique, knowledge creation, and social action that not only informs political strategies and social agendas but also emphasizes the everyday experiences of struggle and oppression that intersect with the complexity of our food system politics.

We begin with reference to Henry Giroux's (1992) scholarship to suggest that this multiplicity of movement activity is an expression of education as **cultural work.** While cultural work has been generally used to refer to the contributions of artists and writers, Giroux extended it to include the performances of educators, asserting the "primacy of the political and pedagogical" (p. 5). In other words, it is the task of educators—broadly defined to include scholars, activists, and practitioners—to work within and across our communities (be they global or local) to nurture a healthy skepticism and scrutiny of the knowledge cultures that govern. Giroux, who has advocated for a praxis of cultural politics, puts forward that the role of cultural workers is that of "radical reflection on our interpretive frames" to focus on the conditions and means in which knowledges and our realities are (re)produced (p. 13). Cultural work, as moments of learning, thus provides us with a useful lens to help us navigate the epistemological and ontological conditions that inform our practices of resistance and change in alternative food system circles.

It is in this context of cultural work and alternative food movements that we bring together conceptual and methodological arguments with instances of stories to illustrate the educative role narratives can play in engendering political praxis and new possibilities. Drawing upon the critical arm of adult education (e.g., Freire 1972), narrative inquiry as methodology (e.g., Clandinin and Connelly 2000), the emergence of "ontological politics" (e.g., Law 2008; Mol 2002, 1999), and the discourse of community food work (e.g., Slocum 2007), we recognize and embrace the generative quality of narratives in the telling, reading, and (re) creating of stories of practitioners and activists striving to transform the food system in ways that purportedly align with a number of alternative food movements. These instances of cultural work comprise stakeholder interests that embody a wide breadth practical strategies and agendas, and emphasize a diversity of political relationships illustrating the complexity and tensions that inform, and are informed by, food system discourses and their material realities. Specifically, we look to our narrative initiative within the Appalachian Foodshed Project (AFP) in the southern USA to provide an illustration of ways in which narratives and storytelling may open means to humanize the "wicked problem" of food insecurity while creating new possibilities in our everyday work of resistance and learning. We put forward that when facing a complex problem like food insecurity, "seeing" the system better means understanding a plurality of perspectives on the issue and ways to engage with it (Hamm 2009). In other words, it is through story that this generative process may flourish.

Our aim here is also inspired by our own hopefulness and critical praxis as educators embedded in the work of community food and alternative food systems. The following sections are therefore a brief foray into the conceptual and methodological literature informing this story making process as a politicized educational project. To do so, we share the frameworks, processes, and moments of story that are a part of the narrative-building work of the AFP. It is important to note that the impetus for creating a narrative project in central Appalachia comes from the movement actors themselves who are eager to develop a regional food systems network to address food (in)security yet struggle with the formative process of crafting and weaving their stories and actions together. What follows are therefore glimpses into their experiences learning for and about the intersections of food system politics and the possibilities for change. First, we give attention to the tradition of adult and community education to explore these experiences through the lens of political praxis. Next, we provide a brief reference to alternative food movement literature to situate our crafting of narratives of community food work in the central Appalachian region. We then explore the epistemological and ontological considerations that inspire the narrative making process and our argument for (re)creating stories as a generative process of learning, knowing, and action. Lastly, we turn to specific instances of story from the AFP as an illustration of the humanizing way in which narratives help us critically engage the "wicked problems" of our food system while also creating spaces of possibilities and hope.

Praxis and Community Food Work

We draw upon the tradition of adult and community education for exploring narratives of community food work as a radical educational project. Adult education has historically focused on catalyzing groups for collective learning and social action (Brookfield and Holst 2011; Cunningham 1992; Foley 1999). The scale and complexity of today's social, cultural, and environmental problems continue to demand lifelong, relational, and reflexive learning processes and frameworks to engender social justice and community resilience (Niewolny and Archibald 2015). For many, these processes are informed by participatory and emancipatory approaches where learners and educators negotiate socially constructed and politicalized knowledges, experiences, and practices (Cevaro and Wilson 2001). Adult and community-based educators amply developed and utilized popular education as a powerful means for transformative action within development agendas and social movements, for the purpose of crafting cultural and social equity (Mayo 1999; Freire 1972). In this view, learning takes on an explicitly critical position that is focused on the complex ways knowledge is (re)produced and controlled, and the ways in which social actors learn for social resistance and change. In community development circles, these processes have been partnered with such discourses as participatory learning (Campbell and Burnaby 2001), action research (Greenwood and Levin 2007), and social movement learning (Crowther 2006; Holst 2002). Although these discourses represent different theories and take up different terms, a thread across each is an engagement with reflectivity toward language, power, and politics in practice.

It is from this perspective we derive our operational understanding of **praxis** through the crafting of narratives as spaces for learning. Praxis is a concept dating back to Aristotle through (post)Marx and feminism that embodies certain qualities of reflexivity underpinning a commitment to the continual and generative interplay between thought and action (Carr and Kemmis 1986; Lather 1991). For Thompson and Pascal (2012), the concept of critical or political praxis provides actors the means to create spaces of possibility in/from/with practice that is performed, theorized, and reflected on, re-imagined, and then re-performed as praxis takes new form. Praxis further arises as a dialogical and intersubjective learning process most notably associated with Freire's (1972) *Pedagogy of the Oppressed*. Here Freire frames praxis as the potential for diverse possibilities to emerge through the process of humanization, which through reflection and action, transforms realities and is the source of knowledge creation.

The political praxis of "narratives as learning" is embedded within and informed by a number of food system discourses and life-world experiences. Across many efforts toward a more sustainable, less "disruptive" food system, these discourses and their social practices vary. Participatory development and education have contributed to the formation of alternative food systems through knowledge claims that celebrate the complexity, diversity, and localization of experience and knowledge politics (Glezner et al. 2011; Hassanein and Kloppenburg 1995; Pretty 1995; Röling and Wagemakers 1998; Stevenson et al. 2007). While understood as unique social movements, collectively calling for an alternative food system, they take on particular expressions of social critique, knowledge creation, and community action that inform the everyday experiences of struggle and oppression that intersects with our global food system politics (Allen 2004; Goodman et al. 2014; Hassanein 2003; Hinrichs 2003).

From a historical lens, alternative food movements take on a number of food access and food availability issues, politics, and priorities. To put it differently, they are shaped by conflicting and intersecting economic, social, material, and cultural aims derived from the Global North and Global South (Julier 2015). For Constance et al. (2014), this conflict and intersectionality can be read through the description of four kinds of alternative food system efforts with emphases and attachments to: the biophysical sustainability of food production; life quality for farmers and agrarian communities; food access, quality, and human health; and emancipatory possibilities for socially just food systems.

The demand for social justice has informed the direction and strategies of alternative food system movements in recent years. The notion of food justice does not necessarily prescribe clear routes to establish a more just food system; instead, it provides a language and vision to open up pathways for action and advocacy (Gottlieb and Joshi 2010). Both academic and grassroots communities are increasingly engaged in food justice work as a means to critique the social, economic, and political hegemony in our food system, calling much needed attention to racial, gendered, and class relationships and intersections in the control over the production and consumption of food (Allen 2010; Alkon and Agyeman 2011; Guthman 2008; Slocum 2007).

For the purposes of this chapter, we have chosen to interact with three alternative food movement discourses according to the intended end goals of our narrative project to engage with the generative possibility of stories as sites of learning and knowing. Therefore, it is not our intention to focus on one alternative food movement (e.g., food security) or social movement sector (e.g., sustainable food production); instead, we embrace the intersections of **community food systems, community food security,** and **community food work** as fluid concepts and "community-level" discourses, to better embrace the multiplicity of "cultural worker" experiences and their possibilities for change in our food systems. We acknowledge, however, a number of scholars who have more adequately provided a comprehensive explanation of the history of alternative food movements (see Allen 2004; Constance et al. 2014; Goodman et al. 2014).

First, *community food systems* is a concept that has been under-theorized and consequently invoked in contradictory ways (Feenstra 2002; Feenstra and Campbell 1996). We view the concept as an attempted response to the "local trap," which is building upon Born and Purcell's (2006) argument challenging the popular notion that local food systems are inherently more sustainable or more socially just simply based on their scale. Whereas the supply chain element of local and regional food systems might be instrumentalized to economic ends and geographical scale, community food systems includes a more explicitly social component. In one article, Feenstra (2002) described a community food system as "a collaborative effort to build more locally based, self-reliant food economies—one in which sustainable food production, processing, distribution and consumption are integrated to enhance the economic, environmental and social health of a particular place" (p. 100). The system described here has the hallmarks of the local and regional food systems with the addition of an emphasis on social health. The meaning of social health is unclear, but it creates an (albeit, small) impediment to economic instrumentalization. In the cited definition, Feenstra (2002) challenged the assumption of community food system as a noun by terming it a process—a verb. This may be read to illustrate the shifting composition of food systems—denoting their nature as one of process rather than a static and pre-determined end.

Related to the discourse of community food systems is *community food security*. Here we point to Hamm and Bellows' (2003) definition as "a situation in which all community residents obtain a safe, culturally acceptable, nutritionally adequate diet through a sustainable food system that maximizes community self-reliance and social justice" (p. 37). Following the emergence of the local food movement in North America, we see a growing concern for our ability to fairly and justly address the "wicked problem" of food security (Hamm 2009). Since the 1990s, publicly and privately funded initiatives have surged to tackle the complex issues of food access and availability with/in limited resource communities under the umbrella of community food security (Allen 2004). These initiatives illustrate the complexity of food system politics that stretch across our urban and rural landscapes (Pothukuchi et al. 2007).

It should be noted, however, that Hamm and Bellows (2003) are perhaps describing an end goal or something to be attained. In the literature, we have found the connections between community food systems and security to be implicit; however, we suggest that community food systems are the process through which the goals of community food security might be achieved. For instance, Abi-Nader et al. (2009) have posited six fields of practice that constitute community food security work: justice and fairness; strong communities; vibrant farms and gardens; healthy people; sustainable ecosystems; and thriving local economies. The first two fields underpin the latter four (Embry et al. 2012).

Lastly, we refer to the description of alternative food movements to be an expression of *community food work*. Drawing from Slocum (2007), we embrace this terminology throughout our own praxis due to its politicized and inclusive meaning that embraces both the processes and end goals of alternative food movement work. Slocum articulated four domains that constitute alternative food efforts, those that focus on: (1) farm sustainability—related to connecting small-scale farmers to markets; (2) nutrition education—with emphases on the prevention of diet-related illnesses; (3) environmental sustainability—related to the development and support of more ecologically sound agricultural production; and (4) social justice—which consists of a bifurcated approach—producer/worker rights and hunger/food insecurity. Slocum termed the integration of these approaches, *community food work*. Tanaka et al. (2015) further acknowledge both movement processes and goals in defining community food work as "facilitating concerned citizens, activists, and professionals to build capacity to define and address food-security challenges in their own communities" (p. 2).

To be clear, these alternative food demarcations are not mutually exclusive, and do, in fact, overlap in many important ways. We value their histories of meanings and their intersectionality. With that said, we argue that the cultural work of community food should include spaces to "unthink" the orthodoxies and the knowledge cultures that are governing our ideas of the possible. In this vein, we now turn to the epistemological and ontological potential of narratives of community food work.

Epistemological and Ontological Considerations of Community Food Work

Our understanding of narratives and their potential for doing community food work hinges upon our critique of essentialist epistemologies. An essentialist epistemology functions from the belief that things have knowable fixed essences that can be defined and captured through language. For example, to be considered community food work, a practitioner might actively seek to counter neoliberal hegemony. This is an essentialist reading of community food work, attributing to it a true essence that can be either affixed or denied to certain forms of food system activism. While this form of reading and understanding practice lends a certain critical aim to scholarship and educational thought, we suggest that it may oversimplify the multiple entanglements of such efforts, and thus mutes the transformative potential of community food work. Since a transformed food system is a fundamental goal of community food work (Slocum 2007), we argue that anti-essentialist approaches to reading these practices bear consideration.

As an epistemological starting point, we ask, "What knowledges are we validating and valorizing through our scholarship and practice?" Consonant with Foucault (1980), Law and Urry (2004), and Gibson-Graham et al. (2001), the ways we enact and produce knowledges have world-making potential. As adult and community educators, do we sift through the swarms of difference and reify essentialized understandings and concepts or do we point to the non-coherence of our social entanglements and seek openings for novel ways of thought and the creation of new generative concepts (Deleuze and Guatarri 1994)?

Our knowledge production is not discrete and isolated, it has direct impacts on the "the conditions of possibility we live with" (Mol 1999, p. 75). The ways that we write and talk about community food work are not about accessing a true essence; rather, these are the lines of thought that we choose to make more real—which in turn, striate a path for future thought—making certain futures more conceivable than others. The scholar/practitioner's choice to striate certain lines of thinking calls attention to the political nature of knowledge production and its impact on the conditions of the possible. This is what some thinkers have termed ontological politics (Mol 1999; Law 1999). As community food cultural workers, how might we ethically engage with the ontological productivity of our work?

We argue that a response to this question involves movement from realist epistemologies that rely on the assumptions of a singular coherent reality that can be captured in essentialized representational language, to creative epistemologies that assume heterogeneity. This means a shift from seeking to understand what *is* happening to explorations of performativity. What worlds are being done or made through our practices, and more importantly, how could they be done differently? This methodological positioning is movement from attempting to understand what is "actually happening" to modes of unknowing (Gibson-Graham 2006). This shifts the educator's relationship with praxis. We view praxis as entangled with theory. The production of and engagement with theory is in itself an ontological, world-making activity. The distinction between theory and praxis carries the implication that the latter acts in the material world, while the former is discrete and removed—belonging to the abstract. But this reading of theory imbues it with what Alfred North Whitehead (1925) termed, misplaced concreteness, "the accidental error of mistaking the abstract for the concrete" (p. 72). This is where narrative enters our work.

What might we, as scholars, practitioners, and activists, learn from the narratives constructed by those connected in our multiple communities? Are such narratives the raw material of epistemological reification and ontological sedimentation or might they be otherwise? We understand narratives as spaces for performative experimentation, for exploring the possible. Rather than a plane for excavation and assessment, they can be grounds for discovering difference and heterogeneity, and a fecund place for experimenting with ways to "make a difference in those differences" (Law 2008, p. 637). For the community food worker, we argue narratives as spaces for learning—less for best practices, more for experimentations with possibilities of the new.

Learning for Community Food Work through Story

Drawing upon these epistemological, ontological, and methodological questions, we turn to one particular example of learning for community food work—the AFP. The AFP aims to address rural issues of alternative food systems and community food security in the Appalachian areas of West Virginia, North Carolina, and Virginia through a regional research, outreach, and educational plan. Funded by the United States Department of Agriculture (USDA), the AFP creatively works with communities, farmers, policy makers, non-profit organizations, and university institutions to build community capacity and organizational cohesion while implementing positive changes across the food system, especially in communities that have been politically isolated and historically underserved.

Since 2013, we, as a scholar/practitioner community, have generated 54 narratives, or "practice stories," from regional activists, educators, and practitioners who operate in community food work and, in some explicit instances, the community food security movement (Niewolny and D'Adamo-Damery 2014; D'Adamo-Damery 2014). These actors are involved in a variety of organizations, but each is in some way connected to the broader issues of food system change articulated in the previous sections of this chapter. The geographic region covered by the AFP is composed of mountains—hollers and hills—which can make travel from one community to another circuitous, time-consuming, and in many instances, downright difficult. On one level, the sharing of narratives of work and practice has been important to our regional community, a way to circumvent the barriers to learning enacted by geographic and geologic boundaries. On another level, we suggest that these narratives have epistemological and ontological connections across our immanently constructed hills and hollers—the essentialist patterns of thought that ossify current connections and make new thought circuitous, time-consuming, and downright difficult.

As we noted in the opening section, the material and corporeal effects of our food system are a maddening and wicked problem. For some, food insecurity is a profound issue that cannot be "solved" with uniform solutions or technical answers but rather by systems and spaces of integration, coordination, and experimentation that are geared toward emergence and the generation of the new (D'Adamo-Damery et al. 2015; Snowden 2002). Particularly, we argue here, by drawing upon a philosophy of difference and possibility (see Deleuze and Guattari 1980/1987), that such spaces are opulent places of new knowledges of community food work that productively contest *and* add to our conceptions of justice and hope, thus opening new possibilities for life-affirming effects with/in the food system. We suggest that narratives contain these spaces. Within the stories we have collected, there lies an ordinary, singular, and unfinished quality that "is not so much a deficiency as a resource, like a fog of immanent forces still moving even though so much has already happened and there seems to be plenty that's set in stone" (Stewart 2007, p. 127). The uneven unfinishedness of the narratives are connected, here and there, as the reader plugs into the narrative, but something ontological is done as the reader of the edited and compiled narratives reads. As Manning (2009) observed, "things aren't as stable as you thought they were" (p. 97). Though they have been constrained through textual representation, narratives retain shreds of heterogeneity of difference, imbued with affect, in which the reader connects to and with.

Before delving into the narrative excerpts, we want to briefly cover some of our thought, methodology, and methods that went into generating the narratives. Our general approach is in the realm of **narrative inquiry** (Connelly and Clandinin 2005). We use the definition of "narrative" to mean both a process and a product in this particular design and approach (Richmond 2002). This includes treating the stories as both a *process* of reflexivity through storytelling and the *products* of engaging, activity and performativity, with everyday knowledges that inform community food work practice. In terms of community direction and involvement in this effort, we followed action research principles (Greenwood and Levin 2007) with regional practitioners participating in the initial design of storytelling prompts, questions, and locations to conduct the narratives. This approach allowed the practitioners to tell their own stories of community food work through a series of "prompting" questions to emphasize their personal meanings and histories. The in-depth interview process took approximately two hours and was oriented for practitioners to share: (1) her/his/their past experiences in the community and/or community food work, (2) a current illustration of community food work that is significantly meaningful, and (3) future hopes, aspirations, and intentions for their community food work. Following our university's Institutional Review Board processes, each narrative was consented to, audio-recorded, transcribed, re-transcribed with editing, and configured as a public "narrative" through a co-reading and framing process with the interviewers and practitioners. This co-authoring process included careful attention to practitioner responses and consent for public use. It is important to note that the narratives have a number of intersections with learning in the region and beyond. This includes the personal and reflexive experiences of the interviewers and practitioners as narrative authors. It also comprises newly crafted knowledges and realities of community food work from across our Appalachian communities through the dissemination of the stories. The narratives also have purpose in generating creativity and idea-making capacity within our university classrooms and public settings in the reading and (re)telling of these stories of cultural work. Lastly, and more broadly speaking, we suggest that the generative quality of the narratives has the capacity to craft productive, "life affirming" possibilities for hope and social change in our learning of community food work from across the central Appalachian region.

In what follows, we have pulled three short excerpts from the narratives of central Appalachian community food work. These examples were selected for various reasons, not the least of which are the multiplicity of resonances, waiting to be taken up by the reader. Consonant with D'Adamo-Damery (2014), we argue that the juxtaposition of multiple, affectively chosen narrative excerpts sets off series of vibrations and resonances between the text and the networked reader (Manning 2009). In moments of engagement with the narrative, meaning is made immanently. To put it differently, the reader populates the excerpts with meaning as s/he/they read the text. The meaning does not exist a priori. This means, making sense of the text as a "middle," not necessarily a beginning or end (Deleuze and Guattari 1980/1987). Although this experience may be disorienting, we have found it useful to enter the text with a degree of unknowing, uncertainty, and openness—reading for resonances, difference—probing the possible.

corner store I think that this corner store project really shows that this work has to be benefitting all of the key players. The store-owner has to be making money off of it; it has to be at a price that the people are willing and able to pay for it, and then it needs to be reliable.... I think food systems work is very segregated, like "We're doing it for obesity," and "Well we're doing it for farmers' rights." And then, "Well we're doing it for animal rights." And it's like "No, no, we're all doing the same thing." If we could just find some common language and start breaking down some of those barriers. Like who doesn't want healthy corner store options that the owner is making money off of? The more money she makes the more taxes she has to pay and the more we get that money back. So it's like every single avenue. The more healthy food she sells the more healthy food she can buy. The more healthy food she can buy the more farmers get to produce them. It's like there's a whole cycle of people who are being affected, but because we so often only think of like "You only care about it being low calorie, you only care about it being local, and you only care..." It's like, "We're all working towards the same thing." Our partners can really look like anything as long as that common goal is shared.

perspective I've found most people coming at farm-to-school come from a health perspective, so they're not thinking about the farmer, and they're not thinking about the economic piece of the work. Because when we actually started this farm-to-school work, our first question was, "Is this a market that's good for farmers? Can farmers make money?" Access to other more lucrative markets would make farm-to-school less appealing to farmers, as it should. Farmers, bottom line, have to make money. We've really come around to thinking that the educational components are what are needed. The elephant in the room around school food is that schools just don't have enough money to spend on food. After they pay everything they have to pay; their salaries, their equipment costs, their indirect costs, they have about a dollar left over per meal. That's just not sufficient, not to do all the things we want it to do. And it's not their fault. And so until we address the basic funding issue we're not going to see it. We can grant support things all day in different parts of the country in different schools, but that's not a long-term solution. So we'd rather focus on the educational components: the school gardens, the cooking, the cafeteria taste tests, and the farm field trips. Even if you drastically change that plate, if there's not the education to go with it, why would the kids respond to it? It's just unknown.

moving forward I am looking forward to not being so mad about decisions that are made for me instead of with me. I'm excited about that. I really do want to live in a world where we are more valued; especially these huge populations of people who are suffering from these systems that we've created. You can't put blame on a person who is operating in a system that's holding them down. And so whether that's ageism or poverty or racism. I'm looking forward to those things being a little less heavy on everything that we're doing. I mean we already do value people, we just do it wrong. The wrong people are getting paid the wrong amount of money for the wrong things. And not everyone. There are a lot of people out there making good dollars, and they should continue making it, but where do we place value? We aren't giving people the skills they need, and then we're mad that they are not able to produce anything. And I'm like "This was your system. They went through your public health care, your public school system, who do you have to blame for that?" I totally believe in those programs. I just believe that it's too little too late. It needed to be done when they were six months old with health care and education and job training for their parents. We are constantly looking for the next policy or environment we can try to change. The youth are the ones telling us, especially because they're the ones living it. And some of its funding. Right now we can get money to do food security work because the need is there. And so, in 10 years, wherever that funding need is, is where the need is, and hopefully it will be more of a holistic view.

Conclusion: Considerations and Possibilities

Our entry into this chapter began with Melissa Orlie's reference to the increasing madness of the industrial food system, and it is our disaffection with the material and bodily inequities of this madness that guides our ongoing connection to community food work. The agri-food studies literature is a burgeoning convergence of interrelated yet distinct social movement discourses calling for an alternative food system that serves as a counter-hegemonic response to the mounting crisis of social, economic, and ecological unsustainability. With that, our aims here are threefold. First, we illustrate the role of narratives as one way to critically navigate, inspire, and create new possibilities for learning and action with emphasis on the fluid and localized sites and processes of community food work. The narratives of the AFP in central Appalachia provide a space to engage with a particular methodology and the voices and realities this work embodies.

We also argue that the collecting, editing, and disseminating of community food narratives is not an apolitical fact of empirical documentation; rather it is cultural and ontological work—a generative process of (re)creating meanings about our food system. To this effort, actor narratives contain potentials and possibilities for emergent and transformative community food work. As noted above, the material and corporeal effects of our food system are a maddening and wicked problem. We argue that such wickedness, including food insecurity, hunger, and ecological unsustainability, are complex problems that intersect with larger systems of oppression and injustice that will not be "solved" by technical and rational "best practices" to be applied across time and space but rather, if engaged and embraced, by new systems of knowing, integration, coordination, and experimentation that both build upon, (de)construct, and deterritorialize our historical approaches to community food work—enabling new possibilities for life-affirming change in our systems and communities.

Lastly, as cultural workers, we make the case for engendering a political praxis through the crafting of narratives as new spaces of learning for and about community food work. This pathway includes embracing one's work as reflexive, mutually informing, and dialogical involving the lifeworld experiences of a multiplicity of food system actors. According to Lather (1991), such praxis is "rooted in our ability to provide a change-enhancing context" that is "grounded in respect to human capacity and, yet, profoundly skeptical of appearances and common sense" (p. 65). We are hopeful that the creating, telling, and sharing of narratives provide us with these kinds of change-making contexts toward a less maddening food system.

> *reward* "The other surprising reward is that people continue to give us ideas."

REFERENCES

Abi-Nader, J. Ayson, A., Harris, K., Herra, H. Eddings, D., Habib, D., Hanna, J., Paterson, C., Sutton, K., & Villanuesva, L. (2009). *Whole measures for community food systems: Value-based planning and evaluation.* Community Food Security Coalition: Portland, OR.

Allen, P. (Ed.). (1993). *Food for the future: Conditions and contradictions of sustainability.* New York: John Wiley and Sons.

Allen, P. (2004). *Together at the table: Sustainability and sustenance in the American agrifood system.* University Park: Pennsylvania University Press.

Allen, P. (2010). Realizing justice in local food systems. *Cambridge Journal of Regions, Economy and Society, 3,* 295–308.

Alkon, A. H., & Agyeman, J. (2011). *Cultivating food justice: Race, class and sustainability.* Cambridge, MA: MIT Press.

Born, B., & Purcell, M. (2006). Avoiding the local trap. *Journal of Planning Education and Research, 26*(2), 195–207.

Brookfield, S. D., & Holst, J. D. (2011). *Radicalizing learning: Adult education for a just world.* San Francisco: Jossey-Bass.

Campbell, P., & Burnaby, B. (Eds.). (2001). *Participatory practices in adult education.* Mahwah: Lawrence Erlbaum Associates.

Carr, W., & Kemmis, S. (1986). *Becoming critical: Education, knowledge and action research.* London: Falmer Press.

Cervero, R. M., & Wilson, A. L. (Eds.). (2001). *Power in practice: Adult education and the struggle for knowledge and power in society.* San Francisco: Jossey-Bass.

Clancy, K., & Ruhf, K. (2010). Is local enough? Some arguments for regional food systems. *Choices, 25*(1), 1–5.

Clandinin, D. J., & Connelly, F. M. (2000). *Narrative inquiry.* San Francisco: Jossey-Bass Publishers.

Connelly, F. M., & Clandinin, D. J. (2005). Narrative inquiry. In J. Green, G. Camilli, & P. Elmore (Eds.), *Handbook of complementary methods in educational research* (pp. 477–489). Washington, DC: American Educational Research Association.

Constance, D. H., Renard, M.-C., & Rivera-Ferre, M. G. (Eds.). (2014). *Alternative agrifood movements: Patterns of convergence and divergence*. Bingley: Emerald Group Publishing.

Crowther, J. (2006). Knowledge and learning in social movements: Issues and opportunities for adult community education. In R. Edwards, J. Gallacher, & S. Whittaker (Eds.), *Learning outside the academy: International research perspectives*. London: Routledge.

Cunningham, P. (1992). From Freire to feminism: The North American experience with critical pedagogy. *Adult Education Quarterly, 42*, 180–191.

D'Adamo-Damery, P. (2014). *Ontological possibilities: Rhizoanalytic explorations of community food work in central Appalachia*. Blacksburg: Virginia Tech.

D'Adamo-Damery, N., Ziegler, P., & D'Adamo-Damery, P. (2015, June). *Re-imagining the commons: Creating the conditions for regional network*. Paper presented at the annual meeting of Agriculture, Food and Human Values, Pittsburgh. Abstract retrieved from http://falk.chatham.edu/foodconference/_pdf/Compiled-Abstracts-Alphabetized.pdf

Deleuze, G., & Guattari, F. (1980/1987). *A thousand plateaus: Capitalism and schizophrenia* (B. Massumi, Trans.). Minneapolis: University of Minnesota Press.

Deleuze, G. & Guattari, F. (1994). *What is philosophy?* (H. Tomlinson & G. Burchell, Trans.). New York: Columbia University Press. (Original work published 1991).

Embry, O., Fryman, D., Habib, D., & Abi-Nader, J. (2012). *Whole measures for community food systems: Stories from the field*. Portland: Community Food Security Coalition.

Feenstra, G. (2002). Creating space for sustainable food systems: Lessons from the field. *Agriculture and Human Values, 19*, 99–106.

Feenstra, G., & Campbell, D. (1996). Steps for developing a sustainable community food system. *Pacific Northwest Sustainable Agriculture: Farming for Profit & Stewardship, 8*(4), 1–6.

Foley, G. (1999). *Learning in social action: A contribution to understanding informal education*. New York: Zed Books.

Foucault, M. (1980). Truth and Power (C. Gordon, L. Marshal, J. Mepham, & K. Sober, Trans.). In C. Gordon (Ed.), *Power/Knowledge: Selected Interviews & Other Writings 1972–1977* (pp. 109–133). New York: Pantheon Books.

Freire, P. (1972). *Pedagogy of the oppressed*. New York: Continuum International Publishing Group.

Gibson-Graham, J. K. (2006). *A postcapitalist politics*. Minneapolis: University of Minnesota Press.

Gibson-Graham, J. K., Resnick, S., & Wolff, R. D. (2001). Toward a poststructuralist political economy. In J. K. Gibson-Graham, S. Resnick, & R. D. Wolff

(Eds.), *Re/presenting class: Essays in postmodern Marxism* (pp. 1–22). Durham: Duke University Press.

Giroux, H. (1992). *Border crossings: Cultural workers and the politics of education.* New York: Routledge.

Glezner, K., Peterson, N., & Roncoli, C. (2011). Introduction to symposium on rethinking farmer participation in agricultural development: Development, participation, and the ethnography of ambiguity. *Agriculture and Human Values, 28*(1), 97.

Goodman, D., DuPuis, E. M., & Goodman, M. K. (2014). *Alternative food networks: Knowledge, practice, and politics.* Oxon/New York: Routledge.

Gottlieb, R., & Joshi, A. (2010). *Food justice.* Cambridge: The MIT Press.

Greenwood, D., & Levin, M. (2007). *Introduction to action research: Social research for social change.* Thousand Oaks: Sage Publications.

Guthman, J. (2008). Bringing good food to others: Investigating the subjects of alternative food practice. *Cultural Geographies, 15*, 431–447.

Hamm, M. W. (2009). Commentary: Principles for framing a healthy food system. *Journal of Hunger & Environmental Nutrition, 4*(3–4), 241–250.

Hamm, M. W., & Bellows, A. C. (2003). Community food security and nutrition educators. *Journal of Nutrition Education and Behavior, 35*(1), 37–43.

Hassanein, N. (2003). Practicing food democracy: A pragmatic politics of transformation. *Journal of Rural Studies, 19*, 77–86.

Hassanein, N., & Kloppenburg, J. (1995). Where the grass grows again: Knowledge exchange in the sustainable agriculture movement. *Rural Sociology, 60*(4), 721–740.

Hendrickson, M., & Heffernan, J. (2002). Opening spaces through relocalization: Locating potential resistance in the weaknesses of the global food system. *Sociologia Ruralis, 42*(4), 347–369.

Hinrichs, C. (2003). The practice and politics of food system localization. *Journal of Rural Studies, 19*, 33–45.

Holst, J. D. (2002). *Social movements, civil society, and radical adult education.* Westport: Bergin and Garvey.

Julier, A. P. (2015, May). *Critiquing hegemony, creating food, crafting justice: Cultivating an activist food studies.* Symposium address at the 10th annual meeting of the Canadian Association for Food Studies. University of Ottawa: Ottawa.

Kirschenmann, F., & Falk, C. L. (2010). *Cultivating an ecological conscience: Essays from a farmer philosopher.* Lexington: University Press of Kentucky.

Lang, T. (2009). Reshaping the food system for ecological public health. *Journal of Hunger & Environmental Nutrition, 4*(3), 315–335.

Lather, P. (1991). *Getting smart: Feminist research and pedagogy with/in the postmodern.* London: Routledge.

Law, J. (1999). After ANT: Complexity, naming and topology. In J. Law & J. Hassard (Eds.), *Actor network theory and after* (pp. 1–14). Malden: Blackwell Publishers.

Law, J. (2008). On sociology and STS. *The Sociological Review, 56*(4), 623–649.

Law, J., & Urry, J. (2004). Enacting the social. *Economy and Society, 33*(3), 390–410.

Manning, E. (2009). 7 propositions for the impossibility of isolation, or, the radical empiricism of the network. In A. Dekker & A. Wolfsberger (Eds.), *Walled garden*. Amsterdam: Virtueel Platform.

Mayo, P. (1999). *Gramsci, Freire and adult education: Possibilities for transformative action*. London: Zed Books.

Mol, A. (1999). Ontological politics. In J. Law & J. Hassard (Eds.), *Actor network theory and after* (pp. 74–89). Malden: Blackwell Publishers.

Mol, A. (2002). *The body multiple: Onotoly in medical practice*. Durham: Duke University Press.

Niewolny, K., & Archibald, T. (2015). Collective impact in/for adult education: A framework for collective action to address community complexity and resilience. In *Proceedings of the 56th Annual Adult Education Research Conference*. Kansas State University: Manhattan.

Niewolny, K., & D'Adamo-Damery, P. (2014). Learning from practice stories & reflective practice: A narrative analysis of community-based activism by community food system practitioners. In *Proceedings of the 55th Annual Adult Education Research Conference*. Pennsylvania State University: Harrisburg.

Orlie, M. (2009). There is no alternative. *Theory & Event, 12*(2), none.

Patel, R. (2009). What does food sovereignty look like? *The Journal of Peasant Studies, 36*(3), 663–673.

Pothukuchi, K., Seidenburg, K., & Abi-Nader, J. (2007). Building community food security: Lessons from community food projects, 1999–2003. Retrieved at: http://www.foodsecurity.org/pubs.html#building

Pretty, J. N. (1995). Participatory learning for sustainable agriculture. *World Development, 23*(8), 1247–1263.

Richmond, H. (2002). Learners' lives: A narrative analysis. *The Qualitative Report, 7*(3), 1–14.

Röling, N., & Wagemakers, A. M. M. (1998). *Facilitating sustainable agriculture: Participatory learning and adaptive management in times of environmental uncertainty*. Cambridge: Cambridge University Press.

Slocum, R. (2007). Whiteness, space and alternative food practice. *Geoforum, 38*, 520–533.

Snowden, D. (2002). Complex acts of knowing—Paradox and descriptive self-awareness. *Journal of Knowledge Management, 6*(2), 100–111.

Stevenson, G. W., Ruhf, K., Lezberg, S., & Clancy, K. (2007). Warrior, builder, and weaver work: Strategies for changing the food system. In C. Claire Hinrichs & T. A. Lyson (Eds.), *Remaking the North American food system: Strategies for sustainability* (pp. 33–62). Lincoln: University of Nebraska Press.
Stewart, K. (2007). *Ordinary affects*. Durham: Duke University Press.
Tanaka, K., Indiano, E., Soley, G., & Mooney, P. H. (2015). Building the capacity for community food work: The geographic distribution of USDA Community Food Projects Competitive Grant Program grantees. *Journal of Agriculture, Food Systems, and Community Development, 5*(3), 97–111.
Thompson, N., & Pascal, J. (2012). Developing critically reflective practice. *Reflective Practice: International and Multidisciplinary Perspectives, 12*(2), 311–325.
Whitehead, A. N. (1925). *Science and the modern world*. Cambridge: Cambridge University Press.

CHAPTER 8

Learning, Food, and Sustainability in Community-Campus Engagement: Teaching and Research Partnerships That Strengthen the Food Sovereignty Movement

Peter Andrée, Lauren Kepkiewicz, Charles Levkoe, Abra Brynne, and Cathleen Kneen

INTRODUCTION

This is a vibrant time for social movement building in relation to **food sovereignty**. A growing number of actors, from farmers' unions to urban food advocates, fisher, and Indigenous activists, are joining together in

P. Andrée
Department of Political Science, Carleton University, Ottawa, ON, Canada

L. Kepkiewicz
Department of Geography and Planning, University of Toronto, Toronto, ON, Canada

C. Levkoe (✉)
Department of Health Sciences, Lakehead University, Thunder Bay, ON, Canada

A. Brynne
BC Food Systems Network, Nelson, BC, Canada

C. Kneen
The Ram's Horn, Ottawa, ON, Canada

© The Author(s) 2016
J. Sumner (ed.), *Learning, Food, and Sustainability*,
DOI 10.1057/978-1-137-53904-5_8

movements to fundamentally reorganize the way food is produced, distributed, and consumed, as well as how it is valued (Desmarais and Wittman 2014; Levkoe 2014; Martin and Andrée 2014). For La Via Campesina (LVC), the global peasant movement that brought the concept forward in the 1990s, food sovereignty was defined as "the right of each nation to maintain and develop its own capacity to produce its basic foods, respecting cultural and productive diversity" (Desmarais 2007: 34). In 2000, this working definition was expanded to include the "right of peoples to define their agricultural and food policy" (ibid.).

While the food sovereignty movement is transnational, it has developed strong roots in Canada. Canada's National Farmers Union was one of the founding members of LVC and, since its establishment in 2001, Union Paysanne has become instrumental in introducing food sovereignty in Québec with an emphasis on sustainable human-scale farms (Desmarais and Wittman 2014). Indigenous activists and scholars have both complicated and enriched the movement in Canada by underlining the necessity for food sovereignty approaches to engage with issues of culture, land, colonialism, self-determination, and practices such as hunting, gathering, and fishing (Morrison 2011). In recent years, Food Secure Canada has become one of the key organizations moving the food sovereignty agenda forward. From 2007 to 2011, leading members of this organization worked alongside a range of other social movement organizations to define a national policy agenda (named the "People's Food Policy") grounded in the principles of food sovereignty, with input from approximately 3000 people across the country (PFPP 2011, also see Kneen 2010; Martin and Andrée 2014).

Meanwhile, in universities and colleges, new ways of teaching and researching are emerging under the banner of **community-campus engagement** (CCE). CCE encompasses **community-service learning** (CSL) and **community-based research** (CBR), as well as other forms of community-campus collaboration. CSL is an "educational approach that integrates service in the community with intentional learning activities" (CACSL n.d.). CBR refers to "a partnership of students, faculty, and community members who collaboratively engage in research with the purpose of solving pressing community problems or effecting social change" (Strand et al. 2003: 3). These models of teaching and research are intended to make campuses more relevant to the communities in which they are based, while giving students meaningful learning experiences.[1] Goals of social and environmental change are at the forefront of many of these initiatives with faculty and students expressing an aim to redistribute power and develop horizontal relationships within the classroom and beyond (Bickford and Reynolds 2002; Friedland 2008; Swords and Kiely 2010).

In this chapter, we consider how movements for food sovereignty and CCE can work together, both in theory and practice. We argue that CCE can, and in many cases already does, strengthen the food sovereignty movement, especially when CCE challenges traditional assumptions about the role of academics—including both professors and students. When undertaken thoughtfully, CCE can: provide academics with important training for critically engaging with food systems; encourage knowledge sharing between social movement actors and academics; and support social movement organizations working toward more just and sustainable food systems. We draw together the lessons from a growing body of literature on food sovereignty with those from CCE and bring them into conversation with our own experiences of, and research with, these movements in Canada.

Our experiences in CCE include a series of nine projects (see Table 8.1) supported by the **Community Food Security** (CFS) hub[2] of the Community First: Impacts of Community Engagement (CFICE) research project between 2012 and 2014.[3] CFICE is a large multi-partner community-based, participatory action research project that studies how community-based organizations define, evaluate, and utilize the value created by CCE; how this work can take place across various scales; and how communities can exert more control over the design of engagement activities (Andrée et al. 2014). This chapter is co-authored by those who served on the management team of the CFS hub, and reflects our experiences supporting these collaborative projects. Three of the authors are academics (two faculty members, and one PhD student), and two have served as representatives of Food Secure Canada, a core partner, on the team. Although only a few of the projects explicitly frame their activities in terms of food sovereignty, all of them are affiliated with progressive food movements (Levkoe 2014) and most are affiliated with Food Secure Canada. In addition, many of the lessons learned from these projects speak directly to the question of how to best undertake CCE in the context of food sovereignty work.

Our chapter speaks to this book's core themes of learning, food, and sustainability in specific ways. One of the pillars of food sovereignty is

Table 8.1   CFS Hub Projects (2012–2015)

Project title	Primary partners	Purpose	Type of CCE
Models of Community University Collaboration (Waterloo, Ontario)	Region of Waterloo Public Health; University of Waterloo	To describe, compare, and share the lessons from two models of CCE that work within Waterloo Region to advance a vision of a healthy community food system.	CSL: practicums and internships sponsored by an academic institution and the public health organization
Campus Food Initiative Study (Pan-Canadian)	Meal Exchange and Ryerson University	To examine how student-led campus food system initiatives begin, how to maintain them, and how partnerships work	CBR: qualitative interviews with actors involved in campus food systems initiatives on six campuses
Cross-Cultural Food Networks: **Building and Maintaining Inclusive Food Security Networks to Support Indigenous and Non-Indigenous Communities** (British Columbia)	British Columbia Food Systems Network; University of Victoria	To uncover the factors which enable cross-cultural relationships around the unifying need for adequate, just, healthy, culturally appropriate food	CBR: participatory evaluation: capturing stories about building and strengthening cross-cultural relationships
Local Food Multipliers (Northern Ontario)	The Food Security Research Network, Lakehead University; the North Superior Workforce Planning Board	To determine the workforce multiplier effects of local food production and processing in Northern Ontario	CSL and CBR
Planning for Change: **Community Development in Practice** (Ontario)	Sustain Ontario: The Alliance for Healthy Food and Farming; University of Toronto	To explore different models and policy initiatives to support regional food procurement among municipalities	CSL and CBR: surveys, interviews, environmental scan, and case studies

Table 8.1 (continued)

Project title	Primary partners	Purpose	Type of CCE
The Seed Community Food Hub (Guelph, Ontario)	Guelph & Wellington Task Force for Poverty Elimination; the Food Access Working Group of the Guelph-Wellington Round Table; the Research Shop, Institute for Community Engaged Research, University of Guelph	Initially, to identify gaps and challenges within the existing emergency food system and assess potential strategies for addressing them; over time, to support the development of a regional community food hub	CBR and participatory action research; developmental evaluation
Edible Campus (Montréal, Quebec)	Santropol Roulant; Department of Architecture and Facilities Department, McGill University	To evaluate the relationship between a community meal program and the university that provides space for its urban agriculture initiative	CBR; developmental evaluation
Community Food Assessment (Regina, Saskatchewan)	Community Food System Steering Committee; the Health Promotion Department of Regina Qu'Appelle Health Region; Regina Education and Action on Child Hunger (REACH) Community Research Unit, University of Regina	To engage in a participatory process to improve the community's food system	CBR: environmental scan, evaluation process using focus groups and telephone interviews
Developmental Evaluation (British Columbia)	Long-term Inmates Now in the Community (LINC); Correctional Service of Canada; District of Mission, BC; School of Nursing, University of British Columbia	To build on: (1) an existing partnership formed around a study of food-related experiences of people transitioning from incarceration; and (2) LINC's agricultural social enterprise (Emma's Acres) that employs survivors/victims, ex-offenders and offenders.	CBR: evaluation of an urban agriculture project to asses short-term outcomes and long-term opportunities

that it "Builds Knowledge and Skills" (International Steering Committee (ISC) 2007), embracing a particular kind of learning that prioritizes the knowledge of local food providers and their communities. Our contribution to the book's first theme is to explore how CCE can contribute to co-produced "learnings" that strengthen the movement. We address the book's second theme by positioning food and food sovereignty movements as particularly fruitful forums for encouraging CCE by bringing people together around tables and bridging academic theory with everyday acts of producing, preparing, and eating. In relation to the book's third theme, we follow the food sovereignty movement in embedding sustainability within a wider set of principles (or pillars) including as follows: "Provides Food for People; Values Food Providers; Localizes Food Systems; Puts Control Locally; and Works with Nature" (ISC 2007).[4] Being rooted in community self-determination, these pillars propose particular paths toward food systems that are not only environmentally sustainable, but also socially just in terms of how their bounty is shared and in terms of the livelihoods supported for food providers.

The food sovereignty movement mobilizes diverse activists seeking to transform the dominant food system, but what role should academics have in this growing movement? Given that academic institutions have a history of exploitative research relationships and often reinforce hierarchical assumptions about whose knowledge "counts," we believe academic practitioners of CCE who claim to support the food sovereignty movement need to critically examine some of the assumptions and practices of their own profession. While this argument is hardly novel, especially from the perspective of community-based activists who have been critical of the role and positioning of the "ivory tower," the attention currently given to CCE by post-secondary institutions, and the opportunities emerging to work alongside food movement actors, suggest that this is an important moment for moving the discussion on praxis forward. Before developing this idea further, we present some historical context on the relationship between the food sovereignty movement and academics.

Academic Engagement with Food Sovereignty

Although the term food sovereignty has been traced back to its use by the Mexican government in its National Food Program in the 1980s (Edelman 2014), its origins as a transnational social movement are rooted in the experiences of farmers and peasants from both the global North and South in the context of **neoliberalism** (Desmarais 2007). While food sovereignty is expressed differently depending on the local context (Desmarais and Wittman 2014), the movement pursues a range of policy goals including: increasing food production for local markets (including for the impoverished) and building mechanisms for fair trade; conserving local knowledge by supporting people who embody this wisdom, particularly women and Indigenous peoples; promoting agroecological production and harvesting; asserting the rights of food providers and harvesters as outlined by existing international agreements; and implementing agrarian reforms including the recognition of customary rights and enabling community control over territories (ISC 2007). These goals stand in contrast to institutions and policies that work to liberalize trade, facilitate corporate control, militarize borders, occupy Indigenous territories, privatize food system knowledge and materials, and promote industrial agriculture and "toxic technology" such as genetically modified organisms and terminator seeds (ISC 2007). Building on these goals, LVC has become one of the world's largest social movements with over 160 member organizations in 73 counties representing an estimated 200 million farmers, fisherfolk, and Indigenous peoples worldwide.

The relationship between academics and the food sovereignty movement involves tensions that go back to the creation of LVC in the early 1990s. Desmarais (2007: 90) documents how LVC emerged in a space "filled by numerous national and international development NGOs [non-governmental organizations] as well as research institutions working on issues of agriculture and food security." One of these, a research foundation called the Paulo Freire Stichting (PFS), was instrumental in bringing farm organizations together for the constitutive meeting of LVC in Mons, Belgium, in 1993. That meeting resulted in considerable conflict when the goal of its organizers (to establish a Research Programme of Farmers Organizations) was put on the back seat by a strong group of peasants and farmers who were more interested in organizing a "farmer-led, autonomous, peasant and farm movement of progressive organizations that would strive to build the capacity to articulate joint positions and policies in opposition to the neo-liberal model advocated by many national governments and international institutions" (94). The conflict between the emerging LVC leadership and the PFS continued for another year (with the PFS serving as its "Technical Secretariat") until the Co-ordinating Commission of LVC eventually severed its relationship with the foundation (98).

This story is relevant here, as academic researchers have often been accused of the same paternalism LVC criticized the PFS for in 1993. The conflict is about voice and power dynamics. In other words, it centers on different perspectives of who has the authority to speak for and enact food sovereignty, and the various power relations they need to confront. LVC was established to be autonomous, to formulate its own positions, and to maintain control over research about it when necessary. This uneasy dynamic remains 20 years later.

The recent literature on food sovereignty reinforces this point. On the one hand, some researchers who are close to the movement have been reticent to criticize it, resulting in work that may be overly "celebratory" (Alkon and Mares 2012). On the other hand, an account of the experiences of two recent food sovereignty conferences, one at Yale University (2013) and a second at the International Institute of Social Studies (ISS) in The Hague (2014)—both of which had a large number of high-profile movement activists in attendance as well as academics—shows that the work of academics continues to be viewed with skepticism by movement actors: "Questions that scholar-activists had raised in the off-the-record interviews with food sovereignty advocates and peasant leaders, or in hushed conversation in university corridors, exploded in fiery polemics" (Edelman et al. 2014: 911–912). Then, "what began as a dialogue in which academics asked 'Does food sovereignty have a future in critical agrarian studies?' was playfully flipped the other way by practitioners to ask 'Do critical agrarian studies have a future in food sovereignty?'" (Edelman et al. 2014: 912).

In reframing this question, food sovereignty activists underlined the tendency of academics to prioritize knowledge produced in the university and highlighted the importance of producing knowledge collaboratively. From the perspective of community-based food sovereignty activists (including within our own author team), the flipping of the central question at these two food sovereignty conferences was more than simply "playful." It provides greater clarity around what is at stake and for whom. It also recognizes that academic studies are ultimately a means to an end: the realization of more sustainable food systems, from the perspectives of those who work in them and who are nourished by them.

The cautiousness with which the food sovereignty movement has engaged academic researchers over the last 20 years has some justification. The agricultural sciences have a long history of developing new technologies for direct use within the food system (Kloppenburg 2005).

These technologies have often worked to facilitate the uptake of industrial food production as well as positioning scientific experts as knowledge producers who disseminate expertise to farmers (Democratising Agricultural Research (DAR) 2012). When scientific methods and technologies have failed, farmers are usually held responsible for their inability to use expert knowledge correctly rather than questioning the research itself (DAR 2012). It was criticisms about these approaches to knowledge production by academic researchers and community members that led, in part, to the contemporary movement for CCE.

ORIENTATIONS TO COMMUNITY-CAMPUS ENGAGEMENT

CCE partnerships are described as "the coming together of diverse interests and people to achieve a common purpose via interactions, information sharing, and coordination activities" (Jassawalla and Sashittal 1998: 239). Notably, these relationships are not always about teaching or research. For example, among our CFS Hub projects, the Edible Campus project began as a way for the community partner to access space on campus for its urban agriculture initiative to grow food for a meal production and delivery program. Central to all types of CCE is the assumption that relationships are mutually beneficial to both parties through an "exchange of knowledge and resources in a context of partnership and reciprocity" (Carnegie Elective Community Engagement Classification 2014). However, the term CCE, while broadly describing partnerships, says little about the content of those relationships and their intended outcomes. To differentiate among partnerships, it is important to identify and articulate the varying motivations and intentions that underlie practices of engagement (Butin 2010). When we do so, we find a spectrum of orientations to CCE, from conventional ones primarily focused on student outcomes or the professor's own research objectives, to transformative orientations that see collaboration as a means of social change.

Conventional orientations to CCE that focus on field experiences (e.g., internships, practicums), content knowledge (e.g., activities that remain driven by academic interests), and cultural competencies have become extremely popular on North American campuses over the past decades. Successful outcomes of these activities include supporting the work of community-based organizations (through administration, front line work, and strategic planning), educating students (research and skill development, practical experience, understanding broader social issues, etc.), and improving the quality of academic research (by grounding that research in lived experiences) (Buys and Barnsall 2007). However, critics have argued that this approach to CCE fails to prioritize community needs, despite the rhetoric of "engagement." With respect to CSL, for example, activities tend to be driven by professionalization, institutionalization, and job readiness for students, and are less focused on supporting grassroots organizations involved in community development and social change (Swords and Kiely 2010; Mitchell 2008; Levkoe et al. 2014). If CCE is to contribute to movement building, these criticisms need to be addressed, either at a system-wide level or in terms of the individual partnerships developed.

By contrast, Paulo Freire's reflections on critical and engaged pedagogy provide a valuable framework for thinking about CCE as a political act and a form of movement building. Instead of merely teaching the instrumental and decontextualized skills of reading and writing, Freire called for teachers (broadly defined to include all who have knowledge or skills to share) to be participants in a political process through education as the path to liberation. Freire wrote of this as "a pedagogy, which must be forged with, not for, the oppressed (whether individuals or peoples) in the incessant struggle to regain their humanity" (2000: 48). What does such a transformative orientation to CCE mean for academic researchers? Drawing on her work in Latin America and Spanish contexts, Zusman (2004) argues that academics should adopt a horizontal approach to their work—where knowledge and accountability is shared among colleagues (whether activists or scholars). Rather than conceive of a CBR relationship as academic-led empirical investigation, Zusman argues that the relationship should evolve out of a commitment to question political, social, and economic conditions, and the recognition that the production of knowledge, and alternative political practice, is a collaborative and mutually beneficial process.

Recognizing that these orientations are two poles of a spectrum with many possibilities in-between—we must now ask how CCE can strengthen the food sovereignty movement. We first address the methodological (especially epistemological) aspects of the issue, followed by some of the practical outcomes of working together in this way.

Cognitive Justice

"The assertion that knowledge is not only mobilized but generated in the community is unfortunately novel, not to say radical."

This comment, drawn from an early manuscript prepared by some of the participants in the CFS Hub, sums up the epistemological issue that food sovereignty activists believe needs to be addressed before we can work productively together. In contrast to mainstream academic assumptions that often place academic knowledges "above" other types of knowledge, food sovereignty movement activists insist that knowledge creation involves multiple perspectives, or "cosmosvisions," that come together to engage in horizontal exchanges (Sandwell et al. 2014: 3). This challenge, and the nature of food sovereignty as rooted in a basic human need as well as a political praxis, positions CCE in this field as a particularly fruitful opportunity for radical change.

As Pimbert (2010: 28) writes, "the issue is not merely about 'using' participation to make research more 'effective' or 'efficient'." Neither is this a question of simply challenging mainstream academic assumptions of who knows what. It is a more fundamental challenge regarding how knowledge is, and should be, produced. The food sovereignty movement calls for ways of knowing that go beyond inclusion or recognition to a process of knowledge production based on connection. Radically transforming the ways we know thus means extending communities' control over research institutions and funding as well as "deep changes in academic cultures, in the self-image of researchers and academics, in teaching pedagogies, in research agendas and methodologies, and in the very role that universities and research institutes play in societies throughout the world" (Pimbert 2010: 23).

Within this model, personal relationships leading to "deeper encounters" are "pivotal for building a robust movement and ultimately for growing a new kind of food system" (Sandwell et al. 2014: 12). The process of realizing such deep encounters must include the collaborative development of codes of conduct and ethics between researchers and activists/ food providers, the creation of safe spaces for knowledge production and discussions, the reversal of roles between researcher and researched, the co-validation of knowledge by both food providers and scientists and the reallocation of resources and use of communication strategies and technologies to decentralize and democratize knowledge production. All of this hinges, first and foremost, on the recognition and practice of cognitive justice, defined as the coexistence of different ways of knowing (Sandwell et al. 2014: 4; see also Pimbert 2010).

The food sovereignty movement's calls for cognitive justice resonate strongly with the calls for a transformative orientation to CCE introduced above. The goal of working together is, after all, to build just, healthy and vibrant communities. When undertaking this work in the context of food sovereignty—which aims at achieving social change by breaking down hierarchical relationships and constructing new types of partnerships—the epistemological perspective discussed here is about ensuring integrity between goals and practices.

From the CFS Hub projects, we have gained a number of insights about what working toward horizontal collaboration looks like in practice. For example, our project on "Cross-Cultural Food Networks in British Columbia" was premised on the fact that Indigenous people occupy a critical space in relation to food systems research, yet such research has often been rejected by Indigenous communities as disrespectful, extractive, and exploitive. This project's purpose was to shed more light on the complexities of cross-cultural relationships, and to identify practices that should inform future research relationships in and with Indigenous communities. It suggested that the starting point of partnership work must be an equal relationship built for the purpose of mutual support and learning, decolonization, and enhancing food sovereignty:

> The key is, it's a relationship. First, getting to know each other, our histories, communities, ways of communicating, stories, listening. An element of 'doing', not 'consultation'. We need less talking, more doing. It sparks energy in relationships and ideas bubble up. (Interview 8)

Indigenous scholars have argued that research *is* relationship (Kovach 2009). Building the relationship is not just one "step" to be completed before entering the "field" (Aboriginal Knowledge(s): Colonialism, Decolonization and Education 2014).

OUTCOMES OF HORIZONTAL ENGAGEMENT

Once CCE partners adopt this methodological approach, what does working toward a horizontal relationship look like across the Indigenous-settler divide as well as across other differences? From our projects, it is clear that each partner brings unique strengths to the table, and that a horizontal approach—including strong communication—ensures that full use is made of each partner's resources and skills.

Sharing Skills and Knowledge

While community partners often provide the practice from which academics collect data and develop theory, academics bring disciplined research skills and access to resources that may not be available to community actors. Academics are also able to give a more concerted amount of time and space to the analytical process because it is part of their training and job expectations. In our projects, academics were often able to reframe issues and understand them in new ways. This was true of the faculty and graduate students involved in the Planning for Change and Local Food Multipliers CSL courses as well as the research from academics in The Seed and Developmental Evaluation project. However, many community-based partners also bring disciplined research skills to the table. This was evident in the cases of the Cross-Cultural Food Networks, the Community Food Assessment, and the Edible Campus projects. In each case, community-based researchers produced extremely high-quality research and reports.

Maintaining the Transformative Orientation

In the context of the food sovereignty movement, often it is the community activists who bring and maintain the ideological orientation of the work they do, as in the Developmental Evaluation project, where community partners had specific motivations for the research and ensured these informed the work from beginning to end. In other cases, however, it is the academics who keep projects focused on the bigger picture. The Planning for Change project showed the ways that students can accomplish key tasks that move community projects forward as well as offer critical perspectives that push more transformational goals. In that case, building on their experiences and reflecting on the theory and practice from the CSL course, students raised critical questions in relation to the tensions between the principles of food sovereignty and the way non-profit organizations are structured, leading to some important lessons for all involved.

Building on Place-Based Knowledge

All food systems happen in a place, and the particularities and nuance of different places are vital to engage with in food sovereignty work, notwithstanding the many commonalities in the work across space and time. Successful models cannot simply be replicated from one place to another, but must be adapted and contextualized over time. Community partners (and sometimes also academics grounded in their communities) bring critical place-based knowledge.

In the Cross-Cultural Food Networks project, different worldviews based in place helped to build stronger cross-cultural relationships. Commenting on how institutional frameworks often fail to account for Indigenous experiences and perspectives, an Indigenous participant explained that neoclassical categorizations of "producer" do not adequately represent Indigenous understandings of and approaches to food systems. Participants also talked about the ways that non-Indigenous peoples have different relationships with land in Canada as well as different histories of coming to this land, resulting in differing worldviews and understandings of food systems. In the Seed project, community partners used their extensive knowledge of the region to help guide academic researchers through a variety of tensions that arose throughout the project. Each of these projects was highly successful in revealing place-based specificities that must be understood for successful CCE.

Networking for Change

Our projects also reveal the importance of network contexts, and this is typically another contributing strength of community-based partners. In the Developmental Evaluation project, LINC played an invaluable role connecting academics with difficult-to-reach prison communities, due to their established relationships and a solid reputation as an ally within these communities. The partnership enabled the collection of accurate and meaningful research in a context where incarcerated individuals, correctional officers, and parole officers rarely feel comfortable speaking with those outside the prison system. The Seed project also benefited greatly from community partners' relationships with participants from marginalized and vulnerable communities as well as the community partners' ability to identify key research goals and priorities. They used their extensive knowledge of the region to link academics to vulnerable communities, and helped legitimate and better enable researchers to collect meaningful data once initial connections had been made.

Working on *Mutual Interdependence*

In the CFS Hub, some of the most successful partnership work is best termed "mutual interdependence" (Andrée et al. 2014). For example, the Models of Community University Collaboration project found that the commonality between two models for defining student placements was the emergence of symbiotic relationships based on implicit understandings that professors, students, and community partners each depend on one another's knowledge and skills. Furthermore, partnerships were established not due to obligation but to a shared vision of healthy community food systems. Again, in the Food Security Research Network project in Thunder Bay, the expertise of different partners "provided the coming together of relevant and complementary sets of expertise in the right place and at the right time. The [community partner] had expertise in workforce planning and an emerging interest in food, but no data; [we] had experience in local food system issues, but had never previously considered the workforce piece" (Nelson and Stroink 2013: 4).

Blurring the Boundaries

Reflecting on our work with the nine CFS hub projects, we have found that some horizontal collaboration emerges because key people have feet in both academic and activist worlds. In the CCE literature, these are termed scholar-activists or activist-scholars (depending on where their primary home is) (Croteau 2005). These positionalities are not uncommon in the food sovereignty movement. In contrast to the division between scientific researchers and farmers as research recipients, academics engaged in food sovereignty research often identify as part of the movement rather than "external scholars [who are] recruited or rejected" (Sandwell et al. 2014: 5), while food sovereignty movement activists are increasingly attending universities to, in part, deepen their knowledge and enhance their efficacy as food systems' interveners. Cloke (2004) argues that we should not fall into the trap of drawing static lines between what is or is not academic research or between our identity and professional lives. The blurred boundaries formed through the research process and from personal contributions are, in reality, impossible to disentangle.

Within the CFS hub projects, most academics and community partners noted an artificial divide between academics and activists as well as the ways that those involved may actually shift their roles. These blurred boundaries were exemplified through the Local Food Multipliers project. The academics involved in the Food Security Research Network adopted an "In Community" methodology, based on the idea that academics "approach the issue of food security as a community member first, one who is immersed in the context of this community and its food security issues" (Harrison et al. 2013: 103). The community partner commented that all of the partners approached the project as people coming together based on a shared concern and a desire to better understand the local food system. In this way "titles and degrees were 'left at the door' and played no part in their interactions" (quoted in Andree et al. 2014: 6).

However, many academics do not go this route, and remain more distant to the social movements they are studying, believing they can serve them best in a more conventional academic capacity. Our next section addresses this approach.

A Place for Conventional CCE?

We end this discussion with an important observation from our work with the nine CFS hub demonstration projects—a point that may appear to counter what we have argued thus far. While we believe there are many limitations with conventional orientations to CCE, we have learned that there is still a place for such approaches when carried out within a relationship based in trust, and when the community has agreed to be less involved in the governance of a project (because they trust the eventual outcome will be useful). Community-based activists often require research because peer-reviewed data can help to further legitimize and support their work in strategic ways (e.g., when applying for grants). While some academics may not see themselves as part of a food sovereignty movement, the critical theory, statistics, documentation, or evidence that they produce can support activist activity. This type of relationship was apparent in the Campus Food Initiative Study and Regina Community Food Assessment.

In the Food Assessment, tensions emerged around expectations of the role the partners would play. Community partners voiced concern that the academics "chose their level of involvement" and did not engage as "full partners." Academics, however, saw their role as "supervisory" and were surprised that concerns had been raised about their level and type of engagement in the project. While community partners had wanted a deeper working commitment from the academic partners, in the end, they were still pleased with the academic research outputs. This case shows that even conventional CCE orientations can have a place in building sustainable food systems, though communication, reflexivity, and an evaluation process all played a part in ensuring the actors were comfortable with that orientation by the time the project was complete.

We also acknowledge that CCE relationships rarely work out as expected, and sometimes do not deliver anything concrete. The transformative path is tough to walk at the best of times, and even conventional CCE orientations take commitment from beginning to end. This is not always possible despite the best intentions. Of our nine projects, some did not make much of a dent on the work that they had hoped to undertake, in some cases because of significant changes in personnel. Even in those cases though, there was learning about how to build relationships that will help the partners move their work forward and reach future goals.

CONCLUSION

> When we start to operate on the basis of power from below, we are moving from the more apolitical interpretation of 'food security' to the more directly political proposals of 'food sovereignty', not just within Indigenous communities, but more generally. (Community co-lead)

The above comment made at a presentation on our first four projects embodies what our argument in this chapter has meant for the work of our hub. The transformative CCE orientation and its associated methodological practices—including blurring the boundaries between academic and community subjectivity—help manifest some of the aspirations of the food sovereignty movement, and has thus taken our work beyond the food security frame which, especially at the international level, has been criticized for being a top-down approach to food systems defined primarily by expert knowledge (Fairbairn 2011). We emphasize here the key difference in the "horizontal" approach to collaboration (Zusman 2004). The most successful CCE projects have involved academics deeply embedded in community-led projects, epistemologically grounded in cognitive justice, with community members and academics functioning as partners with each contributing their strengths to a collectively determined vision.

As a result, we see a need to break down and reimagine power relations and the structures we work within. It is necessary to transform academic assumptions about who produces knowledge as well as how knowledge is produced. Relationships between academics and movement actors must be entered into conscientiously and proactively, with attention to disparities in power relations (Sandwell et al. 2014) as well as a commitment to transforming these relationships. To make horizontal partnerships work when working with social movements, academics need to engage with community actors not as objects of study but as partners. This means that we must not just work toward a politics of recognition, where academics are again given the power to decide who knows and whose knowledge is important, but rather to better understand and break down the structures and histories that place academics in the position to determine who are the objects of study and who constitutes an equal partner in the first place. This will help to ensure that power is shared more equitably, and horizontal partnerships are realized on more than just an individual scale.

While progress is being made to bridge CCE and the food sovereignty movement, we need to be cognizant that there remain challenges faced by movement activists working with scholars. In a report written a day after the 2014 food sovereignty conference at the ISS in the Hague several of these challenges were outlined, including: scholars' inability to meet activists' time-sensitive needs for information due to scholars' multiple commitments; continuing divisions between those who research and those who are "researched"; the potential damage caused by academic publications on internal movement politics; the continuing assumption that the university is the primary hub for knowledge creation; and the inadequacy of funding to support these relationships and the creation of knowledge for food sovereignty (Sandwell et al. 2014: 4–5).

In closing, more work is necessary to ensure constructive CCE is taking place that strengthens the food sovereignty movement. In the Canadian context, organizations like Food Secure Canada are well positioned to play a key role in building the intersection between CCE and the food sovereignty movement, including possible future "bridging" initiatives. Food sovereignty related conferences and gatherings (both academic and community-based) could become powerful spaces to bring people together to share information and strategize about future directions. While this is beginning to happen, it demands securing additional resources and shaping agendas to ensure that these meetings can be accessible and productive for all. It also means working to change structures and processes that place academic knowledge "above" community knowledge and, in doing so, create and support spaces that encourage cognitive justice, horizontal partnerships, and critical reflection. The food sovereignty movement is not unique in its engagement of academics but it does provide important potential to develop a working model for CCE to build food systems that are just and sustainable for all.

NOTES

1. While CSL and CBR are distinct in terms of their objectives, there are overlaps in practice, especially when they involve students working for credit. The most important thing that all CCE modalities have in common, for the purposes of this chapter, is that they involve relationships with external organizations. In the case of food sovereignty movement actors in Canada, CCE partnerships are typically with non-profit or public sector organizations.
2. While our work was initially organized through the frame of "community food security," defined as "a situation in which all community residents obtain a safe, culturally acceptable, nutritionally adequate diet through a sustainable food system that maximizes community self-reliance and social justice" (Hamm and Bellows 2003: 37), we often refer to ourselves as the food sovereignty hub of CFICE, in testament to the values discussed here.
3. For more details on the first four cases, see Andrée et al. (2014).
4. In Canada, a seventh pillar, "Food is Sacred," was added during the development of the People's Food Policy. Drawing on the experiences and guidance of Indigenous peoples, the seventh pillar holds that food is a gift of life which cannot be commodified (PFPP 2011).

REFERENCES

Aboriginal Knowledge(s): Colonialism, Decolonization and Education. (2014). University of Toronto Colloquium for OISE faculty and students. April 10.

Alkon, A. H., & Mares, T. M. (2012). Food sovereignty in US food movements: Radical visions and neoliberal constraints. *Agriculture and Human Values, 29*(3), 347–359. doi:10.1007/s10460-012-9356-z.

Andrée, P., Chapman, D., Hawkins, L., Kneen, C., Muehlberger, C., Nelson, C., et al. (2014). Building effective relationships for community-engaged scholarship in Canadian food studies. *Canadian Food Studies/La Revue Canadienne Des Études Sur L'alimentation, 1*(1), 27–27.

Bickford, D. M., & Reynolds, N. (2002). Activism and service-learning: Reframing volunteerism as acts of dissent. *Pedagogy, 2*(2), 229–252.

Butin, D. (2010). *Service-learning in theory and practice: The future of community engagement in higher education.* New York: Palgrave Macmillan.

Buys, N., & Bursnall, S. (2007). Establishing university–community partnerships: Processes and benefits. *Journal of Higher Education Policy and Management, 29*, 73–86.

CACSL. (n.d.). Canadian alliance for community service-learning. Retrieved from http://www.communityservicelearning.ca/en/welcome_what_is.htm

Carnegie Elective Community Engagement Classification 2014.

Cloke, P. (2004). Exploring boundaries of professional/personal practice and action: Being and becoming in Khayelitsha township, Cape Town. In D. Fuller & R. Kitchin (Eds.), *Radical theory/critical praxis: Academic geography beyond the academy*. Victoria: Praxis ePress.

Croteau, D. (2005). Which side are you on? The tensions between movement scholarship and activism. In D. Croteau, W. Haynes, & C. Ryan (Eds.), *Rhyming hope and history: Activists, academics and social movement scholarship* (pp. 20–40). Minneapolis, London: University of Minnesota Press.

Democratising Agricultural Research (DAR). (2012). Retrieved from: http://www.excludedvoices.org/about

Desmarais, A. A. (2007). *LVCLVC: Globalization and the power of peasants.* Halifax: Fernwood Pub.

Desmarais, A. A., & Wittman, H. (2014). Farmers, foodies, and First Nations: Getting to food sovereignty in Canada. *The Journal of Peasant Studies, 41*(6), 1153–1173.

Edelman, M. (2014). Food sovereignty: Forgotten genealogies and future regulatory challenges. *The Journal of Peasant Studies., 41*(6), 956–978.

Edelman, M., Weis, T., Baviskar, A., Borass, S. M., Jr., Holt-Giménez, E., Kandiyoti, D., & Wolford, W. (2014). Introduction: Critical perspectives on food sovereignty. *The Journal of Peasant Studies., 41*(6), 911–931.

Fairbairn, M. (2011). Framing transformation: The counter-hegemonic potential of food sovereignty in the US context. *Agriculture and Human Values, 29*(2), 217–230.

Freire, P. (2000). *Pedagogy of the oppressed.* New York: Bloomsbury Academic.

Friedland, W. H. (2008). "Chasms" in agrifood systems: Rethinking how we can contribute. *Agriculture and Human Values, 25*(2), 197–201.

Hamm, M. W., & Bellows, A. C. (2003). Community food security and nutrition educators. *Journal of Nutrition Education and Behavior, 35*(1), 37–43.

Harrison, B., Nelson, C. H., & Stroink, M. L. (2013). Being in community: A food security themed approach to public scholarship. *Journal of Public Scholarship and Higher Education, 3*, 91–110.

International Steering Committee (ISC). (2007). Synthesis Report from Nyéléni Forum for Food Sovereignty. Retrieved from: http://www.nyeleni.org/IMG/pdf/31Mar2007NyeleniSynthesisReport-en.pdf

Jassawalla, A. R., & Sashittal, H. C. (1998). An examination of collaboration in high-technology new product development processes. *Journal of Product Innovation Management, 15*, 237–254.

Kloppenburg, J. (2005). *The political ecology of plant biotechnology* (2nd ed.). Madison: The University of Wisconsin Press.

Kneen, C. (2010). Mobilisation and convergence in a wealthy northern country. *Journal of Peasant Studies, 37*(1), 329–235.

Kovach, M. (2009). *Indigenous methodologies: Characteristics, conversations, and contexts.* Toronto: University of Toronto Press.

Levkoe, C. (2014). The food movement in Canada: A social movement network perspective. *Journal of Peasant Studies, 41*(3), 385–403.

Levkoe, C., Brail, S., & Daniere, A. (2014). Engaged pedagogy and transformative learning in graduate education: A service learning case study. *Canadian Journal of Higher Education, 44*(3), 68–85.

Martin, S. J., & Andrée, P. (2014). From food security to food sovereignty in Canada: Resistance and empowerment in the context of neoliberalism. In M.-J. Massicotte, J. M. K. Ayres, P. Andrée, & M. Bosia (Eds.), *Globalization and food sovereignty: Global and local change in the new politics of food* (pp. 173–198). Toronto: University of Toronto Press.

Mitchell, T. D. (2008). Traditional vs. critical service learning: Engaging the literature to differentiate two models. *Michigan Journal of Community Service Learning,* Spring, *14*(2), 50–65.

Morrison, D. (2011). Chapter 6: Indigenous food sovereignty: A model for social learning. In H. Wittman, A. A. Desmarais, & N. Wiebe (Eds.), *Food sovereignty in Canada: Creating just and sustainable food systems.* Nova Scotia: Fernwood Publishing.

Nelson, C. H., & Stroink, M. L. (2013). CFICE FSRN case study report. (on file with authors).

People's Food Policy Project (PFPP). (2011). Resetting the table: A people's food policy for Canada. Retrieved from: http://foodsecurecanada.org/sites/default/files/fsc-resetting2012-8half11-lowres-en.pdf

Pimbert, Michel. (2010). Transforming knowledge and ways of knowing. In *Towards food sovereignty: Reclaiming autonomous food systems* (chapter 7). Retrieved from: http://pubs.iied.org/pdfs/G02493.pdf

Sandwell, K., Kay, S., Hajdu, A., & Hernando, O. (2014). Internal Report on the Day of Dialogue on knowledge for food sovereignty. Retrieved from: https://www.tni.org/files/download/day_of_dialogue_on_knowledge_for_food_sovereignty-1.pdf

Strand, K., Marullo, S., Cutforth, N., Stoecker, R., & Donohue, P. (2003). *Community-based research and higher education: Principles and practices.* San Francisco: John Wiley and Sons.

Swords, A. C., & Kiely, R. (2010). Beyond pedagogy: Service learning as movement building in higher education. *Journal of Community Practice, 18,* 148–170.

Zusman, P. (2004). Activism as a collective cultural praxis: Challenging the Barcelona urban model. In D. Fuller & R. Kitchin (Eds.), *Radical theory/critical praxis making a difference beyond the academy.* Retrieved from: http://www.praxis-epress.org/availablebooks/radicaltheorycriticalpraxis.html

Re: Claiming Food Sovereignty, Reclaiming Ways of Knowing: Food Justice Course Digs Deeper

Deborah Barndt

INTRODUCTION

In May 2014 and June 2015, I co-facilitated, along with Selam Teclu,[1] a three-week certificate course at the Coady International Institute at St. Francis Xavier University in Antigonish, Nova Scotia. Entitled "Creating Just Food Systems: Cultural Tools for Local and Global Activism" and in the second year renamed "Integrating Food Justice into Community Programs," this experimental course allowed us to explore not only the discourse and practice of food justice and food sovereignty but also the diverse learning approaches drawn from participants' backgrounds. This chapter will reflect critically on the challenges of shifting from dominant notions of food security to food justice and food sovereignty consciousness, while also shifting from dominant educational models to popular education methods that honor Indigenous knowledges and holistic ways of knowing. We posit a connection between the content and the process,

D. Barndt (✉)
Faculty of Environmental Studies, York University, Toronto, ON, Canada

© The Author(s) 2016
J. Sumner (ed.), *Learning, Food, and Sustainability*,
DOI 10.1057/978-1-137-53904-5_9

155

that together they promote more democratic, sustainable, and just food production.

STARTING WITH THE SEED

From the first day of the course, we had participants experiencing hands-on the processes of growing food. My co-facilitator Selam led us through an Eritrean ritual of sorting and sprouting teff seeds, accompanied by percussion and song. This simple act was a powerful symbol of the importance of seeds in food sovereignty and the process of recovering practices that were both agricultural and cultural. It also encouraged others to share their own histories and lost practices. Beyond that, participants were asked to nurture their sprouts over the three weeks as they would care for a child, so they developed relationships with their plants, and experienced directly the ongoing attention required to grow food.

Another introductory activity invited participants to tell stories about their own connections to food by selecting from 50 food-related photos one image they could identify with. This storytelling exercise helped us to get to know each other personally and contextually, and planted another kind of seed—grounding us in the realities (soil) within which each participant was growing food justice.

Theoretical Framing

Underlying our course design was the contention that the ideas underlying food sovereignty can be related to worldviews or cosmovisions that honor critical, Indigenous, and holistic ways of knowing and learning. At the core of food sovereignty is a deep connection to the land (simultaneously political and economic, cultural and spiritual) that is maintained by embodied, local environmental knowledges, and organic praxis. The term was created by Via Campesina, a transnational coalition of 164 organizations in 73 countries, led by Indigenous and peasant communities, to offer a regenerative rather than a reductionist vision of food (Morrison 2011). It aims to honor local ecologies and knowledges, dismantle corporate agrifood monopolies, and democratize food systems. In contrast, the corporate food regime built on the notion of food as a commodity is maintained by an increasingly corporatized educational system that has also commodified knowledge. The cultural hegemony of what Paulo Freire (1993) called banking education in the west reinforces the political and economic hegemony of the corporate food regime.

In reflecting on our course, I draw upon two main fields of study: the course content of food studies, in particular food justice and food sovereignty, and the course methodology of popular education, especially community-engaged education honoring arts-based and Indigenous ways of knowing.

Field 1: Course Content—From Food Enterprise to Food Sovereignty

Eric Holt-Gimenez (2011) offers a framework for comparing and contrasting the corporate food regime and emerging food movements. According to him, the discourses of food enterprise and food security support the corporate food regime while food justice and food sovereignty concepts feed a growing alternative food movement.

Food enterprise represents the neoliberal model of monocultural industrial food production, supported by global bodies like the International Monetary Fund (IMF) and the World Trade Organization (WTO) as well as government policies of privatization and deregulation that support corporate concentration. The discourse of **food security** is also considered to be within the corporate food regime but as a reformist approach guiding many development initiatives. While this term is perhaps the most widely used by international institutions, Holt-Gimenez suggest that food security programs often "mainstream less inequitable and less environmentally damaging alternatives into existing market structures," (2011, 323). In other words, they do not challenge the structural underpinnings of the corporate food regime.

Food justice as a discourse and movement has developed primarily in the Global North, in response to inequities in the food system, and championed by community food security and labor organizations, fair trade and slow food movements, and environmental justice and anti-racism groups. Growing out of the environmental movement and led by people of color in North America, food justice initiatives promote small-scale sustainable agriculture, citizen-led community gardens, community supported agriculture (CSA) programs, and food policy councils.

Though the two terms are often used interchangeably, Holt-Gimenez characterizes **food sovereignty** as more radical. Led by the Global South, it promotes the democratizing of the food system in favor of the poor and is often linked to the struggles for land, territory, and local control of food production. The concept was developed by Via Campesina, the transnational alliance that has become the major body challenging the rules of the global bodies governing the corporate food system. Via Campesina has articulated seven principles of Food Sovereignty: (1) Food: A Basic Human Right, (2) Agrarian Reform, (3) Protecting Natural Resources, (4) Reorganizing Food Trade, (5) Ending the Globalization of Hunger, (6) Social Peace, and (7) Democratic Control.[2]

Food security discourse dominates development non-governmental organizations (NGOs) in the Global South, and so it was a challenge for us to know how to promote our course to draw international participants who are often sponsored by civil society organizations or government institutions. In some African countries, for example, it is dangerous to use the language of "food sovereignty." To critique the corporate interests of the seed or agrochemical companies (like Monsanto) and global philanthropists (like the Bill and Melinda Gates Foundation) is to "bite the hand that feeds you." We experimented with different framings: When we concluded that the first year course title "Creating Just Food Systems" might be too ambitious, given the organizational affiliations of participants, for the second year, we renamed it "Integrating Food Justice into Community Programs."

This invited community leaders working on health issues and women's leadership, for example, to consider the connections between their work and the challenges of food justice. Nonetheless, we still had to acknowledge the constraints and possibilities of the particular work contexts of the participants, and the different implications of the terms for their work.

Field 2: Course Methodology—From Colonial Banking Education to Popular Holistic Education

Popular education, the other field informing our course (in particular, our teaching and learning approach) proposes that any educational process must *start with* the participants. It must understand both their specific historical and cultural contexts, as well as their level of consciousness around food issues and their relationship to broader political processes, and appreciate that no learning is neutral and power is operating at every level.

At the start of the course, we introduced Paulo Freire's problem-posing model of education to emphasize that we considered all participants both learners and teachers bringing their own knowledge and experience to a collective process of sharing stories, identifying issues, analyzing structures, proposing strategies, and developing plans for action. This approach may at first be uncomfortable for people who have been educated within a colonial system, which privileges western science and Eurocentric worldviews. Colonial education is characterized by a top-down methodology, what Freire called "banking education," in which the all-knowing teacher deposits rational and often decontextualized knowledge into the heads of passive students who are to digest and regurgitate facts that may not be relevant to their lives, and may in fact contribute to their continued oppression.

Just as food enterprise approaches to the global food system have denied local agricultural knowledges and practices by imposing monocultural industrial methods of food production often controlled by foreign interests and management practices, so too have dominant teaching and learning methods imposed through colonial educational systems, even in the Global South, denied the Indigenous knowledges and multiple ways of knowing inherent in diverse cultures and ecologies. This has often meant that rational and text-based approaches to learning are considered more legitimate than more embodied forms of learning which engage the senses in a more holistic educational process. Dominant educational practices have also marginalized local artistic practices and cultural tools which are and could be powerful forms of learning, organizing, and acting.

In challenging the environmentally unsustainable and socially unjust agricultural practices of the corporate food regime, we are also suggesting that colonial, hierarchical, and text-based teaching/learning is unsustainable in that it does not respond to specific contexts nor empower learners to become active citizens. In the context of our course, then, the food system must be both environmentally and socially sustainable, and the educational approach must be sustainable in its applicability to other contexts and its use of deeply engrained cultural forms of expression and learning. Vandana Shiva (1993) makes the connection between monocultural production practices and ways of thinking with her concept of "monocultures of the mind." In other words, engagement in food production within specific ecologies both reflects and reproduces ways of thinking and knowing. In the same light, we chose popular education approaches in the food justice course, because it promoted vernacular and polycultural rather than monocultural practices and forms of knowledge. Developed out of social movements in Latin America in the 1960s and best articulated by Paulo Freire's (1993) *Pedagogy of the Oppressed,* this approach advocates the development of critical social consciousness that leads to collective action, always appropriate to the particular historical context.

Popular education approaches to teaching community development are already common practice at the Coady International Institute where we co-facilitated the course. There was also support for two other components we integrated into our popular education pedagogy: arts-based and Indigenous ways of knowing. Diana Taylor (2003) in *The Archive and the Repertoire: Performing Cultural Memory in the Americas* traces the imposition of text-based knowing (or the archive) as part of the colonial process in the Americas, often discrediting more embodied knowledges (the repertoire) such as storytelling, performance, music, and dance. These forms of expression are powerful sites of cultural memory, of passing on values and practices, and of creating new understandings. William Cleveland (2002) suggests that these more community-engaged arts can be adapted by social movements to educate and inform, to inspire and mobilize, to nurture and heal, and to build and improve community capacity. The participants in our course were from diverse cultural contexts, many speaking English as a second or third language, so drawing on arts-based approaches and promoting the use of cultural tools in their work tapped a broader repertoire of knowledges and encouraged creative and participatory processes. In effect, it made the course very lively and even fun; this was sometimes viewed in ambivalent ways, as participants in other concurrent courses both envied the energy emanating from our classroom and questioned whether any "serious" learning could actually be taking place.

Institutional Context of the Food Justice Course

The Coady International Institute has been offering community development and leadership training to development NGO practitioners from 130 countries for 55 years. Our three-week food justice certificate was part of a program on "Building Community Resilience," reinforcing Coady's Asset-Based Community Development (ABCD) approach. Such an emphasis counters any top-down or deficit-driven development models and suggests that communities have many strengths that can be tapped for more participatory development processes.

In 2014, we had 13 participants in the Food Justice course, 6 from the Global South (Sierra Leone, Ghana, Ethiopia, Nepal, and Mexico) and 7 Canadian, specifically Nova Scotia (including a Mi'kmaq elder fisherwoman/artist). In 2015, there were four Canadian participants, three of whom were refugees or immigrants (from Bhutan and Argentina), four Africans (Ghana, Zambia, and Burkina Faso) and two Indonesian professors. With both groups, we had to constantly adapt to the range of educational backgrounds, from limited literacy and English skills to a Canada Research Chair in food security; from people working in community gardens and NGOs to managers in government agencies and teachers in universities. Popular education pedagogy advocates that we start with the participants, and build the course organically based on their experiences, knowledge, needs, and skills. The differences—in language, education, and work contexts—which could easily become sources of division more often became sources of rich exchange.

Food Justice Course Design

We designed the course around three themes. *Week One, the Corporate Food Regime,* unveiled the system(s) that we were challenging. We drew on the specific participants' knowledge through participatory processes while using Wayne Roberts' (2013) book, *The No-Nonsense Guide to World Food.* Participants mapped their own organizational and community contexts, before we collectively mapped the history of food justice revealing the forces shaping the current system in both local and global contexts. The Holt-Gimenez framework contrasting the corporate food regime and food movements was introduced through a series of video clips illustrating each of the four approaches he outlines.[3] By touring supermarkets, we explored corporate ownership, the global sources of food, industrial ingredients and health, the illusion of diversity, and the myth of the supermarket nirvana. Through theater forum, we analyzed the power relations from seed to supermarket in Ethiopia. The film "El Contrato" offered a powerful and emotional exposure of the hidden reality of migrant labor.

Week Two, Food Sovereignty and Food Movements, highlighted case studies of rural and urban communities creating alternatives to the corporate food regime. A participant who was a Mi'qmaq elder shared the ways her First Nation community maintains traditional fishing practices. The second year she returned to share her knowledge of native plants as sacred medicine, while another Aboriginal woman survivor of residential schools shared the impact of the recently released Truth and Reconciliation Commission report.

Participants began to imagine new projects mapped in their own organizational, local, and/or national contexts. Global efforts were explored the first year through de Schutter's report (2014) to the UN Assembly on the Right to Food, and the second year through the work of Via Campesina, with case studies by participants from Ghana and Costa Rica. A field trip to Halifax gave us hands-on engagement with community gardens, youth projects, markets, and participatory food research. We capped the week with a collective feast, cooking together and sharing food rituals, like the Ethiopian coffee ceremony.

In *Week Three: Community Projects and Cultural Tools*, teams produced creative learning tools documenting our experiences through power point, slide shows, and a radio show. The artistic forms ranged from Mi'qmaq mask-making to social media. The second year we spent more time working on specific project proposals that participants would initiate back in their own home and work contexts, offering some analytical tools for assessing the constraints and possibilities they might encounter as well as culturally appropriate tools they might apply to encourage more creative participation. The class also produced a collective show for Social Justice Radio on the St. FX campus, synthesizing our learnings at the end of the three-week course.

CRITICAL REFLECTIONS ON KEY ISSUES

For the rest of this chapter, I will reflect on what we considered our most critical challenges in crafting a course on food justice using arts-based methods. I have divided our reflections into two sections, one that focuses more on the content of the course, which I subsume under the title "Education for critical consciousness around food," and the second that focuses on the pedagogy or praxis learning.

Education for Critical Consciousness Around Food

My co-facilitator Selam Teclu introduced us to the mythic Sankofa bird of the West African Akan people, a bird that flies forward while looking backward with an egg in its mouth. She suggested that, in the context of development projects, it might mean that we must return to our roots to recover what has been lost in order to move forward. This idea countered a model of development that frames traditional agricultural practices and knowledges as "backward" and inhibiting "modernization," which was a challenge for some of the Global South participants who were funded by international NGOs or government agencies based on the modernization paradigm.

Dominant approaches to food crises in many development organizations reflect the "reformist" approach associated with "food security." The suggestion in food sovereignty that communities should regain control of their food destinies and honor plants and practices grounded in specific cultures and ecologies contributed to confusion: Were they now being told that traditional knowledges might be healthier and more sustainable than the ideas driving their foreign-funded projects?

Confusion is part of the process of shifting consciousness from food security to food justice and food sovereignty, and we adopted several different pedagogical approaches to move the process forward. First, we invited participants to draw maps of their organizations and communities, identifying their own roles in the organization and showing where food fit within this context. They were encouraged to use any visual forms or symbols, play with colors, and take their time. We then made a gallery out of their drawings on large chart paper, and moved around the room, giving each participant 10 to 15 minutes to introduce us orally to their context. The diverse maps were powerful catalysts for storytelling, reflecting the specific organizations, communities, and nations where they worked as well as the dominant and conflicting perspectives on food production and food issues. They also revealed the unique personalities of the group; one participant, for example, drew a playful monster in the corner of his drawing, which we identified as a "trickster," a role which he continued to play throughout the course. We also considered how participants might carry out their own food mapping in their communities, and offered resources that could be adapted for that purpose (Lewis 2009).[4]

While the individual mapping exercise affirmed the personal experiences and local contexts that participants represented, we used another kind of mapping to assess participants' understanding of the macro context. The Historical Timeline activity invited everyone to identify key moments in the History of the Global Food System—both local and national as well as international events.

Participants were given sticky notes of two colors—one to note developments that helped build the corporate food regime, another for those that contributed to food justice and food sovereignty movements. Everyone placed their contributions on a timeline that arbitrarily began with 1492 (though the philosopher in the group reminded us of the roots of a rationalist food system in the Hellenic philosophy of the Greeks). As we collectively reviewed each note, participants stood by the timeline to elaborate on their contribution to the historical review. Once again the participatory nature of the activity stimulated more stories and interventions, revealing both individual and collective knowledge about the food system and food movements. It also gave us some sense of what information and knowledge was missing; while African participants, for example, were well aware of the interventions of Monsanto and Gates in agricultural initiatives, they knew less about food sovereignty actions by Via Campesina and other activist networks in Africa.

During the first week, we organized two field trips which offered powerful forms of experiential learning. First we broke into groups to visit supermarkets in Antigonish (Walmart, Superstore, Sobeys, and Shoppers Drug Mart), adapting some of the questions used in a Supermarket Tour created by the Ontario Public Interest Research Group (OPIRG).[5]

This tour uses the supermarket itself as a code for examining issues such as the origins and production practices behind meat/seafood, fresh produce, and processed foods; the role of advertising and labeling in convincing/confusing the consumer; corporate concentration in both fresh and processed foods; the psychology of store design; the debates about GMOs, organic, and local/global food, and so on. Participants photographed and took notes of their observations, which they shared with other groups on return, comparing what they found in four different commercial food sites.

In the first year, a major "ah-hah moment" occurred regarding the ubiquitous use of corn starch (to increase the weight of chicken and process most canned foods). We had a unique resource in a participant who had worked for 20 years with the corporate food regime, and was responsible for cornstarch use around the globe. She revealed the inside story of this phenomenon, while also sharing her own story of shifting from being a corporate scientist to becoming a community activist for local and sustainable agricultural alternatives. Global South participants, on the other hand, had ambivalent responses to the supermarket experience, being easily seduced by the color and light, abundance and diversity it offered, while also beginning to understand how the retail sector was now eliminating small producers, crops, shops, and culinary practices in their own contexts.

The day after the supermarket tour, we visited the Antigonish Farmers' Market, where participants talked with farmers, bakers, artisans, and others in this community-building context. Participants were well aware of the contradictions, and did not fall into any easy dichotomizing of the two forms of markets, recognizing, for example, that the farmers' market drew mainly a white middle-class population, and was not accessible to the working class, Aboriginal people, and communities of color. At least one of the larger vendors hires Mexican migrant workers, opening up another issue of global labor in local food movements. This issue is central to food justice struggles and is further elaborated in the next section.

Critical Consciousness and an Intersectional Analysis of Power: Class, Gender, and Race

Labor tends to be a blind spot among food activists, so we introduced the issue of migrant labor during the first week, showing how central it is to the corporate food regime as well as to global food movements. Min

Sook Lee's seminal documentary (NFB 2003) "El Contrato"[6] catalyzed emotional discussion about the personal and structural impacts of migrant farm workers who leave their families behind for months out of the year to grow and harvest our local produce, often under repressive working and living conditions. The migration phenomenon is worldwide, of course, and so participants had their own examples of migration feeding agriculture (e.g., from Burkina Faso to South Africa, from Nicaragua to Costa Rica), as well as within their countries.

One of the more powerful ways we learned about this historical phenomenon came through the sharing of agricultural-related songs that participants recalled from their childhoods. Several referred to migrant workers having to leave their own land to produce food in far-off places for others, and noted that the most exploitative jobs were often shaped by race and gender. For example, a Latin American participant shared "Duerme, Negrito," a lament of an AfroCuban woman rocking her baby to sleep on her back as she cuts sugarcane under the hot sun; the lullaby morphs from a soft and comforting sound to an angry protest song about horrific working conditions.

Another arts-based method we used to explore power differences both between and within food systems and movements was Theater of the Oppressed. A practice developed by Augusto Boal in Brazil and closely related to Paulo Freire's *Pedagogy of the Oppressed*, this tool asks participants to represent situations where they feel oppressed in their own life or work contexts. Facilitated by Coady affiliate Natalie Abdou, the workshop used "theater forum" to reconstruct food-related situations that reveal gender, race, and class tensions in a wide range of contexts. One was based on the experience of an African participant during a visit to Ottawa; in the scenario, he was angrily rebuked when he offered to help an older white woman carry her groceries to her car. When the audience was asked to intervene in the scenario, to suggest alternatives to the actions taken by various actors in the scene, their responses revealed many different ways that race and gender are constructed and challenged. For example, some assumed that the scenario was in the Global South, not Canada; this shift provokes a different interpretation. Some responses focused on the gender dynamic and aimed to protect the white woman, while others assumed the woman was the oppressor, and defended the black man. In any case, the theatrical representation of a personal experience provoked a rich discussion and debate.

Participants found popular theater very compelling, accessible and potentially useful in their education and organizing work around food justice. Toward the end of the course, a group created a scenario that unveiled intergenerational tensions in an African family, centered around a mother involved in local and organic food, while her daughter was drawn to the multinational fast food options often associated with being cool. A local elder as well as a food sovereignty organizer were built into the drama, adding to the complexity of the situation, but true to the nuanced and multilayered situations that participants experience in their work and home contexts.

The most intense conversations came out of moments when differences within our class emerged around race issues, in particular how we represent the historical impacts of colonization on Indigenous populations as well as the legacy of the Atlantic slave trade on African descendants in the Americas. Our hope was that we could create a space where the very real emotions associated with these historical and current injustices could be expressed and heard, and that the differences could catalyze deeper analyses of the systemic inequities which continue to shape not only the food system but also our local and global food movements, as well as our personal and collective lives.

Praxis Learning

Praxis learning begins with experience. Central to traditional agricultural practices is the experiential process of learning by doing; over millennia, Indigenous and peasant elders and communities passed on their knowledge through family and communal participation in growing, cooking, and processing food. For most Indigenous peoples, food is alive, sacred, and medicine; there are rituals and ceremonies honoring its cultural and spiritual significance. In revaluing this kind of learning and recovering practices that had been discredited, we aimed to honor Indigenous knowledges and ways of knowing.

While we were somewhat limited to a six-hour daily schedule within a classroom setting, we tried to integrate activities both inside and outside that would give participants hands-on emotional experience, followed by reflection on what we learned and how it applied to the diverse work contexts represented. These ranged from sprouting and planting seeds on the first day to helping Antigonish food activists plant berries and vegetables around the public library, to creating our own collective feast on the final Sunday afternoon. In the latter activity, we spent six hours cooking our diverse culinary offerings in the university's demonstration kitchen followed by a celebratory meal that integrated different cultural rituals of storytelling and thanking "all our relations," again acknowledging food as a living entity, central to our identities.

Our field trip to Halifax was perhaps the most intense immersion of global participants in a particular local context—visiting urban agricultural projects and immigrant service organizations. Global South participants were moved by the initiatives of black youth in Halifax who produced and sold healthy sauces from their community garden, for example.

Our visit coincided with a public event that offered a visceral introduction to arts-based participatory learning in a multicultural context with over 15 new Canadians sharing their own photovoice stories, while over 50 community members were introduced to the project through simultaneous translations in 7 different languages. The conversations our participants had with these ethnically based storytellers generated a palpable excitement, and gave us a sense of the power of this tool that could never have been grasped through reading or even watching digital stories in the classroom.

But praxis learning requires not only experience but also reflection on experience. The Monday after our supermarket and farmers' market tours, we gathered to compare these two market experiences, identifying the differences between them along four axes that I had used in an earlier study of the corporate food regime (2008). What did each illustrate about the distance between *production and consumption*? How did they threaten or promote *biodiversity and cultural diversity*? How is *technology* shaping the *work* and workers within each context? What is the impact on *human and ecological health* of the production practices behind supermarkets and farmers' markets? This analytical tool, used in smaller groups made up of participants from different countries, generated a lot of international comparisons, debates, and questions about the desired direction in each context.

Of course, the deeper test of how much we generated praxis learning will be revealed over time in the projects that participants proposed to do on return to their own organizations, communities, and countries. As the title for the second iteration of the course was "Integrating Food Justice into Community Programs," we recognized that each context would offer both constraints and possibilities for this to happen. The second year we began the proposal development process earlier, in the second week, so that participants could get feedback, revise, elaborate, and deepen their proposals. We also introduced a tool called "assessing the forces" from the "Naming the Moment" methodology.[7] This tool asks us to identify forces, institutions, and actors in three realms (economic, political, and cultural/ideological) that might support or oppose the proposed projects, as well as those that are undecided or unknown. As a form of political analysis for action, this process embeds the food projects within specific social contexts, and helps project coordinators think more strategically about how they can move their ideas forward—again, a critical part of praxis, or as Paulo Freire names it, the dynamic interrelation of action and reflection.

Throughout the three-week course, we adapted a wide range of art and media forms, many described above. They included embodied practices like drama and music; written forms like poetry, storytelling, and lecture; visual forms like drawing, photography, and video. While low-tech tools like theater were seen as more accessible and engaging, there was a growing passion for the potential uses of Internet-based and digital media. And these two forms of media were not always in opposition. The Internet became a constant participant in the course, with participants finding music and videos (often of embodied cultural forms like dance or music) from their own cultural contexts to show during breaks or as part of the course. An Indonesian participant responsible for one of the daily opening rituals, for example, included a YouTube video of poverty and street children living on $1/day in Java, Indonesia, as a way of introducing an activity asking us to consider how we would spend one dollar if that is all we had to survive daily. These moments revealed that participants had integrated the ideas of praxis learning, and could both design and facilitate creative activities, both embodied and digital, that engaged everyone in experiential education.

One of the best uses of technology was a Skype conversation we arranged to have with Wayne Roberts, the author of the main text of our course. He was in the UK at the time, so we had to juggle time differences. The setup was perfect—participants opened our transatlantic dialogue with a song then in pairs stood and spoke directly to Roberts on the computer screen. A day earlier they had rehearsed presentations on their interpretations of five key features of food sovereignty that we identified in the text; they created not only plain language definitions, but also used drama, drawing, and even their native languages to express the meaning it had for them and their contexts. After each presentation, Wayne engaged the pair in a dialogue, which brought in new information as well as encouragement for participants to contribute cases for the next edition of the book! This direct engagement with a face on a screen was surprisingly intimate and left participants high on the experience. It was a perfect culmination of our three-week course, with participants drawing comfortably on their respective histories, offering their own interpretations of the core ideas, even using their own languages and cultural practices to communicate them confidently.

The ubiquity of cameras in the world today also meant that there were multiple documenters of our own class process. Given that we did more than sit in chairs, listen, and talk, the course methodology provided more interesting visual documentation as well. Toward the end of the third week, we produced three syntheses of the course through three different media.

One was a one-hour live radio show on the campus Social Justice radio program. While we asked a Ghanian journalist to take the lead and host the program, we collectively created questions that would be answered to reflect on the meaning and impact of the course. Participants were paired up so that each would have one opportunity to be the interviewer and another opportunity to be interviewed. In between these dialogues, they searched the Internet for favorite music from their culture. This hastily constructed radio show[8] served multiple purposes: It became a form of course evaluation, it communicated our experience to a sympathetic public, and it engaged everyone actively in its production which left us exhilarated as ten of us tumbled out of the small studio. These collective productions were once again experiences in praxis learning, and emphasized the original subtitle of the course: "Cultural tools for local and global activism."

During the last two days, we also created a slide show of the course, "Harvesting Justice," with images metaphorically organized around the phases of a food cycle: seeds, planting, watering and weeding, harvesting, cooking, eating, cleaning up and composting, celebrating, and thanking. The compilation of these images, however, proved incredibly challenging when everyone wanted to contribute photos they had taken with their cameras, smartphones, or tablets. We selected 90 images from over 1000 photos from 7 different sources. The digital form provided us with a tool at the end which served to remind everyone of what we had done, and thus catalyzed reflection and evaluation, as well as giving participants something to take home to keep the memory of our collective experience alive.

Given that our course had involved so many alternative pedagogical and arts-based tools, the group easily decided to write a collective song for the Coady Institute's graduation ceremony. Even though each course was asked to have one representative speak, we chose one to be the front singer, while the rest were the backup singers. Thus, the final public ritual was collective and performative, illustrating as well as anything that our course had engaged people in creative participatory processes and holistic education.

CONCLUSION

While the future of the course is uncertain, there may be possibilities of offering it regionally, to make it more accessible to more practitioners, to allow us to work in different languages, and to link more directly to agricultural and cultural practices of the participants. There are always trade-offs, in that part of the richness of having participants from various continents is that they learn from both the differences in terms of particular ideas and programs, as well as the similarities in the struggles they experience in trying to contribute to a more just and sustainable food system. There are also contradictions in trying to promote experiential, hands-on and culturally based learning within a neutral classroom which is out of context for everyone, except perhaps for us as Coady facilitators.

The real test of any value of these learning experiences of course can only be shown in the ways that participants integrate any new ideas or shifts in approach to food justice or to praxis learning, when they return home. While some are communicating through a Facebook page, with progress reports on their projects, we cannot really know the impact, nor what challenges they face within their own organizational and cultural constraints. Perhaps quoting an email from Hira, an Indonesian participant, a physician and professor of midwives, in response to an email we sent two months after the course finished, is the best way to end, revealing that sometimes it is the small actions, closest to home, and adapting to local conditions that plant the seeds for broader institutional changes:

My project of starting a school garden may have seemed small when I was in Canada. But, as soon as I arrived home, things happened. I had to spend days in hospital with my son exposed with typhoid fever. It was after I stopped the antibiotics and gave him the juice of a kind of big green pumpkin, three times a day ...that helped him having nights free from fever.

The next thing after the typhoid is the water shortage that is affecting almost every house in my area. We are facing a long dry season.... Now, with that situation, I am refraining myself from approaching the school with the garden idea. Instead I am spending my time doing other things: preparing seeds. Some children from my house area, 3 to 5 children, so 7 with my two girls, are willing to help.

So, I may not directly go to the school garden but am re-routing my steps by starting from my own garden. Good that my well is still having water. I just need to focus on my own garden, first, then I plan to invite the school teachers and show them what happened with my garden.

With your email, it feels like taking me back to the track. It is really invigorating to feel that, when we are kind of losing our way, someone out there is looking at what we are doing. It reminded me of your quoting Aboriginal writer Thomas King, which can be paraphrased for our course:

"Now that you have learnt about food justice, It is up to you for what you are going to do with that. You can either forget it or you can do something about it. You can do anything but one, you cannot say, you know nothing about it."

Notes

1. As a teaching team, we each brought different experiences and skills: Eritrean-born Selam is a holistic nutritionist and urban farmer; while I came with more academic experience in food studies and popular education practice. I want to honor her contribution as invaluable for our teaching/learning process.
2. https://www.youtube.com/watch?v=9fYGCHoP-HY.
3. Food enterprise: https://www.youtube.com/watch?v=kJtyRYrD2Rk; Food security: https://www.youtube.com/watch?v=PiYDG11zIUs; Food justice: https://www.youtube.com/watch?v=xA6p0w2Xoqg; Food sovereignty: https://www.youtube.com/watch?v=5kw_sIu5AyI.
4. http://foodsecurecanada.org/sites/default/files/Mapping_food_matters.pdf.
5. http://www.fairtradebarrie.ca/pdf/wpirg_supermarket_tour.pdf.
6. https://www.nfb.ca/film/el_contrato.
7. Download pdf of *Naming the Moment: Political Analysis for Action* from http://www.popednews.org/downloads/naming%20the%20moment%20.pdf.
8. http://socialjusticeradio.onelouder.ca/shows/SJR/SJR%20June%2018th%20Food%20Justice.mp3.

References

Cleveland, W. (2002). Mapping the field: Arts-based community development. Retrieved September 7, 2015, from http://wayback.archive-it.org/2077/20100906195318/http://www.communityarts.net/readingroom/archivefiles/2002/05/mapping_the_fie.php

de Schutter, O. (2014, 24 January). The transformative potential of the right to food. [Weblog]. Retrieved September 8, 2015, from http://www.srfood.org/images/stories/pdf/officialreports/20140310_finalreport_en.pdf

Freire, P. (1993) [1970]. *Pedagogy of the oppressed*. London: Penguin Books.

Holt-Gimenez, E. (2011). Food security, food justice, or food sovereignty: Crises, food movements and regime change. In A. Alkon & J. Agyeman (Eds.), *Cultivating food justice: Race, class and sustainability* (pp. 309–330). Cambridge, MA: MIT Press.

Lewis, H. (2009). Community food mapping project: South Parkdale, Toronto: Summer 2009. [Weblog]. Retrieved September 8, 2015, from https://westendfood.coop/sites/westendfood.coop/files/wefc/public/2009/events-meetings/community-food-mapping/ParkdaleFoodMappingInformationKit.pdf

Morrison, D. (2011). Indigenous food sovereignty: A model for social learning. In H. Wittman, A. Desmarais, & N. Wiebe (Eds.), *Food sovereignty in Canada: Creating just and sustainable food systems* (pp. 97–113). Black Point: Fernwood.

Roberts, W. (2013). *The no-nonsense guide to world food* (2nd ed.). Toronto: The New Internationalist/BTL.

Shiva, V. (1993). *Monocultures of the mind: Perspectives on biodiversity and biotechnology.* London: Zed Books.

Taylor, D. (2003). *The archive and the repertoire: Performing cultural memory in the Americas.* Durham: Duke University Press.

PART IV

Learning, Food, and Sustainability: Tools for the Future

Youth and Food Literacy: A Case Study of Food Education at The Stop Community Food Centre

Sarah Goldstein

Introduction: What Has Food Education and Food Literacy Got to Do with It?

Of all the ways to interact with our environment, food is perhaps the most universal medium. Throughout the course of our day, the vast majority of us consume at least one meal, and often many more. As North Americans, the way we eat has evolved over time. The current food system is a far cry from that which we experienced only a few generations ago, for there now exists a reliance on fossil fuels, factories, global distribution systems, vast monocultures, corporate concentration, and concentrated animal feeding operations (CAFOs) to facilitate growth and create demand for high-profit manufactured foods. Unquestionably, the food system has undergone remarkable change through the rise of industrial agriculture and subsequent corporatization, and these changes impact what we eat, why we eat, where we eat, and how we eat.

S. Goldstein (✉)
Work undertaken at Faculty of Environmental Studies, York University, Toronto, ON, Canada

© The Author(s) 2016
J. Sumner (ed.), *Learning, Food, and Sustainability*,
DOI 10.1057/978-1-137-53904-5_10

What do we know about food now? What knowledge have we retained among this food evolution, and what does it mean for the future of our food system? The dominant North American food system distances consumers from food's origins, and conceptualizes food as a commodity for profit. Today's eaters are primarily exposed to an industrial foodscape composed of packaged and processed food products, prepared meals, and meals outside the home. These tactics have resulted in a widespread lack of knowledge demonstrated by both children and adults, not only about where food comes from but also about the food system's impact on health and the environment.

With eaters having undergone what Jaffe and Gertler (2006) term a "**deskilling,**" citizens no longer know enough about food and the contemporary food system, for "much of the power of agribusiness ultimately depends on farmers and consumers not knowing" (Kloppenburg et al. 1996, 6). With this takeover of industrial food, "food deskilling has reached a point where it is commonly assumed that the younger generation no longer knows how to manage in a kitchen" (Desjardins et al. 2013, 1).

In response to the effects of deskilling, the popularity of food education programs has grown in recent years as a way to solve food-related social problems (Kimura 2011). Often grounded in experiential learning opportunities through farm to school programs, school and community gardens, and cooking programs, schools, government, health, and community groups seek to provide **food literacy** development opportunities so that children and youth can learn to enjoy growing, preparing, and eating healthy food (Howard and Brichta 2013; Chessen et al. 2009; Davies and Thomas 2010). Most programs maintain common broad goals of reskilling their participants and promoting some level of food literacy, while often touting a relationship between food literacy and food systems change (Jaffe and Gertler 2006; Goodman and Dupuis 2002; Howard and Brichta 2013).

Many of these food education programs are trying to instill food literacy of a sort, but what kind of food literacy? And are they succeeding?

RESEARCH METHODS

The research efforts explored within this chapter seek to answer a series of questions that sprung from one main question: *How, and to what extent, does food education facilitate a reasonable level of food literacy in youth?* Moreover, what are the components of food literacy, and how do we measure and understand food literacy? To what extent can food education programs contribute to food literacy, and what are the challenges of creating and executing an effective program if food literacy is one of the ultimate goals?

In an attempt to begin to answer these questions, I used a mixed methods approach in my research, which centered on a case study of a community-based youth food education program ("Food Leadership for Youth" or "FLY") at The Stop Community Food Centre in Toronto, Ontario. Planned methods of inquiry included a literature review, document analysis, participant observation, semi-structured interviews, and evaluation of The Stop's internal qualitative questionnaires completed by FLY participants at the beginning and end of the program. However, during the 2014 winter semester, staff and volunteers faced an unprecedented problem of both participant retention and lack of regular participant attendance. In order to compensate for the lack of participant questionnaire data, I increased the number of interviews conducted with FLY staff and volunteers. I also chose to interview participants from the current year's program and the 2012–2013 FLY program, which allowed me to collect a rich spectrum of conversations. My research took place between January 2014 and June 2014, and the remarks and opinions of staff, volunteers, and the FLY participants strongly influenced the content of this chapter.

Unpacking the Idea of Food Literacy

Food literacy is a newly prevalent buzzword, described by Cullerton et al. (2012) as a permutable term with no true consensus of meaning. Scores of food education programs either explicitly or implicitly name food literacy as one of their main goals, operating on rather widespread and ongoing assumptions that education efforts are both effective and worthwhile in improving participants' food literacy. As programs proclaim their efforts to teach food literacy, the question holds: What exactly is food literacy, and what are the benchmarks of an individual who has become food literate? A thorough review of the literature reveals that two understandings of food literacy predominate: the neoliberal consciousness model, which maintains a focus on individual consumer responsibility and technical skills to make healthy choices within the current market; and the critical consciousness model, which encourages systems thinking and pursues active engagement with the food system to disrupt problematic practices.

The Neoliberal Consciousness Paradigm: Food Literacy as Individual Responsibility and Choice

In the literature, there appears a trend where food literacy is deemed an individual responsibility. While there are subtleties within each researcher's definition, as a whole this rather prevalent understanding of food literacy is remarkably narrow. It places the burden of both literacy and action on the individual by defining food literacy as an increase in individual skills or in one's ability to make healthy choices. In scrutinizing the definitions alone, the language used reinforces this assumption; it is often defined in "the capacity of the individual" (Coveney et al. 2012, 634) and in eaters' ability to "make healthy choices throughout their lives" (Sustain Ontario 2013, 2). When conceptualized as the ability to pursue individual healthy choices, food literacy is also often measured through functional, skills-based markers and the ability to improve one's own food situation within the current system. A range of reports on food literacy programs (e.g. Thomas and Irwin 2011; Cullerton et al. 2012; Brooks and Begley 2013) evaluate food literacy based on technical, measurable skill sets with a focus on functional knowledge, including criteria like food safety, food selection, food preparation, food budgeting, fruit and vegetable consumption, and general nutrition.

Paralleling this trend, a consortium led by Queensland University of Technology in Australia sought to establish a more global definition of food literacy (Vidgen and Gallegos 2011), with components of the definition—planning and management, food selection, preparation, nutrition—intimating a more functional and skills-based measure of food literacy. Consistent with most researchers, the Conference Board of Canada's Centre for Food in Canada published a 2013 study on food literacy where the term was defined as "an individual's food-related knowledge, attitudes and skills" (2). Throughout the report, food literacy is billed as an intensely individual undertaking rooted in nutrition and quantitative science—for example, understanding food pyramids and nutritional labeling. Bublitz et al. (2011) and Block et al. (2011) argue that an individualized, functional understanding of food literacy can also be engrained in larger notions of health and well-being. They write that food literacy serves as one component of the concept of "food well-being," with food literacy defined as being able and motivated to navigate the current paradigm of industrial food with the intention of seeking or maintaining personal health.

In the minds of many, to be food literate is to make healthy choices to benefit oneself. The definition and benchmarks in this rendition of food literacy assume that a food literate individual operates within the current food system. That is, rather than having the awareness and "know-how" to advocate for larger, more structural food systems change, this type of food literacy promotes knowledge and skills acquisition for one's own betterment, while leaving the roots of problems within the food system untouched. It is a more restrictive definition of food literacy, tethered to the neoliberal ideology of self-reliance, sometimes viewing food as a nutritional input and often ignoring the larger impacts of the modern industrial food system on the functioning and health of current society as a whole.

The Critical Consciousness Paradigm: Food Literacy as Active Engagement and Transformative Learning

For a number of researchers and authors (e.g. Stinson 2010; Wilkins 2005; Sumner 2012; Kimura 2011), to truly be food literate means to engage in democratic practices in the food system, to actively take part in nurturing ecological health, and to have the ability to disrupt current food systems practices while taking into account social, cultural, economic, and environmental factors. To researchers such as Stinson (2010), food literacy is part of a larger idea of ecoliteracy or environmental literacy: To be food literate is to understand the role of food in our interactions with the environment, and to understand more deeply how food teases out social, political, and cultural issues in our lives.

How does the definition of food literacy by these researchers differ from the definition and measures of food literacy put forth by so many others? These authors move beyond equating food literacy to improving one's own well-being through healthy choices. Instead, food literate individuals and communities are defined as having "an increasing ability to disrupt ingrained notions of how food is supplied and consumed within a local area or region" and as having "a stronger voice in expressing what kind of food system they want enacted" (Stinson 53). Here, food literacy is not founded on directing individuals to make changes in their own lives, or on how to navigate the current system for one's own benefit. As Sumner says, "food literacy must move beyond individualized prescriptions and notions of blame to become a concept that can analyze current foodscapes and model sustainable alternatives" (320).

To be truly food literate in these authors' minds means to recognize the realities of contemporary environmental practices and choices, to be able to engage as an active citizen, to exercise democratic rights, and to possess the willingness and empowerment to seek changes and share a voice in the current system. Food literacy facilitates participation within the food system in a way that supports the development of a new or alternative system, rather than simply navigating the current system. Kimura highlights this more macro definition of food literacy in her study on food education and food literacy in contemporary Japan. She also pushes for an alternative framework for food education and food literacy that "does not shy away from challenging policies and the structure of economy" (480). To be food literate through this lens is to have the knowledge needed to act and seek change at a systems level. It is a type of food literacy that facilitates food citizenship (Wilkins 2005), **transformative learning**, and emancipatory knowledge (Sumner 2012).

Measuring Food Literacy

If one of the primary purposes of this research is to evaluate whether, and to what extent, the FLY program fosters food literacy in its participants, it is prudent to develop a collection of benchmarks against which to compare their experiences. Operating with two main paradigms—the "neoliberal consciousness" and the "critical consciousness"—the former is most widespread in the literature, and is generally supported by those in the fields of nutrition and dietetics, health studies, consumer research, and some non-profit research organizations. The latter is often found in the fields of education or various social sciences, with authors critical of predominant understandings of food literacy. Table 10.1 consolidates by category the benchmarks and measures of food literacy identified in the literature reviewed.

Understandably, the benchmarks of a more individual, functional approach to food literacy are more easily measured. They rely primarily on functional knowledge and technical skills such as preparing healthy meals, knowing nutrition facts, or opting to consume more fruits and vegetables. In comparison, the benchmarks for the broader understanding of food literacy are more qualitative and grounded in a change of values or outlook. Nevertheless, this understanding of food literacy can be evaluated based on the language an individual employs to describe their opinions on and relationships with food and the food system.

Table 10.1 Benchmarks of food literacy as identified in academic and organizational literature

	Benchmarks of neoliberal consciousness paradigm: individual, consumer-oriented, functional approach to food literacy[a]	*Benchmarks of critical consciousness paradigm: contextualized, systems-based, and politically/socially motivated approach to food literacy*[b]
Frequent[c]	Increased nutrition knowledge Improved cooking skills Cooking more meals from scratch; ability to cook for oneself Ability (and desire) to purchase healthy foods Improved food safety behaviors Ability to budget/plan meals	Knowledge and awareness of the multiple dimensions of food (broader engagement) Ability to reflect critically on food and the food system, interest in seeking change
Often[d]	Increased consumption of fruits and vegetables	Awareness of socio-political impacts of the food system and ability to analyze associated discourses Interest in active citizenship as it relates to food
Sometimes[e]	Interest in trying new foods Confidence and motivation to use food knowledge to make healthy choices Ability to make informed decisions and judge marketing, new products, and quality of food Ability to influence family/friends in purchasing/cooking/eating decisions Satisfaction, creativity, confidence, resilience because of food knowledge and skills Ability to cook with substitutes Knowledge of where food comes from and various food terminology (e.g. GMO)	Ability or attempts to disrupt current food system through informed actions Exercising food-related behaviors that support a democratic, socially, and economically just food system Knowledge and awareness of food and agricultural systems and their relationship to environment and health

[a]Out of ten scholarly articles fitting this paradigm

[b]Out of five scholarly articles fitting this paradigm

[c]Identified in at least 60% of the literature with the indicated food literacy paradigm

[d]Identified in 26–59% of the literature with the indicated food literacy paradigm

[e]Identified in 25% or less of the literature with the indicated food literacy paradigm

COMMUNITY-BASED YOUTH FOOD EDUCATION AT THE STOP'S "FLY" PROGRAM

On a mostly residential street punctuated by shoebox-sized convenience stores, The Stop's primary location sits on the ground floor of a high-rise community housing building. It is an organization that bills itself as a community food center, described by the former executive director as "truly a place where people come to cook, grow, eat, learn about and advocate for good food" (Saul and Curtis 122). Having begun out of a church in the 1970s as a community advocacy center turned food bank, The Stop has, from its conception, sought to position itself as something other than a band-aid fix. Claiming to have retained its activist roots throughout the organization's multiple transformations, The Stop explains its main work as advocating for and with low-income people about food issues, and providing people with the tools and knowledge to critically engage as vocal and politically aware citizens. The Stop centers its model on food access, supported by its food bank and healthy drop-in meals program; food skills, supported by cooking and gardening programs and food literacy for children; and engagement and education, supported by programs that facilitate community involvement in food and social justice issues (Saul and Curtis 2013).

The FLY program takes the form of weekly sessions from October to May, where newcomer and low-income youth gather on Wednesday afternoons. It is an after-school cooking and leadership program for high school girls who want to learn to cook while engaging in issues related to nutrition and environmental sustainability (Food Leadership for Youth, The Stop 2012). In concept, the FLY program makes use of cooking to not only teach food skills but also initiate discussions around food systems issues. Participants spend at least an hour cooking—first watching a demonstration by the program coordinator or a volunteer on key food skills for the week, and then working independently or in pairs to prepare ingredients and follow the week's recipes. After cooking, all participants gather to dine communally and enjoy what was prepared. For a food education program that strives to instill food literacy, there are glimpses of conversations on food systems issues that punctuate the dominant discussions and hands-on action around food skills. Yet, the primary driver of Wednesdays at 1884 Davenport is the week's recipes, the focus on chopping, tasting, and improvising throughout the cooking process.

The FLY program is grounded in its internal logic model and work plan, which define the program's audience as teenage girls (13–17) in Toronto's Davenport West area who have low income or are newcomers. Specifically, the program's goal is "to develop healthy, *food literate*, confident, and empowered young women" (emphasis added), and the program goals adopt two forms: one, to increase self-confidence and inner strength through food and community; and two, to facilitate an increase in food literacy. One specific objective around food literacy (The Stop Community Food Centre 2013a) is "to increase participants' skills, knowledge, and behaviors around healthy food." The model asserts that participants' progress can be inferred based on: observed discussions of participants making healthier food choices, participants demonstrating new cooking skills, participants cooking without a recipe, or feeling comfortable cooking with substitutes. These measures closely parallel the most widely used individual measures of food literacy. In contrast, the logic model's second food literacy-related objective is "to increase program participants' capacity to apply new knowledge to take effective action on food systems issues in their community," which speaks to a food literacy of critical consciousness. Assumed outcomes of this objective include "increased participant knowledge of food systems, social justice, and AOP [anti-oppression] concepts and issues," along with "active participation in actions to address systemic issues."

The FLY program's work plan serves as a more detailed outline of program goals and activities compared to the logic model, and incorporates both food literacy paradigms identified in this chapter (The Stop Community Food Centre 2013b). For example, the individual, consumerist paradigm is present through the goals of "increasing the food skills of participants through hands-on programming" and "building knowledge and positive attitudes towards healthy eating principles." Yet, the critical and engaged citizen paradigm is evident in the goals of "fostering the leadership capacity of participants to promote food issues to their peers and their families," "building knowledge of local and global food issues," and "increasing knowledge of poverty and food systems issues and creating opportunities...to take effective action on these issues."

The logic model and work plan demonstrate that FLY understands food literacy from a dual perspective; that is, while FLY has a foundation of skills-based food literacy that aligns with individual behavior modification, the program also seeks to enable participants to critically engage and instigate change in systemic food issues. It is unsurprising that the FLY program seeks to approach food literacy from both paradigms, given

The Stop's philosophical underpinnings. Nevertheless, only some of the objectives and outcomes came to fruition during my time as a participant observer and volunteer with the FLY program.

FACILITATING FOOD LITERACY IN FOOD EDUCATION

Drawing on benchmarks of food literacy identified earlier in this chapter, six benchmarks predominated in the FLY program. In particular, language, conversations, and assertions of increased nutrition knowledge, cooking skills, and ability to teach others and influence friends and family were most frequent. Other benchmarks were present, though not quite as prevalent. A visual summary of the six most prominent types of food literacy gained by FLY participants is found in Chart 10.1.

1. *"I'm Not Afraid to Cook": Improved Cooking Skills, Cooking More Meals from Scratch*

For a food education program whose main focus is cooking, it is unsurprising that the most prominent benchmark of food literacy that emerged was improvement in the girls' cooking skills and their cooking more meals from scratch. Whether we were demonstrating chopping and stove skills when making jerk chicken and coleslaw or facilitating a "snack challenge"

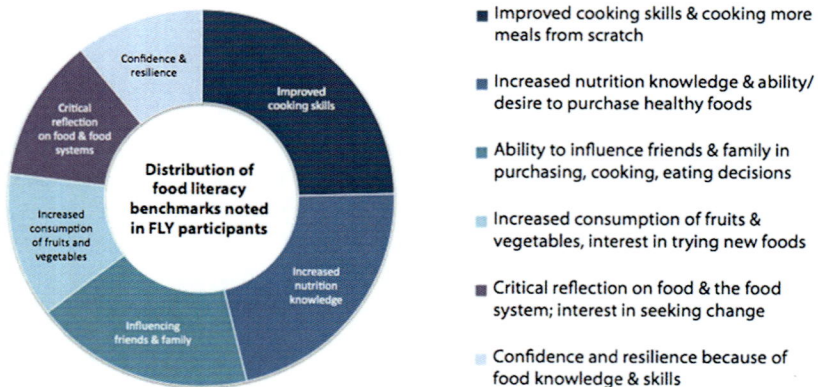

Chart 10.1   Distribution of the six most prevalent food literacy benchmarks in FLY participants as coded in research data

to encourage improvisation in the kitchen, the week's goals were frequently centered on building functional and technical cooking skills.

Before the program, I was probably like a 4 or a 3 [out of 10]. I wanted to cook but I didn't know how. And now I'm pretty good. Like an 8.—FLY participant March 2014

I think before I didn't care what knife I was using. Now for sure I know there's a bread knife, meat knife.—FLY participant March 2014

My knowledge grew on little things like oils and salt and spices and things like that.—FLY participant April 2014

I definitely saw, and heard, the kinds of comments like… 'I'm not afraid to cook' or you know, some comments like 'I wish I had more people to cook for at home'.—FLY volunteer March 2014

2. *"I Want the Good Stuff": Increased Nutrition Knowledge, Ability/ Desire to Purchase Healthy Foods*

During one FLY session, we explored healthy options to fast food by making our own burgers and discussed the nutritional makeup of fast food versus homemade alternatives. Of note was the participants' keen interest in nutrition, supported by a strong presence of commentary in interviews on how the FLY program made participants more aware of or able to judge healthy foods.

Before the FLY program, I think I was cooking a lot but I wasn't cooking well… but now ever since, I cook for myself three or four times a week and I think that's because I am so keen on getting great ingredients, I want the good stuff.—FLY participant March 2014

When I go to the grocery store I always read labels a lot more than I used to, like if things say 50% less sugar or organic or things like that. So I always choose food now based on things like that.—FLY participant April 2014

Now, my lunch choices are different. I love packing my lunch…I got more creative with it…the kale salad I just made on Monday.—FLY participant March 2014

3. *"I'm Trying to Teach My Brother": Ability to Influence Family and Friends in Purchasing/Cooking/Eating Decisions*

Based on the girls' interests, our conversations during the interview process turned to how the FLY program facilitated their ability and interest in passing on their newfound knowledge to their families and friends.

One of my friends doesn't eat French fries anymore because I made her kale chips.—FLY participant March 2014

I try to convince my mom to switch to better foods. I'm kind of strict with her just because she's my mom.—FLY participant April 2014

I'm still trying to keep really healthy. Obviously it's hard because the food industry—the fast food industry—is just everywhere, it can sometimes be more convenient, once in a while. But I still do try to keep it up a lot, especially for my grandfather, my grandparents. Even I'm teaching them new things they can do.—FLY participant April 2014.

Interviews with FLY staff and volunteers also tangentially moved toward how the program enables participants to influence their families' eating habits.

I definitely saw, and heard, the kinds of comments like... oh when I go to the grocery store now, I look at where food comes from, or I have influenced my parents to buy local food or to buy healthier food.—FLY volunteer March 2014

She took control over that [shopping for the family's produce] and is able to do that in her family, and her mom is super proud of her.—FLY program coordinator May 2014

4. *"They Usually Come Out of It Liking Kale!": Increased Consumption of Fruits and Vegetables and Interest in Trying New Foods*

Staff and volunteers never forced FLY participants to eat new foods, but the program was structured to introduce the girls to new ingredients every week, and to encourage the consumption of fresh produce.

I also liked that we were trying things that I wouldn't have tried otherwise. I mean I love trying new food but there were things that I'd never worked with before.—FLY participant March 2014

It's definitely been effective...watching their expressions when they see a vegetable they've never seen before. Or [FLY participant] adding vegetables for the first time to her sandwich.—FLY volunteer May 2014

Exposure to new foods [is what they got most out of the FLY program]. They usually come out of it liking kale!—FLY program coordinator February 2014

5. *"We Should Be Doing Better, Right?": Ability to Reflect Critically on Food and the Food System; Interest in Seeking Change*

In my interviews with FLY participants, the participants showed an interest in change, though not an interest in *seeking* change. I include this benchmark of food literacy with a caveat; while the FLY program undoubtedly instilled the girls with an ability to reflect on problems in the food system and to express a desire for an alternate reality, the critical analysis present in the girls' thoughts was completely grounded in the individual and in change occurring through personal choices. Thus, the conversations did not reflect the ultimate essence of the critical consciousness paradigm under which this benchmark falls.

We should really be putting a lot of money into, or care into [food]. It's nurturing our lives. But if we realize that then I think people would make more conscious decisions on what we eat...we should be doing better, right?—FLY participant March 2014

I just think if it [good food] is something you really care about, you make an effort to look, because it's here, it's everywhere...it has to take the person to decide that they want to go out and look for it.—FLY participant March 2014

While our conversations demonstrated their ability to reflect on the food system, the girls were not often aware of the larger sociopolitical web that impacts how we eat. They blamed the individual rather than the system for the resulting problems, and approached the issues from a consumer mindset.

6. *"It Made Me Feel Better About Myself": Confidence and Resilience Because of Food Knowledge and Skills*

FLY believes strongly in fostering participants' confidence and empowerment, and both participants and staff noted how the program transformed the girls' confidence.

I went into the program and I was learning all these sorts of things...and I was cooking at home and I was learning about real ingredients and...from that I definitely, I feel like I got more confident with food. And food is something that I love, so in turn it made me feel better about myself somewhere down the line.—FLY participant March 2014

When I cook, I just feel like I am good at it. I'm not trying to be egotistical. And I just feel really happy when I'm cooking. Like I get into my own little world.—FLY participant April 2014

That's where the empowerment piece comes from, seeing themselves in that food because it came from them.—FLY program coordinator February 2014

The Discord Among Beliefs, Intention, and Reality

Analysis of primary research conducted during the FLY program reveals that the main benchmarks of food literacy that the participants demonstrated included improved cooking skills and cooking more meals from scratch; increased nutrition knowledge and the ability or desire to purchase healthy foods; and the ability to influence family and friends in purchasing, cooking, or eating decisions. It is clear that the FLY program facilitated the acquisition of food literacy in its participants. However, participants acquired a specific type of food literacy in line with the individualized, consumerist paradigm rooted in functional knowledge and technical skills.

The approach to food literacy that encourages the individual to live well and enjoy healthy food within the current confines of the market was also evident in the type of language used when talking about food and food systems. The language of individual choice was employed when participants discussed making healthy lunch *choices, choosing* food based on nutrition labels, making *better decisions* when shopping, and when participants emphasized the need for individuals make *an effort* to seek out produce, or the need to act as examples by making the *right choices.*

On paper the FLY program claims to define and instill food literacy from a dual paradigm approach. However, in practice and in execution, the understanding and approach to food literacy that guides programming is rooted more in encouraging healthy choices and individual behavior modification. This is not a critique of the program, for the participants gain food literacy. However, the food literacy acquired clearly aligns with only one of two food literacy paradigms that the program seeks to pursue in theory. It is unsurprising that the program demonstrates this discord between theory and reality, for it is simpler and easier to teach concrete food skills and individual behavior modification for health and well-being than to shape active citizens who can critically engage with contemporary food systems issues. As one FLY volunteer noted in our March 2014 conversation, "it's hard to move from food skills to larger issues of justice and food systems issues...because of the complexity of each of the issues, it was hard to have enough time, or even to create a safe enough space to push the issues a bit further."

BUILDING A STRONGER FOOD EDUCATION PROGRAM FOR FOOD LITERACY

For all the programming, meal preparation, and activities that FLY offers, the program is not without struggle. The 2013–2014 FLY program faced an unprecedented lack of regular participant attendance, coupled with poor participant retention. It is difficult to discern the cause of these problems, though it is not the intent of this chapter to do so. Nevertheless, the general consensus among staff and volunteers attributed lack of attendance to a combination of terrible winter weather that made it difficult for teenagers to travel, some participants having to choose paid work that conflicted with the FLY schedule, other participants needing to care for younger or older family members, and a lack of institutionalization between the FLY program and participating schools. It is essential to recognize this year's lack of attendance, not only because it impacted the data collected, but also because with lower attendance came the revelation of some barriers to creating effective food programming for food literacy. As one volunteer noted, "the attendance was a bit unstable. Which then affected the curriculum because there is a continuity" (FLY volunteer March 2014). When attendance is low or participants cannot regularly attend on a weekly basis, it becomes more challenging to build on skills and concepts and to delve into more complex food systems issues.

The barriers to programming most frequently present in the analysis of my data were lack of resources and lack of time. While the FLY program is free to participants, The Stop is unable to incentivize the program due to funding constraints. By not providing resources to the girls—transportation tokens, sibling care, or a program honorarium—access to food education programming becomes limited based on one's socioeconomic status. Moreover, a significant number of references were made to a lack of time in the program to fully explore food systems concepts through a critical lens. As volunteers and staff surmised, due to time constraints it becomes easier to pursue the familiar: In this case, individual behavior modification and functional food skills.

The barriers of resources and time impacted both participant attendance and FLY's ability to expand programming to move beyond a dominance of functional food skills and individual, consumer-driven food literacy. It may be difficult to remove these barriers; however, they are important to note, for addressing them could improve attendance by way of eliminating socioeconomic driven hurdles to participation.

Does Food Literacy Mean Food Systems Change?

As food education programs have expanded in number, the assumption remains that food education will create a food literate population, and with food literacy will come impactful change (see Jaffe and Gertler 2006; Goodman and DuPuis 2002; Howard and Brichta 2013 for examples). This chapter established that a food education program like FLY can impart food literacy in its participants, though the food literacy gained predominantly follows a specific paradigm. A food literacy based on the critical consciousness paradigm was unable to fully flourish in the FLY program, despite the goals and intended outcomes of the program. Given this conclusion, one of the next logical questions is whether the food literacy gained can contribute to the promotion of some type of wider food systems change.

Transformative Learning in Food Literacy for Change

There is little evidence that links the acquisition of food literacy to wider food systems change. To question whether food literacy gained in a program like FLY can facilitate change, it thus becomes necessary to move into a broader selection of literature. For example, asking what type of *learning* can instigate change leads to a significant body of literature on transformative learning and its role in fostering wider, systems-based change. Originally put forth by Jack Mezirow (1997, 2009) as a process of adult learning, transformative learning occurs through critical reflection, engaging in discourse, and taking action. It is a process that represents a change of consciousness and impacts "how the learner perceives and makes sense of the world" (Kerton and John Sinclair 2010, 401). Transformative learning is not comprised of simply gathering functional skills or knowledge for individual change, but is rather a learning that shifts one's frame of reference to effect change.

The execution of transformative learning in practice combines critical awareness and reflection, discourse, and broader social engagement, and theory asserts that it is this combination of outcomes that fosters change. Strikingly, these three benchmarks of transformative learning are some of the same benchmarks of the more politically and socially aware, systems-based and critically conscious food literacy paradigm identified earlier in this chapter. What we can glean from the similarities demonstrated is that the broader, more critically conscious food literacy is indicative of a process of transformative learning, something to which Sumner (2012) alludes as well in her conference paper on food literacy and education.

If a food education program like FLY strives to teach food literacy with an end goal of fostering some type of change beyond influencing individual choice, or if food education programs are created with the goal of instilling food literacy for wider change, then the program must instill not only the dominant paradigm of individual, consumer-driven functional food literacy, but also the broader, more engaged and aware paradigm of food literacy. If a food education participant acquires the type of food literacy present in the paradigm of critical consciousness and broader engagement, they will have, to some extent, undergone a process of transformative learning.

Re-evaluating the FLY Program

Is it beneficial to continue pursuing the current FLY program model considering it imparts only one type of food literacy in its participants, which on its own may not foster wider food systems change? While food literacy is gained, this is accompanied by the ability to reach only a small number of participants on a significant human and physical resource investment. The outcomes noted in this year's FLY program, coupled with program's barriers and constraints, thus suggest that the FLY program is not a particularly scalable model, particularly since the program's outcomes and challenges exist within a fairly well-resourced organization compared to others involved in food efforts.

Given the problematic participant attrition and attendance encountered by the program, it may be worthwhile to more heavily invest in outreach and recruitment at the beginning of each program year. Enrolling more girls would not only improve attendance, but also, by extension, could help facilitate a program environment more conducive to community-based projects and learning activities that foster a critical awareness of the food system. It may also be advisable to implement more rigidity in curriculum structure, such that activities that support transformative learning and critical engagement with food systems issues are not set aside in favor of functional cooking skills-based activities. This could foster a more balanced curriculum that incorporates advocacy and community engagement activities identified in the FLY internal logic model and work plan, including zines, videos, and peer-led food systems awareness presentations. These preliminary possibilities are prospects that could be explored in future work and research efforts.

Conclusion

This chapter evaluates conversations around food literacy that exist in academic and organizational literature and establishes two primary food literacy paradigms and associated benchmark measures. One of the primary goals of this research was to evaluate whether, and to what extent, food education programs like FLY can instill food literacy in their participants. With the aforementioned food literacy definitions and benchmarks serving as a foundation, this case-study research establishes that FLY primarily facilitates the dominant food literacy paradigm of a neoliberal consciousness that will not necessarily lead to wider change, for it focuses on individual behavior modification within the current food system. This outcome occurs despite the program's expressed interest in, and intention of, facilitating both food literacy paradigms identified in this work.

The research summarized in this chapter furthers the conversation on what exactly is meant by the term food literacy, and begins to answer the question of what types of food literacy are instilled in participants of programs like FLY. Nonetheless, discussion must continue on what the best form of food education may be if a more critical and engaged food literacy is desired, and if a reskilling of eaters and a reclamation of the food system is the goal.

References

Block, L., et al. (2011). From nutrients to nurturance: A conceptual introduction to food well-being. *Journal of Public Policy and Marketing, 30*(1), 5–13. Print.

Brooks, N., & Begley, A. (2013). Adolescent food literacy programmes: A review of the literature. *Nutrition and Dietetics*. doi: 10.1111/1747-0080.12096.

Bublitz, M. G., et al. (2011). The quest for eating right: Advancing food well-being. *Journal of Research for Consumers, 19*, 1–12. Print.

Chessen, J., Hey, D., Nicholson, L., & McDermott, A. Y. (2009). What's cooking on the central coast with the pink and the dude chefs? *Health Education & Behavior, 36*, 975–977. Print.

Coveney, J., Begley, A., & Gallegos, D. (2012). 'Savoir Fare': Are cooking skills a new morality? *Australian Journal of Adult Learning, 52*(3), 617–642. Print.

Cullerton, K., Vidgen, H. A., & Gallegos, D. (2012). A review of food literacy interventions targeting disadvantaged young people. *Queensland University of Technology*, 1–43. Web. 30 January 2014.

Davies, L., & Thomas, H. (2010). *Cook It Up! How-to manual: Planning, implementing & evaluating a community-based cooking program*. London: London Community Resource Center. Print.

Desjardins, Ellen et al. (2013). Making something out of nothing: Food literacy among youth, young pregnant women and young parents who are at risk for poor health. Locally Driven Collaborative Projects Food Skills Ontario, Technical Report November 2013, 1–89. Web. 4 March 2014.

Food Leadership for Youth (FLY) Program. *The Stop Community Food Centre*, 2012. Web. 4 June 2014.

Goodman, D., & DuPuis, E. M. (2002). Knowing food and growing food: Beyond the production-consumption debate in the sociology of agriculture. *Sociologia Ruralis, 42*(1), 5–22. Print.

Howard, A., & Brichta, J. (2013). What's to eat? Improving food literacy in Canada. *The Conference Board of Canada's Centre for Food in Canada*, October 2013. Web. 13 November 2013.

Jaffe, J. A., & Gertler, M. (2006). Victual vicissitudes: Consumer deskilling and the (gendered) transformation of food systems. *Agriculture and Human Values, 23*, 143–162. Print.

Kerton, S., & John Sinclair, A. (2010). Buying local organic food: A pathway to transformative learning. *Agricultural and Human Values, 27*(4), 401–413. Print.

Kimura, A. H. (2011). Food education as food literacy: Privatized and gendered food knowledge in contemporary Japan. *Agriculture and Human Values, 28*, 465–482. Print.

Kloppenburg, J., Jr., Hendrickson, J., & Stevenson, G. W. (1996). Coming in to the foodshed. *Agriculture and Human Values, 13*(3), 33–42. Print.

Mezirow, J. (1997). Transformative learning: Theory to practice. *New Directions for Adult and Continuing Education, 74*, 5–12. Print.

Mezirow, J. (2009). An overview on transformative learning. In K. Illeris (Ed.), *Contemporary theories of learning* (pp. 90–105). New York: Routledge. Print.

Saul, N., & Curtis, A. (2013). *The stop: How the fight for good food transformed a community and inspired a movement*. Toronto: Random House Canada. Print.

Stinson, E. (2010). Eating the world: Food literacy and its place in secondary school classrooms. Master of Education thesis. University of Victoria. Print.

The Stop Community Food Centre. (2013a). FLY program logic model. Internal Documentation, The Stop Community Food Centre. Electronic.

The Stop Community Food Centre. (2013b). FLY work plan. Internal Documentation, The Stop Community Food Centre. Electronic.

Sumner, J. (2012). Learning for life: Food literacy and adult education. In S. Brigham (Ed.), *Canadian Association for the study of adult education: Proceedings of the 31st annual conference* (pp. 316–323). Waterloo: University of Waterloo. Print.

Sustain Ontario. (2013). Backgrounder on food literacy, food security, and local food procurement in Ontario's schools. Sustain Ontario and Ontario Edible Education Network, October 2014. Electronic.

Sustain Ontario. (2014). *A Discussion about food literacy within the context of the Local Food Act. Draft for discussion*. Toronto: Sustain Ontario & Ontario Edible Education Network, June 2014. Electronic.

Thomas, H. M. C., & Irwin, J. D. (2011). Cook It Up! A community-based cooking program for at-risk youth: Overview of a food literacy intervention. *BMC Research Notes, 4*(495), 1–7. Print.

Vidgen, H. A., & Gallegos, D. (2011). *What is food literacy and does it influence what we eat: A study of Australian food experts*. Brisbane: Queensland University of Technology. Print.

Wilkins, J. (2005). Eating right here: Moving from consumer to food citizen. *Agricultural and Human Values, 22*(3), 269–273. Print.

CHAPTER 11

School Food and Nutrition Policies as Tools for Learning

Mary McKenna and Sharon Brodovsky

INTRODUCTION

Why did my school stop selling chocolate chip cookies the size of my head? Why does not my school sell pop anymore? Why does all the pizza come with a whole-wheat crust? Why is there so much local food at school now? If students studied school food and nutrition policies (SFNPs), they could answer these questions. Teaching about policy in schools takes it from the hidden curriculum—part of the unspoken academic, social, and cultural messages communicated to students (Hidden Curriculum 2014)—and makes it explicit. It takes students from being passive recipients of policy to active participants throughout the policy process—from identifying the need for policy change to developing, adopting, implementing, and evaluating it.

Weaver-Hightower (2011) provides compelling arguments that food in schools warrants greater attention from the educational community. This chapter makes the case for engaging students in a neglected aspect of school food, learning about SFNPs. The chapter begins by summarizing

M. McKenna (✉)
Faculty of Kinesiology, University of New Brunswick, Fredericton, NB, Canada

S. Brodovsky
Sharon Brodovsky Consulting, Toronto, ON, Canada

© The Author(s) 2016
J. Sumner (ed.), *Learning, Food, and Sustainability*,
DOI 10.1057/978-1-137-53904-5_11

the current state of SFNPs in Canada. It then provides context for studying SFNPs in relation to comprehensive school health (CSH), student engagement, and citizenship education. Next, the chapter reports on nutrition education initiatives that are related to teaching students about SFNPs, suggests questions that curricula on SFNP could address, and identifies considerations for teachers who want to incorporate SFNPs into their teaching. The chapter concludes with a brief summary of potential benefits of teaching and learning about SFNPs.

SFNPs in Canada

Across Canada, all provinces and the Yukon Territory have adopted school nutrition policies or guidelines that contain requirements or recommendations for school foods. These policies are designed to improve food environments that will lead to improved food choices by students and, in turn, contribute to improved student health. Although evaluations conducted in a number of provinces indicate some improvements to the nutritional quality of foods in schools, results are inconsistent (Downs et al. 2012; Fung et al. 2013; Watts et al. 2014). Results also show that after policy adoption, more students may opt to bring food from home or purchase food from non-school outlets (Fung et al. 2013; Vine et al. 2014) and that schools face considerable resistance from a range of stakeholders to implementing the policies (Downs et al. 2012; Vine and Elliott 2013; Taylor et al. 2011). Common challenges include concerns about lost school revenue due to decreased sales of food, conflict regarding the food-related roles and responsibilities of schools relative to parental roles, and students' negative reactions to changes to schools foods (Downs et al. 2012; Taylor et al. 2011; Vine and Elliott 2013). In order to enhance implementation of SFNPs, researchers have recommended numerous solutions (Downs et al. 2012; Mâsse and de Niet 2013; Quintanilha et al. 2013; Vine et al. 2014) including involving parents and students in the development and implementation of SFNPs (Downs et al. 2012; Vine et al. 2014). Teaching students about SFNPs operationalizes this recommendation.

Setting the Context: CSH, Student Engagement, and Citizenship Education

It is important to situate SFNPs within the context of the classroom. The connection between SFNPs and health (reflecting the four pillars of the CSH framework) is evident. Less evident is that SFNPs can also help students learn about policy and the political process, an important aspect of citizenship education. Moreover, as a pedagogical approach, teaching about SFNPs can encourage student engagement because it is a real-life, meaningful topic.

CSH

In Canada, CSH is the primary health promotion framework in schools, which is recognized internationally. The framework simultaneously supports students' education while addressing school health in a planned, integrated, and holistic way. The framework, as shown in Fig. 11.1, addresses the whole environment of the school and consists

Fig. 11.1 CSH framework (Joint Consortium for School Health 2015)

of four inter-related pillars: social and physical environments, teaching and learning, healthy school policy, and partnerships and services (Joint Consortium for School Health 2015).

All four pillars of CSH can significantly impact the food and nutrition experiences of students (Bassett-Gunter et al. 2012). The social and physical environments of schools impact the types of food outlets and specific foods available in and around schools, and include facilities that enable students to learn about the food chain, from growing, preparing, and preserving food to dealing with food waste. Social environments include norms and values and the culture of food and nutrition within the school, for example, offering foods that reflect students' cultural backgrounds. Teaching and learning about food includes the formal and informal opportunities for students to learn about food and nutrition and the extent to which students have access to hands-on practical learning experiences within the school environment, such as on-site food labs or kitchens, gardens, and/or greenhouses. Healthy school policy, in this case SFNPs, "provide a framework by which schools can plan, implement, and evaluate nutrition-related actions using a coordinated approach that reflects current dietary guidance" (McKenna 2010, p. S14). SFNPs have the potential to underpin all actions and programs pertaining to school food and nutrition. Food and nutrition partnerships and services allow schools to capitalize on expertise within the community pertaining to food and nutrition and can extend the impact of school-based activities into the larger community. For example, public health nutritionists can provide input into menu planning, local farmers may supply foods, and community groups can support breakfast and other food programs. In addition, school-based health services make it easier for students to seek help for food- and nutrition-related health problems.

Conceptually, all aspects of CSH are inter-related. Supportive food and nutrition environments facilitate and reinforce effective teaching and learning that, in turn, is underpinned by constructive policies; all are supported by effective partnerships and services that maximize health and learning outcomes. Teaching about SFNPs, specifically, intersects two pillars, Teaching and Learning and Healthy School Policy. However, because these policies impact the types of food and food services offered in school environments and because the policy process entails partnerships, teaching about SFNPs addresses all aspects of CSH.

Citizenship Education

"Our future public policy depends on the commitments of young Canadians and thus deserves the attention of educators and policy-makers" (Llewellyn et al. 2007, p. 1). Citizenship education provides students with knowledge of the political, legal, and economic functions of modern society, along with the social and moral awareness to function effectively (Citizenship Foundation n.d.). Interest in citizenship education stems at least partly from concerns about low voter turnout rates by young people (Chareka and Sears 2006). Knowledge of social policies, the policy process, and relationships between policy and politics are all components of citizenship education. The potential benefits are numerous: It can help develop students' self-concept, encourage political engagement, and increase their tolerance for others (Morgan and Streb 2001). It may improve voter turnout and increase political knowledge interest, attitudes, civic participation, and an individual's intent to vote (No author 2015). Studies have shown that citizenship education may increase students' capacity for community engagement, their understanding of how to help others, and their interest in politics and political issues (Westheimer and Kahne 2007).

Chareka and Sears (2006) observe that young people want to know that their political involvement can actually result in change. Learning strategies proposed by Llewellyn et al. (2007) include project-based learning, community service learning, simulations and workshops, exposure to activist role models, developing communities of support and of civic practice, and examining contemporary social problems and conflicts. The study of SFNPs by students—learning about how SFNPs are created, factors influencing their development and implementation, supports and challenges associated with the SFNP process, and evaluation strategies—provides the basis of projects that offer a useful segue for examining more abstract constructs within citizenship education that are vital to students' roles as future citizens and leaders.

Student Engagement

Student (or youth) engagement consists of involving them in sustained and meaningful activities that are focused outside of themselves (Pancer et al. 2002). Much has been written about strategies for engaging students so they are motivated intrinsically to learn. Facets of engagement include the degree of attention students give a topic, their levels of curiosity and interest, and the optimism and passion they bring to their learning (Hidden Curriculum 2014). Student engagement may take several forms, including, (1) academic, (2) cognitive, (3) behavioral, (4) psychological, and (5) social (Parsons and Taylor 2011). In order to enhance student engagement, Friesen (2009) recommends that work be designed with students, not simply for them, but that it is relevant to students and that it connects to their world inside and outside of school. Also, it is important to involve students in meaningful conversations that address perspectives from within and across disciplines. Parsons et al. (2014) posit that challenging, authentic, collaborative, and student-directed learning promotes student engagement. When student engagement succeeds, students experience positive classroom learning environments that support academic achievement and positive student behaviors.

The Joint Consortium for School Health (2014) recognizes the important connection between engagement and health and has created a toolkit to assist schools and others with engaging youth. Certainly, SFNPs offer a ready-made avenue for engaging students. Eating is a very personal act, and young people are in the process of developing their lifelong eating habits. A SFNP that impacts the availability of food in schools will undoubtedly get students' attention, especially if it entails replacing favored foods with foods that are perceived as less appealing choices (a common response). It may be an 'easy sell' to engage them in decisions that will affect their school food environments.

Nutrition Education Initiatives: Teaching and Learning about SFNPs

SFNPs offer a rich teaching and learning opportunity for students, linking education and policy. Moreover, linking the two fits well within a multi-component (or whole school) approach that includes behavioral, environmental, educational, and policy components and is often cited as the most effective approach to improve students' food habits (Waters et al. 2011; Story et al. 2008). But, while the literature often recommends the two components, they rarely connect them; SFNPs are seldom proposed as a classroom topic. For example, Finland implemented a comprehensive approach that includes policies to support school nutrition, nutrition education, and free school meals for all students. Finland regards meals as "pedagogical tools to teach good nutrition and eating habits" and as a means to increase consumption of vegetable and fruits, whole grains, and low fat milk (Sarlio-Lahteenkorva and Manninen 2010, p. 172). Finland's nutrition education, however, does not explicitly address SFNPs. Laurence et al. (2007) reported on a whole school intervention in four Australian schools to increase fruit and vegetable intake by students. It included a nutrition education component and a policy component but did not mention student involvement with the policy. Other multi-component initiatives are similar (e.g., Black et al. 2015; Rowe et al. 2010: Scherr et al. 2014; Woodgate and Sigurdson 2015). Likewise, programs designed to engage students in social justice education that involve students in working on problems within their social context have the opportunity to include SFNPs but tend not to do so (e.g., Cammarota and Romero 2011). The Heart and Stroke Foundation of Canada recommends that governments strengthen nutrition education in schools and develop SFNPs but does not connect the two (Heart and Stroke Foundation of Canada 2013).

Although rare, a number of education modules either directly focus on SFNPS or propose learning activities that could be adapted easily to include them. For example, Alberta Health Services (n.d.) includes a lesson that asks grade nine students to develop a food policy for their school. The lesson encourages students to consider various aspects of SFNPs, such as providing the basis for guidelines on the sale and availability of food items and supporting the availability of healthy food choices. The 'Food Environments' lesson plan from Johns Hopkins University (n.d.) uses lectures, discussions, activities, and a group project to help students examine how food environments in homes, schools, restaurants, stores, and communities affect what they eat. All students examine food in school (and may examine food costs and availability as a project), recommend improvements to school food, and identify challenges to making these improvements. The Public Health Advocacy Curriculum from Stanford University (Curran et al. 2012) is designed for high-school students and consists of ten experiential learning lessons to teach students how their neighborhood conditions affect their health and to engage students in health-related advocacy efforts. Three of the lessons focus on health advocacy in which students learn several tools, such as writing advocacy letters; developing public service announcements; assessing health environments using photovoice, mapping, and inventories; and facilitating brainstorming sessions for individuals and small and large groups—teaching and learning strategies that lend themselves to engaging students in studying about SFNPs.

No evaluations were found on the effectiveness of these specific lessons or modules. In general, however, evaluations of nutrition education in schools indicate that interventions that address student knowledge, attitudes, behaviors, and eating environments are more likely to have a positive impact on students' eating habits than knowledge alone (Waters et al. 2011; Story et al. 2008). A couple of research studies support the positive potential of teaching about SFNPS. A small study that examined the simulated fast food meal preferences of ten students before and after a 30-minute nutrition education program found that it mainly improved post-education selections: The choices contained significantly fewer calories, as well as less cholesterol and carbohydrates, but also less fiber (Allen et al. 2007). Likewise, a larger study (n = 1476 intervention students and 656 control students) that used a constructivist approach to nutrition education (but did not include the study of SFNPs) achieved significant improvements in students' knowledge, efficacy, and eating behaviors (McCaughtry et al. 2011). Six one-hour lessons focused on students as active learners, helped them connect nutrition education with existing knowledge and their lives outside school, and encouraged group work, sharing, discussing, and debating.

Just as curricular materials can link to policy, similarly, policy documents may include a mandate for student involvement. The Saskatchewan Ministry of Education does not explicitly link policy to curricula but recommends that schools engage students in the "development, implementation and evaluation of school level administrative procedures" that align with the nutrition policy of the school division (Saskatchewan Ministry of Education 2012). Researchers from the USA examined 539 wellness policies from school districts to assess the extent to which they addressed student involvement (Jomaa et al. 2010). The document analysis revealed that 65% of the policies had a goal to share nutrition information with students, 63% reported involving students in annual policy reviews, 49% reported conducting surveys with students, and 44% reported involving students in menu selection. The researchers did not report on whether they assessed if classroom learning was examined as a facet of student involvement.

Engaging Students in Teaching and Learning about SFNPs

The potential teaching topics connected to SFNPs are extensive. Most Canadian students, whether they realize it or not, attend schools that have a SFNP adopted by their province or territory, district, or school. Potential topics for study include all the components of Canadian SFNPs (SFNPs from other countries and agencies could also be studied to compare and contrast approaches). All Canadian provinces address nutrition standards and school food outlets and one or more policies address: meal scheduling/eating environments, food intake of staff, nutrition education/information, nutrition training of staff/volunteers, family/community involvement, food safety, food rewards/punishment, special events/celebrations, fundraising, food/nutrition monitoring, and school nutrition committees. In addition, many schools offer multiple food outlets that are covered by SFNPs, each of which could be a site for student investigation, such as vending machines and canteens, lunch programs available through a local restaurant or catering company, school food programs such as breakfast programs that provide free or subsidized food, and/or cafeteria food services.

The steps in the policy process (identifying the need for policy and policy development, adoption, implementation, and evaluation) offer an organizational construct for teaching the topic. It is important to note that the status of a SFNP will vary among schools. Some schools may have already adopted a policy, in which case the questions below provide a basis for examining the history of the SFNPs process and identifying potential next steps for future policy actions. In schools without SFNPS, the questions offer opportunities to involve students throughout the process—with an official SFNP as a potential outcome. Although this process is presented in a linear fashion, in reality it is often iterative, moving back and forth between steps in the policy process.

(a) *Identify a need for policy and set the stage for policy development*

- What types of people/groups are interested in raising awareness about SFNPs and what is the nature of their involvement in the process? Are there other people/groups who could be involved?
- What are the reasons people identify a need for a SFNP?
- What needs do SFNPs respond to—who is likely to support SFNP development and who is likely to challenge the need for them?
- What are the current eating habits and food skills of young people, their nutrition knowledge/food literacy levels, current health issues related to their eating habits, and their knowledge of how their current eating habits may impact their long-term eating habits?

- What are the attitudes and views of school-based stakeholders (e.g., students, teachers, administrators, food service personnel) toward SFNPs, current foods served in schools, nutrition education, food skills training, and the role of food in schools?
- What is the overall food environment within the school and the surrounding area (e.g., number of school food outlets and types of foods available nearby) and what conditions within the school food environment might support (e.g., school garden) or challenge (e.g., food rewards for student accomplishments) SFNPs?
- What steps have stakeholders taken to create awareness of the need to improve school food and what advocacy strategies could further increase awareness?

(b) *Develop a SFNP*

- Who develops policies and what steps are involved? How long does it take to develop a typical SFNP?
- What types of groups are usually involved in SFNP development?
- How is the policy development process communicated and to whom?
- Is there a SFNP that applies to this school (from the province/territory, district, and or school)? If not, are there policies that are relevant to this school (e.g., the school is in a province that recommends but does not require policy adoption)?
- How does this policy and resources to support the school's SFNP compare and contrast with SFNPs from other jurisdictions? What policy components and resources from other jurisdictions might be applicable to a SFNP for this school?
- How does the SFNP document meet the needs of this school that were identified in the 'identifying the need' section?
- How can a SFNP connect with other related policies and programs at a school?

(c) *Adopt a SFNP*

- How are SFNPs adopted (e.g., through legislation or other means)?
- At what levels can they be adopted (e.g., country, province/territory, district, school)?

- Who needs to be informed that a policy has been adopted and how is the adoption of a policy communicated? Should special communication be targeted to groups likely to support and oppose the policy?
- What steps would be needed for a SFNP to be adopted by this school?
- (If a policy exists already) What is the degree of awareness of the policy within the school community? What are the attitudes toward it by students, parents, and the broader school community? What was the response to policy adoption (e.g., in the local media)?

(d) *Implement a SFNP*

- What steps occur during the implementation of a SFNP? What groups are typically involved in SFNP implementation?
- What strategies are likely to enhance policy implementation (e.g., make changes during holidays, engage stakeholders in the change process)?
- How will this school implement its policy, for example, which components will be implemented first?
- What resources will be available to support implementation? How will implementation be linked to other food and health programs and activities within the school?
- How can the larger school community be engaged in SFNP implementation?
- Who will have overall responsibility and accountability for policy implementation?
- (If a policy exists already) To what extent are all components of the policy being implemented? What resources, if any, exist to support policy implementation? What steps have been taken to achieve policy implementation? What steps could students take to assist with implementation?

(e) *Evaluate a SFNP*

- What does it mean to evaluate a SFNP? Why are evaluations conducted and what are potential outcomes of these evaluations? What evaluations of SFNPs have been conducted in this school or elsewhere, with what results? What can be learned from evaluating SFNPs?

- How will the policy process be monitored and what roles can students play in the monitoring process? What specific indicators will be used for each of the various components of the policy?
- What will be done with the evaluation results? How will they be communicated to the larger school community? Who is accountable for the overall policy process?
- (If a policy exists already) Are any aspects of policy implementation monitored? If so, what are the results? How often is the policy reviewed and what happens with the results?

These questions provide the basis for extensive learning that could occur in relation to SFNPs. The topic lends itself to active learning strategies, which can engage students and promote citizenship goals. Students could, for example,

- establish a food and nutrition committee, either within the class or within the whole school, to assist with the SFNP process; include regular updates to students who are not on the committee.
- create an inventory of current foods available and the food environments in and around the school (e.g., using a survey and photovoice approach) and identify potential healthier (and tasty, appealing, and economical alternatives via taste-testing and other methods) in relation to the SFNP nutrition standards.
- facilitate brainstorming sessions to identify student and school community suggestions for improving school food.
- Role-play as nutrition experts to analyze the nutritional quality and appeal of food outlets in and around the school, and make expert recommendations in accordance with the SFNP from their school (or if there is no SFNP, a SFNP from another jurisdiction).
- develop recipes for foods that meet the SFNP and could be served in school. This activity could be part of a contest such as the US-based Kids 'State Dinner' (see: http://www.letsmove.gov/kids-state-dinner).
- develop a social marketing campaign to support the need for a SFNP and/or its adoption and implementation, including creating public service announcements, advocacy letters, and identifying local and international champions to promote healthy eating (e.g., Jamie Oliver and Michelle Obama).

- research effective strategies to implement SFNPs that help students eat healthy food and determine the feasibility of implementing them (e.g., lower the price of healthier foods).
- include a school garden/greenhouse as a component of the SFNP and implement the change to increase the availability of healthy foods and help students learn more about food.
- participate in food preparation in the school cafeteria (as part of the curriculum or on a volunteer basis) as part of policy implementation.
- invite guest speakers (e.g., public health nutritionists, local chefs and farmers, representatives from food-related organizations) and/ or participate in field trips to nearby schools/farms/food outlets to learn strategies to assist with policy implementation and evaluation.
- assist with monitoring policy compliance.
- conduct surveys during various phases as part of evaluating the policy process (e.g., awareness and attitudes of the school community toward the SFNP).

CONSIDERATIONS

SFNPs have the potential to have far-reaching positive effects on student learning and health. For the topic to be taught effectively, however, important aspects must be considered.

1. Pedagogical approaches—active and engaged learning by students is foundational to this topic. The list above provides examples of strategies for achieving engagement. In addition, teachers will need to consider parameters for the actual changes that might occur as a result of teaching about SFNPs (is the topic an 'academic exercise' or something that could result in actual change?). Some students may be very receptive to learning about SFNPs and improving the nutritional quality of food in their school from the outset, but others may question the initiative. Teachers will need to be prepared to teach learners with diverse perspectives and experiences.
2. Scope and sequence and curriculum objectives—all aspects of SFNPs and all school food outlets covered by SFNPs can be topics. The potential scope is broad. An overall contribution that teaching about SFNPs can make is to help make healthy eating a normal expectation in schools. Teachers will need to ensure that certain aspects of SFNPs,

such as school food programs that entail offering free or subsidized food, are not taught in a manner that might stigmatize or cause discomfort among students. In terms of sequencing, schools can address this topic as soon as students begin school. It is important that initial lessons on SFNPs are simple and straightforward; complexity may increase with students' age and maturity. Coordination among teachers is important in order to build on students' previous knowledge and skills from year to year. Lastly, in order to justify including this topic, it will be important for teachers to link the study of SFNPs to required learning outcomes of students, which will vary from province to province.

3. Stand alone and/or integrated curricula—this topic lends itself to being taught using an integrated approach and from a 'problem solving perspective.' For example, the topic can cover mathematics (e.g., calculations for nutrient standards), sciences (e.g., policy components as a reflection of biological requirements), language arts (e.g., writing about policy, communicating information about SFNPs, and debating the role of the policy), media studies (e.g., response to the policy by the media), drama and the arts (e.g., learning advocacy strategies and conducting photovoice projects), and citizenship education/social studies/political science (e.g., advocating for improved school food and nutrition, learning the policy process, and conducting surveys). Alternatively, the topic could be covered in health or nutrition courses where the students could use a problem-based approach to answer some or all of the questions about the policy process that were posed above.

4. School- and community-based opportunities—because nutrition education is likely to succeed best when it is part of a multi-component approach, it is helpful for schools to link teaching about SFNPs to other school food and nutrition and CSH initiatives (especially promotion of physical activity), citizenship education activities, and student engagement activities. Community partners are potential contributors.

5. Communication—teachers and school administrators and school councils will find it helpful to inform members of the school community that they are covering the topic as it might have an impact outside the classroom. Since healthy eating is not yet a normal expectation for all schools, teachers who address this topic may receive some negative feedback.

6. Assessment of student learning—teachers will need to determine how to assess the active learning strategies associated with this topic, such as problem-based learning and assessment, group work, presentations, and hands-on projects. If school food or other components of a SFNP change due to the students' learning, it will be important to capture these changes.

7. Teacher training—in terms of content, it is important that teachers understand policy and the policy process in general, SFNPs specifically, the CSH framework, and the school food and nutrition environment in their school and nearby community, and can make connections with other topics, such as citizenship education. They also require pedagogical skills that enable them to make the topic relevant by linking policy, which is more abstract, to concrete examples and outcomes, and to interest and actively engage students in learning about policy. Teachers would benefit from assistance on both the content of SFNPs and approaches to teaching the topic. Most provinces will have employees who work with SFNPs and could serve as excellent resources to help teachers.

8. Potential supports and concerns—support for teaching about SFNPs may come from within the school community as well as concerned parents, health professionals, chefs, environmental groups, farmers, school funding organizations, and others within the larger community. Literature and resources are becoming more available (e.g., the Nourishing School Communities and Power Up projects in Canada both address school-based policies).

The topic is not without challenges. Common concerns apply, such as, not enough time in the curriculum, inadequate teacher preparation, and insufficient resources for teaching this topic. Perez-Escamilla et al. (2002) surveyed over 100 elementary teachers in Connecticut and reported that lack of curricular flexibility was a key factor for teachers who did not teach nutrition in the classroom. Only 1% of the teachers strongly agreed that enough nutrition is taught in the classroom (n = 3).

Because this topic is based on situational learning, it requires careful planning, as well as flexibility and backup plans when situations change. Students' initial responses to learning about SFNPs may vary from indifference to strong positive responses and strong negative responses; teachers will need to be prepared to integrate all responses into their teaching. In addition, Manning and Edwards (2014) caution against only involving students in a token way (e.g., serving on advisory committees). Jomaa et al. (2010, p. 378) note that "further studies are needed to identify barriers for student involvement, the best practices for schools to adopt student engagement activities, and factors needed to ensure the sustainability and efficacy of these efforts [toward student involvement] on the long-term dietary behaviors of youth." Overall, it is fair to say that while teaching about SFNPs offers considerable opportunities for meaningful learning, it also offers some potential risks for teachers.

CONCLUSION

Schools educate by the foods they offer day in and day out, for better or worse. Although SFNPs have spread across the country since 2005, Canada is still not at a point where all students attend schools where healthy eating (and full implementation of SFNPs) is the norm. The modern food supply is too complex to be captured by a set of nutrient standards. Adopting SFNPs that reflect a CSH approach can help schools fulfill not simply the 'letter' of a policy (following its nutrient standards), but its 'spirit' (providing foods that will optimize student health and learning). Educating students about SFNPs will help them to better understand the 'spirit' of SFNPs and to contribute meaningfully to all aspects of the policy process. Moreover, teaching about SFNPs capitalizes on an opportunity that already exists in most Canadian schools. It offers a meaningful opportunity to engage students in learning more about food and nutrition decision-making, interactions between policy and food environments and food choices, and the policy process. Potential health-related benefits are that it may increase students' sense of ownership of healthy eating in schools, which may have a positive impact on their food choices (Jomaa et al. 2010). More buy-in from students and potentially less resistance to SFNPs are additional benefits and, by capitalizing on student input and engaging them in meaningful ways, improved SFNPs and more effective policy implementation may result. Jomaa et al. (2010) indicate that student involvement in SFNPs may even help with the prevention of obesity.

The use of active learning strategies to support student learning about SFNPs and a comprehensive approach can have a long-lasting impact on students, equipping them with important skills to help them make informed food choices, influence food environments, and shape policy decision-making over the long term. Potential transferable skills from studying SFNPs include: problem solving, decision-making, advocacy, critical thinking, teamwork and cooperation through group projects, positive and constructive influence and persuasion, debating, and inter-personal communication, both with other students and policy stakeholders. Overall, students who learn about SFNPs in school are better positioned to achieve better health and to become active and engaged citizens.

References

Alberta Health Services. (n. d.). Nutrition resource kits: Grade nine – Lesson plans. Retrieved from: http://www.albertahealthservices.ca/assets/info/nutrition/if-nfs-nr-kit-gr9.pdf

Allen, K. N., Taylor, J. S., & Kuiper, R. (2007). Effectiveness of nutrition education on fast food choices in adolescents. *The Journal of School Nursing, 23*(6), 337–341. doi:10.1622/1059-8405(2007)023[0337:EONEOF]2.0.CO;2.

Bassett-Gunter, R., Yessis, J., Manske, S., & Stockton, L. (2012). *Healthy school communities concept paper.* Ottawa: Physical and Health Education Canada. Retrieved from: http://www.phecanada.ca/programs/health-promoting-schools/concept-paper

Black, J. L., Velazquez, C. E., Ahmadi, N., Chapman, G. E., Carten, S., Edward, J., Shulhan, S., Stephens, T., & Rojas, A. (2015). Sustainability and public health nutrition at school: Assessing the integration of healthy and environmentally sustainable food initiatives in Vancouver schools. *Public Health Nutrition, 18*(13), 2379–2391. doi:10.1017/S1368980015000531.

Cammarota, J., & Romero, A. (2011). Participatory action research for high school students: Transforming policy, practice, and the personal with social justice education. *Educational Policy, 25*(3), 488–506. doi:10.1177/0895904810361722.

Chareka, O., & Sears, A. (2006). Civic duty: Young people's conceptions of voting as a means of political participation. *Canadian Journal of Education, 29*(2), 521–540.

Citizenship Foundation. (n.d.). What is citizenship education? Retrieved from: http://www.citizenshipfoundation.org.uk/main/page.php?286

Curran, N., Ned, J., & Winkleby, M. (2012). Public health advocacy curriculum. Stanford Prevention Research Center. Stanford Medical Youth Science Program. Retrieved from: http://smysp.stanford.edu/education/phac/documentation/fullCurriculum.pdf

Downs, S. M., Farmer, A., Quintanilha, M., Berry, T. R., Mager, D. R., Willows, N. D., & McCargar, L. J. (2012). From paper to practice: Barriers to adopting nutrition guidelines in schools. *Journal of Nutrition Education and Behavior, 44*(2), 114–122. doi:10.1016/j.jneb.2011.04.005.

Friesen, S. (2009). *What did you do in school today? Teaching effectiveness: A framework and rubric.* Toronto: Canadian Education Association. Retrieved from: http://www.galileo.org/cea-2009-wdydist-teaching.pdf

Fung, C., McIsaac, J. L., Kuhle, S., Kirk, S. F., & Veugelers, P. J. (2013). The impact of a population-level school food and nutrition policy on dietary intake and body weights of Canadian children. *Preventive Medicine, 57*(6), 934–940. doi:10.1016/j.ypmed.2013.07.016.

Heart and Stroke Foundation of Canada. (2013). Schools and nutrition (Position Statement). Retrieved from: http://www.heartandstroke.on.ca/site/c.pvI3IeNWJwE/b.4672097/k.2126/Position_Statements__Schools_and_Nutrition.htm

Hidden Curriculum. (2014). In S. Abbott (Ed.), *The glossary of education reform.* Retrieved from: http://edglossary.org/hidden-curriculum

Johns Hopkins Center for a Livable Future. (n. d.). *Food environments lesson plan.* Retrieved from: http://www.jhsph.edu/research/centers-and-institutes/teaching-the-food-system/curriculum/food_environments.html

Joint Consortium for School Health. (2014). *Youth engagement toolkit.* Retrieved from: http://www.jcsh-cces.ca/ye-book/

Joint Consortium for School Health. (2015). *What is comprehensive school health?.* Retrieved from: http://www.jcsh-cces.ca/index.php/about/comprehensive-school-health

Jomaa, L. H., McDonnell, E., Weirich, E., Hartman, T., Jensen, L., & Probart, C. (2010). Student involvement in wellness policies: A study of Pennsylvania local education agencies. *Journal of Nutrition Education and Behavior, 42*(6), 372–379. doi:10.1016/j.jneb.2009.07.012.

Laurence, S., Peterken, R., & Burns, C. (2007). Fresh Kids: The efficacy of a Health Promoting Schools approach to increasing consumption of fruit and water in Australia. *Health Promotion International, 22*(3), 218–226. doi:10.1093/heapro/dam016.

Llewellyn, K. R., Cook, S., Westheimer, J., Girón, L. A. M., & Suurtamm, K. (2007). *The state and potential of civic learning in Canada: Charting the course for youth civic and political participation.* Ottawa: Canadian Policy Research Networks. Retrieved from: http://www.cprn.org/documents/48798_EN.pdf

Manning, N., & Edwards, K. (2014). Why has civic education failed to increase young people's political participation? *Sociological Research Online, 19*(1), 5.

Mâsse, L. C., & de Niet, J. E. (2013). School nutritional capacity, resources and practices are associated with availability of food/beverage items in schools. *International Journal of Behavioral Nutrition and Physical Activity, 10*(26). doi: 10.1186/1479-5868-10-26

McCaughtry, N., Fahlman, M., Martin, J. J., & Shen, B. (2011). Influences of constructivist-oriented nutrition education on urban middle school students' nutrition knowledge, self-efficacy, and behaviors. *American Journal of Health Education, 42*(5), 276–285. doi:10.1080/19325037.2011.10599198.

McKenna, M. L. (2010). Policy options to support healthy eating in schools. *Canadian Journal of Public Health, 101*(Suppl 2), S14–S17.

Morgan, W., & Streb, M. (2001). Building citizenship: How student voice in service-learning develops civic values. *Social Science Quarterly, 82*(1), 154–169. doi:10.1111/0038-4941.00014.

No author. (2015). *The impact of civic education on voter turnout. Canada's Democracy Week*. Retrieved from: https://www.democracy-democratie.ca/content.asp?section=res&dir=rsrch/icevt&document=icevt&lang=e

Pancer, S. M., Rose-Krasnor, L., & Loiselle, L. D. (2002). Youth conferences as a context for engagement. *New Directions in Youth Development, 96*, 47–64.

Parsons, J., & Taylor, L. (2011). *Student Engagement: What do we know and what should we do?*. Edmonton: University of Alberta. Retrieved from: https://education.alberta.ca/media/6459431/student_engagement_literature_review_2011.pdf

Parsons, S. A., Nuland, L. R., & Parsons, A. W. (2014). The ABCs of student engagement. *Phi Delta Kappan, 95*(8), 23–27. doi:10.1177/003172171409500806.

Pérez-Escamilla, R., Haldeman, L., & Gray, S. (2002). Assessment of nutrition education needs in an urban school district in Connecticut: Establishing priorities through research. *Journal of the American Dietetic Association, 102*(4), 559–562. doi:10.1016/S0002-8223(02)90130-6

Quintanilha, M., Downs, S., Lieffers, J., Berry, T., Farmer, A., & McCargar, L. J. (2013). Factors and barriers associated with early adoption of nutrition guidelines in Alberta, Canada. *Journal of Nutrition Education and Behavior, 45*(6), 510–517. doi:10.1016/j.jneb.2013.04.002.

Rowe, F., Stewart, D., & Somerset, S. (2010). Nutrition education: Towards a whole-school approach. *Health Education, 110*(3), 197–208. doi:10.1108/09654281011038868

Sarlio-Lähteenkorva, S., & Manninen, M. (2010). School meals and nutrition education in Finland. *Nutrition Bulletin, 35*(2), 172–174. doi:10.1111/j.1467-3010.2010.01820.x.

Saskatchewan Ministry of Education. (2012). Nourishing Minds: Eat Well, Learn Well, Live Well: Towards Comprehensive School Community Health: Nutrition Policy Development in Saskatchewan Schools. Regina: Author. Retrieved from: http://www.education.gov.sk.ca/nourishing-minds/

Scherr, R. E., Linnell, J. D., Smith, M. H., Briggs, M., Bergman, J., Brian K. M.,..., Zidenberg-Cherr, S. (2014). The Shaping Healthy Choices Program: Design and implementation methodologies for a multicomponent, school-based nutrition education intervention. *Journal of Nutrition Education and Behavior, 46*(6), e13–e21. doi:10.1016/j.jneb.2014.08.010

Story, M., Kaphingst, K. M., Robinson-O'Brien, R., & Glanz, K. (2008). Creating healthy food and eating environments: Policy and environmental approaches. *Annual Review of Public Health, 29*, 253–272. doi:10.1146/annurev.publhealth.29.020907.090926.

Taylor, J. P., Maclellan, D., Caiger, J. M., Hernandez, K., McKenna, M., Gray, B., & Veugelers, P. (2011). Implementing elementary school nutrition policy: Principals' perspectives. *Canadian Journal of Dietetic Practice and Research, 72*(4), e205–e211. doi:10.3148/72.4.2011.e205.

Vine, M. M., & Elliott, S. J. (2013). Examining local-level factors shaping school nutrition policy implementation in Ontario Canada. *Public Health Nutrition, 17*(6), 1290–1298. doi:10.1017/S1368980013002516.

Vine, M. M., Elliott, S. J., & Raine, K. D. (2014). Exploring implementation of the Ontario School Food and Beverage Policy at the secondary school level: A qualitative study. *Canadian Journal of Dietetic Practice and Research, 75*(3), 118–124. doi:10.3148/cjdpr-2014-003.

Waters, E., de Silva-Sanigorski, A., Hall, B. J., Brown, T., Campbell, K. J., Gao, Y., Armstrong, R., Prosser, L., & Summerbell, C. D. (2011). Interventions for preventing obesity in children. *Cochrane Database of Systematic Reviews,* (12), 1–224. CD001871. doi:10.1002/14651858.CD001871.pub3

Watts, A. W., Mâsse, L. C., & Naylor, P. J. (2014). Changes to the school food and physical activity environment after guideline implementation in British Columbia, Canada. *International Journal of Behavioral Nutrition and Physical Activity, 11*(50). doi:10.1186/1479-5868-11-50

Weaver-Hightower, M. B. (2011). Why education researchers should take school food seriously. *Educational Researcher, 40*(1), 15–21. doi:10.3102/00131 89X10397043.

Westheimer, J., & Kahne, J. (2007). What kind of citizen? The politics of educating for democracy. *American Educational Research Journal, 41*(2), 237–269. doi:10.3102/00028312041002237.

Woodgate, R. L., & Sigurdson, C. M. (2015). Building school-based cardiovascular health promotion capacity in youth: A mixed methods study. *BMC Public Health, 15*(421). doi:10.1186/s12889-015-1759-5

Learning to Transgress: Creating Transformative Spaces in and Beyond the Classroom

Angie Carter, Claudia M. Prado-Meza, and Jessica Soulis

INTRODUCTION

Our chapter is rooted in an interdisciplinary approach to understanding justice in food systems. We are all sociology students in or graduates of the Iowa State University Graduate Program in Sustainable Agriculture (ISU GPSA), the first graduate program in sustainable agriculture in the USA established in 2001 (Kirschenmann 2004). The program offers graduate degrees in "the evaluation, analysis, design, and implementation of sustainable agricultural systems" (Delate 2006:445). The focus on sustainability and specifically sustainable agriculture offers promise that academia is engaging in pressing questions related to systemic change; however,

A. Carter (✉)
Department of Sociology, Anthropology and Social Welfare, Augustana College, Rock Island, IL, USA

C.M. Prado-Meza
Facultad de Economía, Universidad de Colima, Villa de Álvarez, Colima, México

J. Soulis
Global Greens, Lutheran Services of Iowa, Des Moines, IA, USA

© The Author(s) 2016
J. Sumner (ed.), *Learning, Food, and Sustainability*,
DOI 10.1057/978-1-137-53904-5_12

we found that students and faculty often lack a language and the space to engage together in questions of justice, especially when these questions may be critical of existing dominant epistemological and philosophical approaches to questions of sustainability. We were part of a group of students who, with the mentorship of several of our faculty, successfully led an effort to institutionalize a social justice cross-disciplinary concentration area within our program curriculum (Carter et al. 2014). We draw upon our personal experiences within our graduate program as well as intersectional social science literature and pedagogy to propose alternative frameworks for understanding justice in, and ultimately transforming how we learn about, food systems. Together we learned to hear the silenced and we began to make visible the invisible. We acknowledge with gratitude the many other students and several faculty with whom we struggled in our work; however, in this chapter, we speak only of our own experience in an effort to join a larger conversation within and beyond our program, and beyond this book, about what it means to be agents of change in a broken system.

We share with you the process through which we learned to unlearn the colonization of our learning about sustainability by corporate, capitalist agriculture and began to heal, finding both strength to question and power in our community. This chapter is an act of resistance and also an exercise in vulnerability. We are learning alternatives in order to not let our hearts or minds be colonized (Shiva 2015). This chapter is our orange paper: warm, bright, and alive. We named it "orange" four years ago when we first discussed the possibility of its existence in contrast to a previous case study we wrote and referred to as "the blue paper." In this chapter, we try to avoid that cold, professional, academic voice that we found we so often use when discussing social justice because we want to be taken seriously, to be respected as scientists and scholars. This orange paper presents us with an opportunity to share our whole selves; a chance to be true to who we are as individuals and who we are as a group; "writing this unconventional [chapter] is a form of resistance against cultural and academic hegemony" (Mayuzumi 2006:22).

As we write this, Angie is still a graduate student within the ISU GPSA program, Jess is employed in local food systems work in the state of Iowa, and Claudia, who was an international student, is now a professor in Colima, México. We chose to analyze our experiences and positionality as students and graduates of our program through **autoethnography** (Ellis 2004; Ellingson and Ellis 2008). Autoethnography has provided us a liberating methodology through which to understand and share our experience as graduate students who found solace, transformation, and, ultimately, healing through community as we successfully integrated social justice within our program's curriculum. This autoethnography, this orange paper, is also an act of resistance to the often taken-for-granted norms of scientific discourse (Ellingson and Ellis 2008:450). We explore our engagement in nonconventional pedagogical approaches rooted in community and social justice as students in an interdisciplinary graduate program in sustainable agriculture. Through these approaches, we discovered new ways of knowing, thinking, and learning about sustainability, as well as about our own positionality in our work and research. Most importantly, we found a safe space within academia to question our own positionality as researchers and the weight of our compromises and struggles as agents of change. The power we found in our community of students continues to feed us today in our scholarship, activism, and community engagement.

The following questions have guided our reflection during these four years: What was involved in our own process of unlearning and relearning about systems of power in agriculture and food systems? How do we avoid replicating dominant systems of oppression in our learning of sustainability? Building upon those experiences, how do we create transformative spaces for ourselves, our colleagues, and our students to continue the process of unlearning in and beyond the classroom?

Drawing upon the work of bell hooks (1994), we argue that learning to build sustainable food systems demands liberating and transformative pedagogical approaches that call the **banking system of education** and its preservation of the status quo (Freire 1993 [1970]), as well as our own privilege, into question. Engaging teaching that transgresses boundaries, dismantles power structures, and creates an environment in which students might empower themselves as active agents is not often rewarded in the traditional education system. It is, as we have learned, subversive and not without consequence. In fact, as hooks writes, such pedagogy is political activism, as it challenges the hegemonic narratives of education and power (1994:203). In this paper, we share our journey of alienation and healing as we learned to unlearn through resistance and community.

Our Academic Experience

The ISU GPSA is the first graduate program in the USA that explicitly stated in its name that its focus was sustainable agricultural practices (Kirschenmann 2004). ISU is a public, research-intensive, **land-grant university** (Mast

2012) located in Ames, Iowa. Throughout its history, ISU has gained a reputation as a leader in agriculture, engineering, veterinary medicine, consumer science, and for a commitment to university extension (Osei-Kofi et al. 2010:328). Its mission is to "create, share, and apply knowledge to make Iowa and the world a better place," and, to do this, ISU has committed to being a leader in the development of "more sustainable ways to produce and deliver safe and nutritious food, water, minerals, and energy" (Iowa State University n.d.).

Land-grant universities are often considered "hegemonic institutions in the sense that they develop and transmit ideas, discourses, and practices that constitute the 'common sense' of the agrifood system" (Allen 2004:55). This "common sense" then marginalizes even the question of other ideas, systems of knowledge production, or alternative practices, and results in a "monoculture of the mind" that limits our science and its practice (Shiva 2003). While most definitions of agricultural sustainability emphasize the equal value of social, economic, and environmental components (Robinson and Tinker 1995), many leave out analysis of power relationships, such as who is, or is not, included in decision-making (Allen et al. 1991:35). Therefore, it is especially important that agricultural research oriented toward finding solutions to ecological and social problems include consciousness of power and privilege lest we work in a "luxury of obliviousness" (Johnson 2005:22) that perpetuates existing oppressions (Allen 2004:88).

Well-intentioned, we, along with other students in our program, often fell back to the mythology of opting out of the capitalist agrifood system (e.g., I grow all my own vegetables! I will just start my own off-the-grid farm!) or using personal choice (e.g., I would never shop at WalMart!) as an answer to the injustice of our food system. Dixon (2014) calls this contemporary narrative categorically false, and argues, "unless we see how choices about food are constrained we may not be in positions to correct for these obstacles to free agency in respect to food" (178). She explains that knowledge about how to eat is not enough, because "[t]he kinds of circumstances that constrain the freedom to eat nutritious food include: lack of money, lack of time, no transportation, no accessible place to shop, diminished physical mobility, or ineffectual public policy at the local, state, federal, or global level" (178). We were privileged as students, able to create boundaries between our topics of study and research and our real lives. It was easy to remain unaware of the structural processes of inequality in the agrifood system, and perhaps also easier to blame others, since we were in the privileged position to be able to make decisions about what, when, how, and with whom we eat.

The institutional culture in which we worked as students convinced us that we needed to "adjust our lenses" if we wanted to learn to act on behalf of food justice (Dixon 2014:184), and so we worked together to create opportunities for students and faculty to discuss social justice and inequality in the agrifood system. These conversations, however, often left us feeling at a loss, angry, and hurt. It was as if we were supposed to leave our values and our passion at the door and exchange them for value-free, objective "scientific" research; yet we knew, as feminist standpoint theory teaches us, that there is no value-free knowledge, that questions asked (or, most often, not asked) by science reflect systems of power (Smith 1974; Collins 1991). As Mohanty reminds us, "There can, of course, be no apolitical scholarship." (1984: 334).

As students, we knew, it was rare to have the power to incorporate our own knowledge and ideas within the curriculum, but the GPSA was open to this. We wanted to change the curriculum because what we were learning was not what we needed to change the system and, in many cases, sustained injustice. Our efforts were intended to improve our program and the culture of our university, thereby providing a framework for future cohorts of students to engage in systemic change more directly. Our program did not have a framework that could help us to identify tools for engaging questions of injustice at their heart, and so we turned to our community of students for inspiration and courage as we asked hard questions about systems of power and challenged institutional hegemony. As we began to work purposively together, we reflected about what brought us to this group and what inspired us to propose changes in our program. As students, we gravitated toward opportunities in our local communities and on our campus to explore this consciousness of power and privilege. We met resistance to our efforts and faced intimidation as individuals. We also found opportunities, together, to share our experiences of having grappled with power and privilege in other contexts in our lives.

In our efforts, we found support from campus resources and mentors. ISU offers a Social Justice in Higher Education Certificate Program with professors who were eager to engage in our questions about justice in the agrifood system and epistemological questions about our research. We each took classes in this program, and successfully worked to include many of them within our program's new social justice cross-disciplinary concentration area. They helped us to find the language needed to understand

and explain our reality and the challenges that we were facing during our efforts to integrate social justice within our own program curriculum. We took a risk and successfully applied for a Provost Diversity Grant even though several of our faculty suggested that it was not yet the right time. This grant provided funding and also credibility for our work. Further, we were able to use the university infrastructure to meet, providing opportunities to create safe spaces for our discussions and initiatives as other students involved in this endeavor held us accountable to our original goals and purpose. We had the fortune to find a professor in our department and program, Dr. Betty Wells, whose concern with our inner well-being (hooks 1994:17) inspired her to regularly attend our meetings, giving us insight into how the system worked, and suggestions to fight back, or win people over to our cause. As we reflect now on the beginning of our efforts, we realize that our student group and those meetings became an important, communal place that enhanced the likelihood of collective effort in creating and sustaining a learning community (hooks 1994:8). Through these efforts, we began to create community, and thanks to these efforts we are continuing to learn how we—as students, and now, professionals engaged in activism, scholarship, and food systems work—can be agents of change in the food system as we engage with issues of injustice on our campus and in our work.

In this group, we reflected upon past experiences, sharing moments, ideas, and strategies that helped us to learn better. We discussed not only the materials we wanted to include in our efforts, but also, the learning strategies. We attempted to share these approaches with the larger community of students and faculty in our sustainable agriculture program through targeted interventions and course modules. We knew we would eventually graduate and leave our program, and so we were purposeful and strategic in engaging new student cohorts and new faculty allies to participate in our work with us. We were learning to unlearn, looking for better ways to teach about social justice. It was a demanding effort, but **"engaged pedagogy"** always is (hooks 1994:15). It was only later that we became aware that we were engaging in a progressive, holistic education.

These efforts were motivated by not only wanting to adjust our lenses, but also trying to change the institutional culture in which we worked. To illustrate this culture, we explain briefly an event that drew national attention and critique to our university during our time as students.

In the summer of 2011, we learned about our university's partnership with AgriSol Energy's international development project in Tanzania, which promised to provide "wealth and development" to the 162,000 refugees who were or were in the process of being displaced in the company's planned establishment of "world-class, sustainable and environmentally responsible farming methods" upon the refugees' farmland (Oakland Institute 2012). Bruce Rastetter, co-founder and managing director of AgriSol Energy, was also at the time the Iowa Board of Regents Pro Tem[1] and is a major donor to our university. The partnership was called a land grab by many organizations, including Food and Water Watch and the Oakland Institute (Oakland Institute 2012; Schwab 2012). We began to discuss what we felt were concerning questions about the nature of the proposed partnership and the cultural assumptions of the proposed project. Our Dean remained silent. Tenured and emeritus faculty spoke only off the record or behind closed doors. On the surface, it appeared a misuse of power on the part of our Regent Rastetter—his private corporation stood to profit from the partnership with the university which he helped govern and to which he had donated $2.25 million dollars (Furfaro 2012). As public pressure to halt the project escalated, ISU eventually backed out (Wintersteen 2012), and the project remains stalled. Still, our requests for the university to make public the guidelines used in vetting the project were never answered. While we found allies in fellow students, faculty, community members, and community organizations, we were disheartened by those faculty who would speak only behind closed doors or our friends who inquired, "why are you still talking about that?" We were discouraged that many people on our campus remained silent despite the seeming conflict of interest that had resulted in the displacement of refugees for the establishment of a conventional, corporate agricultural plantation.

The AgriSol case is just one extreme example of the everyday hegemony of the dominant agricultural system within the land-grant institution and the outcomes of an approach rooted in Western ideology. Our situation, we fear, is not unique. The emergence of sustainable agriculture programs across the country does not coincide with increased engagement in the complex and pressing problems of our agrifood system, such as hunger, poverty, gender subordination, and racial oppression; rather, these problems are usually framed without questioning the economic and social structures responsible for their continuation (Allen and Sachs 1991:2). We echo the question posed by Patricia Allen and Carolyn Sachs, "Who and what do we want to sustain?" (1991:1).

We have learned through our work together that we must look beyond agriculture as a practice and look to institutions of education, economy, and health within the larger social structure. We bring our personal experiences to our process of unlearning as we focus beyond changes in practices to changes in systems. The conversations that we have been having since we began working together have made us reflect and recognize that while we do not have answers, we are becoming more comfortable with the questions.

OUR STORIES

While we were intentionally working to achieve the institutionalization of social justice within our graduate program's core areas, we were also simultaneously creating a community of students and **scholar activists** (Sudbury and Okazawa-Rey 2009) who met frequently to discuss challenges we faced both as individuals in our research and as a collective in our efforts. As we worked to document our efforts through autoethnography, we realized that it was our community that held us accountable as critical scholars as we "unlearned" objectivist conceptualizations of sustainability and, through our mutual support, questioning, and exploration, learned to adapt a social justice lens to our work.

While there are three of us writing this chapter, we consider it important to acknowledge the individual stories of our experience when participating in this project. Our different life experiences, both prior to and during the ISU GPSA, brought us together. We were drawn to one another by a common vision and commitment to engage in praxis. These commonalities and differences, as well as the way we interacted and worked together—always trying to be just and peaceful with each other—made for a strong bond. As we continued to meet, work together, and create this community, it became a liberating space—a place where we could be ourselves, but where we could also question our identities; a place where we were encouraged to be courageous, but where it was also okay to just "be"; a place where we could expect to have our assumptions challenged, but where we also felt safe if we made a mistake; and a place where we could heal and transform, knowing that this is a lifelong process. Because we have created and continue to nurture this collective space, we are better able to share our individual stories. In the following discussion, we reflect on how this process changed us individually.

Claudia

Kintsugi is a Japanese art form that means golden joinery, also known as Kintsukuroki or golden repair, and from what I have read it is a method used to repair broken pottery. Kintsukuroki reminds me of me and the work that I had the chance to do when participating in the initiative of integrating Social Justice in the ISU GPSA.

While being proud of having the opportunity to be enrolled in the program, and doing interesting research as part of my assistantship, I was feeling broken. I disliked the stillness of some of my classmates and felt suffocated by their desire to have access to healthy food without questioning other aspects of the food system. Was I feeling burned out before my 30s? Was I a broken pot? Trying to find meaning in what I was going through, I went to counseling and decided to take a **sentipensante pedagogy** class with Dr. Laura Rendón (Rendón 2008) within the ISU Social Justice in Higher Education certificate program. Finally, there it was. I found myself being part of a challenging course. I was encouraged by my professor to create change, but what it meant, at the beginning, was not entirely clear to me.

Riyad A. Shahjahan, another professor who was in charge of one of our postcolonial classes, had no problems challenging my decision to enroll in the GPSA. He asked me, "So, you are in Iowa and you are in sustainable ag. What relationship do you have with Native Americans? And how do you take their input when you study sustainable practices?" My response, "What? What do you mean? We don't even talk about them like they exist [in our GPSA classes]." So, I decided to enroll in the ISU Social Justice in Higher Education certificate program to have the language to be able to be more vocal about why I was so unhappy, and why studying sustainable agriculture practices by themselves was not enough to create systemic change.

The classroom then became a communal place that enhanced the likelihood of collective effort in creating and sustaining a learning community (hooks 1994:8). I had the opportunity to meet those who would help me to heal, and now, looking back, it was like they became my golden joinery, and were helping to repair the broken me. I have found allies in the margins—those whose work has been similarly questioned or set aside. And even today, I find allies in the writing of this chapter, in this book.

We were given the tools to be empowered by the process, but also, while being part of the group of students working to integrate social justice within the GPSA, I realized that our struggle was about not only a sustainable agriculture, but also a commitment to eradicating systems of class exploitation (hooks 1994:27). Through our work in this group, we started wondering if our research and our work was helping to promote a perverse vision of freedom that makes it synonymous with materialism. Were we taught to believe that domination is "natural," that it is right for the strong to rule over the weak, the powerful over the powerless (hooks 1994:28)? Now that I think back, the postcolonial courses that I took helped me to understand what a system is, and what systemic changes are for. It was then that I understood that my efforts would have to be significantly different if I really wanted a different world; that was when I decided to take part in the efforts to integrate in a better way a social justice lens when discussing sustainability issues.

Participating in this experience allowed me to identify where my pain was coming from, to name it, and, best of all, to have a community that accompanied me during my healing process, because while I was healing, there was still so much pain, so much sadness, and so much anger; some of it still remains.

I could finally tell that the injustices I was seeing and experiencing in the food system that I have always known were not invented by my hurt heart and mind, and they were not a product of some spontaneous generation. They emerged from a system that was oppressing us all, and that was a relief. There was no need to fight against my neighbor. They, like me, were somehow victims, and that changed the way I embraced food in my life. Potlucks and community gardens were places and spaces about changing the world, about knowing people who have always worked in changing it through food. Our collaborative work, and the safe spaces that we had created for ourselves, were developed by the same philosophy that we had about our food, nature, and our planet. We were all important. There was no room for domination, but it was about being part of the world, where we all were working collaboratively as hard as we could to change our graduate program in the hopes that future graduates would have a social justice framework to analyze the world and better tools to create just food systems.

Jess

I remember the feeling I had when I first read about the GPSA on ISU's website. The more I read, the more I knew this was where I needed to be. It just felt so right. I wanted to explore questions about healthy food, hunger, and the environmental and social impact of our agrifood system. When I started grad school, though I have always felt different—even radical—and had some great teachers and educational experiences, I was still so well socialized to the banking model of education that I found myself resisting anything else (hooks 1994). This resistance did not spring from doubting that I had good ideas and questions, but rather from doubting that it was my place to share or ask them. I would get frustrated by other students who would disrupt the typical flow of the classroom to challenge something that was said and critique the status quo, even though I believed strongly in the need to do so. This contradiction shows how powerful socialization can be, but some of my frustration also stemmed from my desire to stay optimistic, and the fact that being critical of attempts to make things better can be really uncomfortable for me. I do not want to hurt people, and I do not want to discourage those who are working for change. But as I began my coursework in the ISU Social Justice in Higher Education certificate program with Dr. Nana Osei-Kofi, I started to understand the possibilities of a different kind of education and learning community.

In Nana's classes, there was a lot of intention around how we interacted. She has a way of creating a sense of community and encouraging students to participate fully in this creation. These communities were places where I felt held while also feeling challenged. For the first time, I really began to have words for so much that I had struggled with, by discussing and learning about systems of oppression and alternative pedagogies with an amazing group of people. Through these classroom experiences, I not only got to live some of my ideals about education, but also to heal.

At around this same time, I was invited to join the group that was forming to explore ways to further incorporate social justice into the curriculum of the GPSA. These initial conversations were so powerful for me. I was in. Whatever we were doing, I was going to be a part of it—I felt such a kinship, and it was such important work.

Early on, we read an article by Paul Kivel (2007) about the difference between working for social change and doing social service work. Prior to going back to school, I had been in social work, and I felt like this article shone a light on so many of my core frustrations with this field. I worked at a wonderful shelter for homeless women in Denver, but this article helped me articulate the frustration that even if you address homelessness at a citywide level, with a really holistic and respectful model, when you are in this system that will always marginalize people who do not fit, how will you truly change things? And unless you are addressing the root causes of homelessness, there will always be people who are homeless. Making these connections, and connections to the questions about justice in the agrifood system that brought me to the GPSA, helped me to know that, in this group and in my social justice classes, I had found spaces that were special and really vital to me.

At the same time, it was unsettling to be a part of these spaces where we studied power in higher education and then go to another class where the professor flexed that power. It was so hard for me to just sit there like I had been taught and allow a professor to bully me. And it was really hard to sit in other classes and just let professors fill my brain with their expert thoughts. I began to more fully understand why some students were so willing to openly challenge and question the status quo in the classroom. Once you have experienced a liberating classroom, it is painful to go back. And this made it even more clear how important our work was—everyone should have opportunities to explore and resist the banking model and to experience transformative education.

Community is the common factor in the spaces, places, and relationships that have been most dear and life-giving for me. In describing a healing community, Mayuzumi (2006) stated, "This relation involves sharing a space and spirits, and it becomes healing when the space is full of respect, humbleness, and care" (13). The community our group created was full of these qualities, and I believe that is why it was, and continues to be, so important to me. We are not done with this work yet, and our community is an ongoing source of inspiration and healing as well as an affirmation of my initial feelings about the GPSA—it was exactly where I needed to be.

Angie

I shared in my application essay to the ISU GPSA that I wanted to engage in community research. As the fourth generation of my family to attend ISU and the seventh generation of my family to live in Iowa, I felt compelled to engage in the hard questions about inequality in our agrifood system in the hopes that we could create a more just system. I did not yet understand the power of engaging in praxis: now I do. For me, praxis has been liberating and transformative—finding a community of students with similar spirits—as well as exhausting and difficult—experiencing intimidation and retaliation for my activism and research. Our student group has fed both my heart and mind as we struggle with our experiences as students and what they mean for us as future scholars.

I enrolled in Dr. Nana Osei-Kofi's Pedagogies of Dissent course in the ISU Social Justice in Higher Education program in the spring of 2013. During our work raising awareness of our university's partnership with AgriSol, my then-advisor came into my office and told me to stop, to be quiet, and warned me that I was jeopardizing my career as a scholar. She later called my community-based dissertation research with women farmland owners in Iowa "bitch sessions." Feeling alienated, I had only shared these experiences with close friends and a few faculty mentors; yet within this class, I learned to see the institutional narratives all around me that were silencing or discrediting the work of others engaged in critical research. I began to find and develop my voice as a scholar, and to learn a language that identified systems of power, hegemony, and colonization.

My learning about the colonization of our agrifood system has been a journey that began in my childhood. As a new student in the ISU GPSA, I was not naive to the consequences and realities of corporate influence within agriculture; my return to Iowa and participation in this graduate program were inspired by my childhood experiences growing up in rural Iowa during the 1980s Farm Crisis.[2] I had grown up believing rural Iowa became someplace to be *from*. Returning to Iowa for graduate study, and understanding its landscape changes through the knowledge I gained in my graduate program, inspired the passion and anger that have fueled my praxis. I am angry because the same systemic forces that forever changed my childhood home are now still actively transforming the landscape into someplace toxic, eroding, and polluted; someplace that harms the health of those working in its hog confinements and drinking its water. The most fertile soil in the world is now used to produce ethanol to power cars and grow food for hogs to feed the rich in China. I am angry because this system of agriculture is being exported as "progress." The externalized costs—the loss of community, the ecological degradation, the public health impacts—are part of my history and my daily lived experience, and in them, I find myself linked to the stories of people fighting for the autonomy of their local food systems and against the invasion of corporate control of their natural environments the world over. I am angry, and learning how to identify my experience within systemic injustice has helped me to transform my anger into questions and action.

As students in the ISU GPSA, we witness the construction of a destructive agricultural system everywhere we go on campus, from Grant Wood's mural in the ISU library "Where Tillage Begins, Other Arts Follow" depicting the plowing of the Midwestern prairie to the profiling on our website of our faculty actively lobbying on behalf of the GM industry. The rhetoric of agribusiness is omnipresent. Yet together we have succeeded in integrating social justice within our program curriculum, pressuring the university to back out of the AgriSol partnership, and supporting one another as we pursue critical research. In the spring of 2015, we welcomed Vandana Shiva to campus and filled our Great Hall in the Memorial Union with over 800 people. It is not just us, we realize. We are not alone. Our agrifood system is broken: it feeds corporations rather than people. Our soil is depleted: it grows fuel rather than food. Our hearts are hungry for community, for transformation, for a new sort of power, and there are many more of us than we realize. Our community is growing.

Thanks to this community of students I have found a space in which I do not have to stand guard over my anger or my frustration—it is shared—and I do not have to fear mistakes. As hooks writes, "If we fear mistakes, doing things wrongly, constantly evaluating ourselves, we will never make the academy a culturally diverse place where scholars and the curricula address every dimension of that difference" (hooks 1994:33). Together we have implemented change and created space for critical questioning that was nonexistent before. Most importantly, we have stopped hiding. We will write orange knowing that our unlearning is a process and that we will continue to change. These words on the page are where we are today, here and now, as we reflect on our journey together and realize that we must find places to resist, heal, and transform even in, especially in, our scholarship.

Conclusion: Learning To Unlearn

In this chapter, we shared our efforts to intervene critically in our lives and the lives of future GPSA students. Meeting together and creating community was our resistance—in it, we found strength and healing. The creation of the social justice cross-disciplinary concentration area was our intervention—it legitimized the space and discussion we had been having within our program and with one another. Just as we first struggled to find a language together to name our shared anger and hurt, to find strength to push for change, we struggled in the writing of this chapter. Our personal testimony and personal experience are fertile ground for the production of liberatory feminist theory (hooks 1994) and we hope our journey is helpful to others. As Audre Lorde (2007) reminds us, our silence will not protect us—in sharing our experiences through this chapter, by writing orange, we hope to open up space for others to speak about their experiences as scholars engaged in transformative social justice work within the food system.

Through our community, we were able to create and, most importantly, to maintain a space in which we were safe to be both self-reflective and critical. Our learning was also a healing process as we developed an understanding together through sharing our experiences and exploring the discomfort that arises during discussions of privilege, power, and inequities. Our experience taught us the importance of taking risks, both personal and professional, to pursue alternative methods of engagement and modes of inquiry in order to cultivate these spaces.

Our community granted us permission to be angry, hurt, and afraid. Our space and time together empowered us to continue to question, to learn from one another, to unlearn what we had been taught were the important questions or the right approaches: "We must intervene to alter the existing pedagogical structure and to teach *students how to listen, how to hear one another*" (hooks 1994:150). Our learning to unlearn led us to identify ways to transgress dominant ideologies of agriculture and food systems in our lives and work through the power of our community. We invite others to be creative as we challenge existing conceptualizations and teachings of sustainability together. We encourage others to create new ways of knowing in our classrooms, on our campuses, and within larger communities of knowledge and practice. We hope that our experience will be helpful in inspiring others to believe that such spaces are possible and to find power through community to make these spaces real.

Notes

1. The Iowa Board of Regents is a group of nine citizens appointed by the governor and confirmed by the Iowa Senate to govern Iowa's five public educational institutions (Board of Regents, n.d.). At the time, Rastetter was President Pro Tem, or "pro tempore," the board member who acts as president in absence of the board's president. Rastetter is now the president of the Board of Regents.
2. The Farm Crisis occurred during the 1980s in the USA and describes an economic recession that, for agricultural communities, was worse than the Great Depression.

REFERENCES

Allen, P. (2004). *Together at the table: Sustainability and sustenance in the American agrifood system*. University Park: The Pennsylvania State University Press.

Allen, P., & Sachs, C. (1991). What do we want to sustain? Developing a comprehensive vision of sustainable agriculture. Sustainability in the Balance: Issues in Sustainable Agriculture: Issue paper #2. June 1991.

Allen, P., Van Dusen, D., Lundy, J., & Gliessman, S. (1991). Integrating social, environmental, and economic issues in sustainable agriculture. *American Journal of Alternative Agriculture, 6*(1), 34–39.

Carter, A., Prado-Meza, C. M., Soulis, J., & Thompson, D. (2014). Students creating curriculum change: Sustainable agriculture and social justice. *Journal of Critical Thought and Praxis, 3*(1): Article 5.

Collins, P. H. (1991). *Black feminist thought: Knowledge, consciousness, and the politics of empowerment*. New York: Routledge.

Delate, K. (2006). Incorporating organic and agroecological approaches into the university curricula: The "Iowa State University" graduate program in sustainable agriculture. *HortTechnology, 16*(3), 445–448.

Dixon, B. A. (2014). Learning to *see* food justice. *Agriculture and Human Values, 31*, 175–184.

Ellingson, L. L., & Ellis, C. (2008). Autoethnography as constructionist project. In J. A. Holstein & J. F. Gubrium (Eds.), *Handbook of constructionist research* (pp. 445–465). New York: The Guilford Press.

Ellis, C. (2004). *The ethnographic I: A methodological novel about autoethnography*. Walnut Creek: Alta Mira Press.

Freire, P. (1993 [1970]). *Pedagogy of the oppressed*. London: Penguin Books.

Furfaro, H. (July 20, 2012). Rastetter breaks his silence. *Ames Tribune*.

hooks, b. (1994). *Teaching to transgress: Education as the practice of freedom*. New York/London: Routledge.

Iowa State University. (n.d.). Strategic plan 2010–2015. Retrieved June 30, 2015 http://www.president.iastate.edu/sp

Johnson, A. G. (2005). Privilege, oppression, and difference. (Chapter 2). *Privilege, power, and difference. 2nd Edition*. Boston: McGraw Hill.

Kirschenmann, F. (2004). A brief history of sustainable agriculture. *The Networker, 9*(2). Retrieved June 30, 2015, from http://www.sehn.org/Volume_9-2.html.

Kivel, P. (2007). Social service or social change? In Incite! Women of Color Against Violence (Ed.), *The revolution will not be funded: Beyond the nonprofit industrial complex* (pp. 129–149). Cambridge, MA: South End Press.

Lorde, A. (2007). "The Transformation of Silence into Thought and Action" in *Sister Outsider* (pp. 40–44). Crossing Press.

Mast, T. (July 5, 2012). Morrill Act leaves long legacy. *Iowa State Daily*. Retrieved September 10, 2015 http://www.iowastatedaily.com/news/article_754cdcba-af28-11e1-aef2-0019bb2963f4.html.

Mayuzumi, K. (2006). The tea ceremony as a decolonizing epistemology: Healing and Japanese women. *Journal of Transformative Education, 4*(1), 8–26.

Mohanty, C. T. (1984). Under Western Eyes: Feminist Scholarship and Colonial Discourses. Feminist Review. *Boundary 2, 12*(3), *13*(1), On Humanism and the University I: The Discourse of Humanism (Spring–Autumn, 1984), 333–358.

Oakland Institute. (2012). Land deal brief: Lives on hold. Retrieved June 20, 2015 http://www.oaklandinstitute.org/land-deal-brief-lives-hold

Osei-Kofi, N., Shahjahan, R. A., & Patton, L. D. (2010). Centering social justice in the study of higher education: The challenges and possibilities for institutional change. *Equity & Excellence in Education, 43*(3), 326–340.

Rendón, L. I. (2008). *Sentipensante (sensing/thinking) pedagogy: Educating for wholeness, social justice and liberation*. Sterling: Stylus Publishing.

Robinson, J., & Tinker, J. (1995). Reconciling ecological, economic, and social imperatives: Towards an analytical framework. Presented to IDRC Workshop on Integrating Environmental, Social and Economic Policies. December 4–5, 1995. Singapore.

Schwab, T. (2012). Iowa State: The Land-Grab University? Food and Water Watch. August 4, 2012. Retrieved June 30, 2015, from http://www.foodandwaterwatch.org/blogs/iowa-state-the-land-grab-university/

Shiva, V. (2003). *Monoculture of the mind: Perspectives on biodiversity and biotechnology*. London: Zed Books.

Shiva, V. (2015). The future of food. Lecture at Iowa State University, Ames, Iowa. March 11, 2015. Retrieved June 30, 2015, from http://www.event.iastate.edu/event/32739

Smith, D. (1974). *The everyday world as problematic: A feminist sociology*. Boston: Northeastern University Press.

Sudbury, J., & Okazawa-Rey, M. (Eds.). (2009). *Activist scholarship: Antiracism, feminism, and social change*. Boulder: Paradigm Publishers.

Wintersteen, W. (2012). Dean Wintersteen ends advisory role in Tanzania plans. February 10, 2012. Retrieved June 30, 2015 http://www.cals.iastate.edu/features/2012/dean-wintersteen-ends-advisory-role-tanzania-plans

Afterword: Food 360: Seeing Our Way Around Learning About Food

Wayne Roberts

Though people have enjoyed and worried about food, learning and teaching for tens of thousands of years, this is one of the first books to deal comprehensively with food and education. I am sure there are countless books about teaching nutrition or horticulture and about learning how to cook or how to store vegetables during the winter. But bringing together the whole nine yards of food, education and sustainability is a fresh and bold undertaking.

So the first thing to say in an afterword to this book is: congratulations and welcome!!! I am going to devote my space here just to savor this moment and to outline some of the exciting and transformative opportunities before us—now that someone has taken the first step on booking in the topic.

It is high time someone took teaching and learning about food seriously. Teaching ourselves *how* to learn about food is the perfect match to teaching ourselves *what* to learn about food. The two are wrapped up together, in somewhat the same way as "a question well-asked is a question half-answered." Teaching without the use of experiential teaching methods, for example, makes it hard for students to really understand, remember and "really get" that food engages all the senses, including the senses of fun and imagination. "Nothing would be more tiresome than eating and drinking if God had not made them a pleasure as well as a necessity," Voltaire famously said. Our teaching and learning methods must be held to the same high standard.

© The Author(s) 2016

J. Sumner (ed.), *Learning, Food, and Sustainability,*

DOI 10.1057/978-1-137-53904-5

239

MAKING FOOD VISIBLE

Before discussing good methods of learning and teaching about food, let me focus your attention on a prior issue: the invisibility of food within the educational system and across society at large. My proposition that food has been rendered invisible will seem preposterous at first. Think of all the food ads in the media, all the stores that sell food, all the time people spend eating, all the art and photography that deal with food, all the "food porn" on the Internet and at supermarket displays that highlight food's curvaceous lusciousness.

But the bald fact is that food has been rendered invisible or pushed to the side of conventional schooling, especially the schooling of professionals and specialists in fields related to food and health. What thoughts are triggered by my mentioning "fields related to food"? Are you thinking of nutrition, food safety inspection and farming? That is what I mean by rendered invisible or at best marginalized. What about the food-related careers in medicine, dentistry, psychiatry, psychology, career counseling, social work, water quality, energy, transportation, waste management, culture, immigration, city planning, human rights—even teaching and learning and the balance between sound minds and sound bodies?

Unless it is about a specialized occupation or issue, food is simply left out of most public discussions, including discussions about educational curriculum and services. Consider a few examples. The countries, regions and cities in the world that have an actual food policy are rarer than hens' teeth. Almost every country, region and city has a policy on such matters as water, energy, air, health, culture, transportation and waste. But food, which looms large in all of these matters, does not warrant a policy. When it comes to how governments departmentalize services, food is almost always an add-on and afterthought—as in ministries of agriculture, food and rural affairs or departments of agriculture and agri-food. Indeed, most government bodies embed a conflict of interest in such departments, giving them responsibility to serve both the groups that grow, process and retail food on the one hand and all the people who eat food on the other. In other areas of public life, where the subject is visible, it would not be considered proper to have one ministry in charge of both promoting and regulating, as is standard with food.[1]

The low level of public discussion and discourse suggests the invisibility cloak that has been cast over food. The power of the invisibility cloak is most easily revealed by two cases: the international debate around the failed Kyoto Treaty of the 1990s to limit global warming emissions[2] and the universal way governments collect and present statistics of employment in the food sector. In both cases, numbers are added up in charts that render food and agriculture impacts invisible. Employment statistics list food processing workers under general manufacturing or industry, for example, while food retail workers are organized under general retail and food service workers are listed under service. Wave the magic wand of charts and poof!, the clear and unmistakable direction of industrializing society is to reduce the proportion of people who work in food!! The global warming debate tilts to the same side. Charts lump refrigerators and ovens, commonly the major users of electricity in North American and European homes, in with all home uses, while the energy to process and transport food is listed under all manufacturing and all transportation. Wave the magic wand again and poof!: agriculture and food are responsible for less than 20 per cent of fossil fuel-derived energy use. Such charts, which have been used to guide public discussion, hide more than they reveal and serve to keep food as an issue that is sidelined in public policy.

I had the good luck to have a front-row seat on food's slow recovery from almost total invisibility. I joined Toronto Public Health as coordinator of the Toronto Food Policy Council in 2000—as I tell my younger daughter, long after the earth cooled and well after cars, TVs and computers were in common use. I was one of only a handful of people in the English-speaking academic, government and health worlds to have food in my job title. There were nutritionists (pardon me, dietitians), food safety inspectors, agronomists and a basketful of other specialties, but full-frontal food was not on many people's titles, degrees, calling cards or office doors. Back in 2000, most media, governments and public servants discussed sex, homosexuality and AIDS openly, intelligently and compassionately. That led me to argue that food, not sex, was in fact the last taboo topic that dared not state its name or lay a claim to public importance.

My first break came in 2001 when I met leaders of University of Toronto's New College program on equity studies. I took a glance at the brochure that Principal David Clandfield and Vice-Principal June Larkin proudly showed me. "You have nothing here about food," I said. They gasped and immediately agreed to fix that. That is how I ended up teaching one of the first university research seminars on food security in Canada. New College subsequently made up for any lost time by hosting the first and biggest local and sustainable cafeteria service in North America and later launching a global food equity program that encompasses all levels of learning and teaching. Food is now being taken into account in appropriate landscaping, which has provided room for a student-run garden. Food is highlighted in several college co-curricular activities—what used to be called extra-curricular, as in outside the curriculum, but now more properly identified as an adjunct to the formal learning curriculum, even though not always graded—such as annual public events on World Food Day and a yearly food-related tour to Belize.

Such co-curricular opportunities foster student participation in what is now listed as "community-engaged learning"—what used to be called "service learning." Sometimes, such learning through direct participation in an organization takes the form of volunteering, and sometimes it takes the form of internships or work-study contracts. Whatever the form, the experience can be noted on student transcripts, in effect defining the student as having been introduced to generic employment-readiness skills such as time management, scheduling and personal responsibility. More formal courses and learning programs are still evolving but at this time feature an introductory New One lecture course adapted to the special needs of first-year students, many of them also first-year newcomers to Canada, as well as a third-year course called "theory and praxis in food security." Both courses are taught by people with formal academic qualifications, as well as extensive practitioner experience.

Such course offerings require innovation in teaching methods. The food stream within the New One program, for example, is based on an understanding that most first-year students need to learn the ABCs of how to take lecture notes, write a university-level reflection paper or response paper, make a class presentation, engage and debate with students and instructors and so on. However much first-year students *do not know* about university, they *do know* about eating, working at food outlets and so on. So food has a place in a first-year course introducing the basics of university-level inquiry and analysis because it can leverage the experience, self-confidence and competence that students bring with them to university. They are not just people with knowledge deficits; they are also people with knowledge assets. They are not just vessels to be filled but lamps to be lit, as the old saying goes. For my money, this is a very creative way to introduce food into a university curriculum—not just as an additional course but as a course that adds value to the whole university experience by leveraging everyday experience with food into an understanding of university-level learning and teaching methods. As food becomes more and more visible in the academic world and as food studies acquire legitimacy as a cross-cutting field akin to women's studies, labor studies and so on, the blossoming of innovative teaching and learning opportunities beckons.[3]

After retiring from my Toronto Food Policy Council job in 2010, I was able to keep my food finger in the educational scene when I evaluated a national program to increase the presence of local and sustainable foods in Canadian universities by a student group called Meal Exchange. Working with Meal Exchange organizers Sarah Archibald and Caitlin Colson, I came up with a new way of formulating a two-part food question that can be posed to any university—a two-part interrogation that can, with minor modifications, be adapted to elementary schools, cities, hospitals or whatever. Instead of leading with the question "What can universities do for food?" I argued that we need to first ask, "What can food do for universities?" That two-part question turns the table on the whole framing of institutional food programs. Instead of students having to make the case that the university should spend more money to address student preferences for healthier, more local and sustainable food, the new framing begins by identifying institutional benefits of making food a visible and positive force.[4]

The benefit list is impressive: improved reputation and relationships with farmers and processors in the university's catchment area, higher "earned media" profile arising from journalistic interest in local food or university sustainability programs, increased opportunities to provide experiential learning relating to health and sustainability, attraction of students interested in food issues ... The list of benefits took a full chapter of my report. Opening an assessment of possible institutional policies on food by asking first "What can food do for the institution?" rather than "What can the institution do for food?" opened up a whole new approach to food advocacy for me. It is akin to a salesperson learning to sell shoes by telling potential customers, "Here's what a new pair of shoes can do for you" rather than "Here are the reasons why I want you to buy a pair of shoes from me." As all marketing texts insist, start with the client's needs, not yours. Food advocates need to do the same. When addressing institutions responsible for education, start with the ways an educational institution benefits from a food perspective. Reframing food advocacy as solutions to problems faced by the organization, rather than grievances of a client group desiring better services from the organization, can become an important feature of food advocacy—itself a form, lest we forget, of public and adult education and not just an expression of political organizing that mobilizes behind a cause.

Making Food Visibility Teachable

The idea of preparing a class on the invisibility of food seems daunting. How to explain to students who joke that they are on a seefood diet—whatever they see, they eat (the joke is based on the identical sound of seafood and seefood)—that the Photoshopped picture in their mind is hiding things from them? The discussion quickly goes beyond a lesson on food; it becomes a lesson on how you trust your own senses when believing is seeing, as much as the other way around. Such discussions are inevitable because the lesson plan on food invisibility is really about critical thinking, one of the generic life skills needed in society today. It is a huge advantage of featuring food in the curriculum that it is rich in opportunities to practice critical thinking and evidence-based decision-making.

However much students may think they accurately see food with their very own eyes every day, they have had experiences which taught them that looks can be deceiving. Most people have learned not to judge a book by its cover, nor to judge a person's vitality by absence of lines and wrinkles that may just show the power of makeup or plastic surgery. Maybe the way to whet student appetites for what you will say about food visibility is to start with an exercise that lets students discuss all the ways the wool has been pulled over their own eyes so they approach the class with an awareness that appearances can be deceiving.

Investigative reporters supportive of the modern food movement deserve credit for breaking the real story behind the appearances of many foods. A shiny red tomato does not tell the story of virtual slave labor conditions that prevailed in Florida's tomato fields until at least 2012, one writer has proven, and a delicious chocolate candy does not tell the story of the child slavery that commonly goes into African chocolate today, as organizations like Oxfam have shown.[5] For obvious reasons, the tomato and chocolate bar could tell nothing about these problems. More disturbing, retailers, government officials and the mass media kept silent until investigative reporters broke the news. At this point, a teacher can make the connection between critical thinking and investigative reporting; both are essential skills in making food truths *transparent* rather than *apparent* and visible rather than invisible. This is also the time when students can discuss controversies over the right to know and the right to have food labels that tell the truth—including the truth about toxic fungicides that make sure tomatoes and apples have no skin blemishes, unlike any person that high school students know. With a little luck, there will be a lot of "aha moments" in this class.

There are many other stories that cannot be seen by looking at the surface level of food. Neither the apple nor the sticker on the apple says that it has traveled all the way from China. The birthplace and subsequent transportation of food have minimal visibility on food labels. Nor is the amount of water in a food item identified. Few people, for example, know that one typical 5-ounce burger expresses 2400 liters of "virtual" or embedded water that went into growing the grains and other foods eaten by the steer. An excellent book, Stephen Leahy's *Your Water Footprint*, documents the amount of water that goes into everyday products. The book not only explains what the untrained eye does not see in terms of embedded water in food, it makes water an important topic of public conversation in an era when drought will be a significant factor in food production and availability.[6] Making students aware of this invisible "virtual" water is part of preparing students for the debates that will drive the policy agenda of their generation as a world in the throes of climate change copes with drought; drought will almost certainly affect most of today's "breadbaskets" located in drylands, such as the North American plains or prairie, and the dependence of North America's favorite foods on stable climate will suddenly become highly visible.

The list of factors that are not visible on the surface of food is long. There is no surface indication of nutrients and fiber, no sign that the potato or tomato were among the majority of vegetables developed by Indigenous people of the Americas before Columbus ever set sail in 1492, no sign of the meaning of a food to a culture or of the science that went into its domestication and genetics, or no sign that the sultana raisin was a forced tribute of Greek peasants to Turkish sultans or that many food traditions and relationships are shaped by colonialism. Indeed, there's enough hidden information in any basic food to keep a classroom busy for an hour, a day, a year, or a lifetime as shown by absorbing and revealing books that tell the story of such items as salt, coffee and oranges. Food is not just a pretty face.

On top of stories and facts about individual foods that are largely invisible, there is the invisibility of food connections—rendered invisible by the way powerful forces have framed the food picture. Connections can be Photoshopped out of the picture as readily as blemishes. Showing food connections is admittedly a higher-order skill for teachers. It took me 15 years of learning, teaching and working as a practitioner to get to the point where food connections are as visible to me as they are now—not that I am sure I am seeing correctly now. Back in the year 2000, when I started at the Toronto Food Policy Council, it was considered quite extreme for me to say that the big project was to link food to a larger system, not subdivide it into smaller parts and specialties such as nutrition and agriculture. We need to think bigger about the food system, I would say, and sometimes taunt people by quoting US farm philosopher Wendell Berry to the effect that people are fed by the food industry, which pays no attention to health, and are treated by the health industry, which pays no attention to food.[7]

Think bigger, I used to say, but forgot we really need to think wider. Today, I look back on the pint-sized view of food I had in 2000 as being every bit as segmented and every bit as guilty of mistaking the part for the whole (the fallacy of misplaced concreteness as science philosopher Alfred North Whitehead called it, or reification as Marx called it) as specialties such as nutrition and agriculture. Fifteen years later, I strive to see food as a life force straddling natural living systems of land, water, air and biodiversity, as well as systems for organizing human services such as transportation, energy, economics, health, spirituality and culture. In my view, food is a central node in a network that can only be seen in the right light when it is linked to all these larger systems. That means food is as much about soul as soil, as much about celebration as stoop labor.

A broad food system understanding obviously starts with foragers, fisherfolk, farmers and processors who produce food. But if all the work that goes into our ability to eat food is truly visible, the food sector is much bigger than that. It includes the people and things that go into direct food production (fertilizers, tractors, assembly lines, agricultural researchers and so on). It adds on the truck drivers, trains, ships, docks and warehouses needed to get food from point A to point B. It includes the people who make things, from refrigerator trucks to stoves that keep food safe while it goes from point A to B and the people who make freezers and shelving for the cooks and staff in the food service and food retail industries. There are also people and materials required to outfit homes for eating—kitchen renovators, makers of dining room tables, knives and chopsticks, sinks, fridges and dishwashers. Then come the people and things involved in managing food leftovers, such as toilets, garbage trucks, composters, sewage pipes and sewage plants. Then come the products that make up for deficient foods, such as food supplements, over-the-counter pills for heartburn, constipation and dietary aids, not to forget dentists and public health workers. The next generation of food workers must be trained, and that means teachers, researchers, writers, artists and school buildings.

Instead of being depicted as a shrinking sector of the modern economy, the food sector needs to be seen as the largest, most varied and dynamic sector of a modern economy. Peasants are the largest occupational group in today's world, restaurant workers are leading members of almost every city's service economy, food processors are bastions of any manufacturing economy, while food artisans, teachers, researchers and chefs are important within any creative economy. If vocational training and career guidance are part of pedagogy, then there are practical as well as academic reasons why the scope of food systems needs to be made visible.

Having said that, a strong case can be made for teaching food connections and visibility through osmosis, as distinct from formal class instruction. The community can be a classroom, teaching visibility and much else. This was the norm before 1950. Farmers markets, once the main place where food was bought, were invariably sited at the center of downtown, right beside the City Hall and most majestic churches. This is obvious in any major center that goes back to pre-automobile days. In an auto-centered city, food was placed beside other shops, and all shops were hived away in plazas and malls—no longer part of the visible commons of community life once situated in city centers. Likewise, before the 1950s, when the cost of food started to drop—from about a quarter of the expenses of a typical family down to about 10 per cent in North America today—growing of food in front and back yards was much more common. During the 1950s, many cities actually banned growing food on front lawns, lest people think the lack of lawns was a sign of the dodgy residents' poor taste and poverty. The rise of television mass marketing to kids also climbed during and after the 1950s. Food ads almost never feature fruits, vegetables or cooking from scratch since such products and activities cannot be patented by corporations that pay for ads, so such portrayals of food become invisible in the minds of children sculpted by informal education from a television, rather than a community.

In effect, the invisibility of food in the school curriculum mirrors the invisibility of food in the properties, buildings and media around them. So public life and the commons are where visibility must be renewed. This is one reason why I believe the development of community food centers should be treated on par with other standard neighborhood infrastructure, such as libraries, fire halls, elementary schools, playgrounds and main street shopping. Not only do such centers make food visible, they serve as forces of neighborhood cohesion, personal self-improvement and skill-building, public education and public safety and deserve to be as visible as other essential public services.

Such community centers—the best-known model of which is THE STOP community food center in Toronto[8]—orient many of their programs to children, beginning with breastfeeding programs and proceeding to after-school gardening programs. They teach many food production, processing and preparation skills to many people, adults as well as children, but the most important thing they teach is personal and community empowerment—a neglected topic in the mainstream education system as well as conventional food literacy. Relevant empowerment is encouraged by beginning with skills which provide people with the competence to negotiate daily life, especially the ability to feed oneself good food—a competence denied many people, most notably people on low income. Such centers also provide follow-up along a continuum of empowerment, up to and including personal skills to speak, write and campaign around common needs that deserve to be recognized by the community and government. One of these sponsored activities, which I had the privilege of participating in, is a week-long food bank diet when a normally well-fed family learns what it is like to rely on a food bank for several days a month—a life-changing experience that ends the invisibility of food. Since a goodly number of poor children already come to school on such a diet—children are the most numerous users of food banks in most communities, invisible though they seem to be to politicians—why not make that diet an experience all students and teachers go through for a week as a teaching technique to make food system disparities visible? Perhaps the exercise could coincide with a week when students study the prevalence of food waste (usually about 40 per cent) in their city so two truths of a food system can be seen side by side.

Meanwhile, back in school, food is a gateway for returning education to core skills of competency and thriving, few of which are provided any more through osmosis of public or family life. Since much of this learning agenda historically belonged in the family and community sphere, it presents an opportunity to develop "schools without walls," whereby schools serve as hubs to rebuild community competence and capacity. The most obvious start-up project is a school-based garden, since schools monopolize the largest amount of unoccupied land in most neighborhoods, both in the school yard and on roofs, and leave these grounds idle for most weekends and summers when families could make use of them. Far from being an agenda that takes away from the school function to provide skills of classical education for professional careers, this agenda creates new opportunities to make life as a learning journey come alive—as anyone can attest who sees the delight in children's eyes when they work in gardens and at food preparation. These are precursors not only to healthy eating—distaste for vegetables ends after children harvest their first carrots and tomatoes—but to studies in personal and public health, soil science, land use planning and social studies.

Beyond school walls, one of my favorite social enterprises in Toronto is ChocoSol, which calls itself a learning enterprise. When ChocoSol founder Michael Sacco first told me about calling his company a learning enterprise, my mind flipped back 30 years to a time when I prepared a 1981 discussion paper for the Toronto Board of Education on linking high school technical courses to apprenticeships. The paper used the term "teaching industries," which had been coined by Board technical education coordinator Charles Taylor to describe companies so good at training employees that they deserved recognition as part of the educational system. Such companies should be hired by the Board of Education to help teach apprentices, our Board of Education work group argued.[9]

ChocoSol is such a teaching industry. Using horizontal and direct trade mechanisms to ensure a fair price is paid to peasant producers, ChocoSol brings the original cacao of Indigenous Mexico to Toronto, where it is made into chocolate for drinking, cooking and snacking. The foundational part of ChocoSol's learning agenda is accomplished as Toronto staff and Mexican peasants learn about chocolate and how best to grow and process it without using fossil fuel energy or losing any of its Mayan heritage as a product of forest gardens, the most eco-friendly form of food production.[10] But from the point of view of ChocoSol as a business, an important aspect of its learning agenda is accomplished through public and school-based workshops featuring the production of chocolate, in the course of which participants learn from ChocoSolista staff about the cacao story: its nutrients, its Mexican peasant origins, its forest garden methods of food production, its ecological methods of processing cacao so more carbon is safely stored in the soil after the cacao has been eaten than before it was grown, and most importantly, the use of cacao as an embodiment of an intercultural food that allows people to not only respect the food culture of others but learn from, share and adapt them. The schools of the future should surely have a budget that allows learning enterprises such as this to flourish in every region—not only for foods that can be grown outside during the summer but also for foods that usually have to be imported but can now be greenhouse-grown or at least processed close to the customer—an ideal way to educate shoppers, reduce packaging waste and increase employment. The schools and businesses of the future can be built without the mental walls of the past.

How can teachers make visible the shape and scope of food systems in less time than it took me to see them? We may not be able to go too far with logic as our only guide. What is the logic to one culture seeing dandelions as disgusting weeds to be sprayed with poisons, while the much-revered Italian cuisine sees them as delicious and healthy salad greens? What is the reason why insects, rich in minerals and lean protein, are eaten by two-thirds of the world's peoples but sprayed with toxins by one-third? Why is seaweed seen as slimy by some cultures and left on the beach to rot, while fine dining in Japan requires sea greens? In the 1800s, salmon and lobster were often used to feed North Americans in Dickensian poor houses, but now they are seen as prize catch. By contrast, macaroni was seen as food for snobbish Yankee Doodle Dandies in the late-1700s and then for lowlifes and now for hipsters. Obviously, there is no accounting for taste, or visibility.

But teachers can create conditions that allow vision to improve. Annabel Slaight is the founder of child-oriented *OWL* magazine and one of the visionaries behind Ladies of the Lake, protectors of Ontario's Lake Simcoe, who produced the delightful children's book called *Do Fish Fart?* That is the book which startled me into recognizing that I could no longer look at food separately from water because food is almost as directly a solid form of water as ice is. At a get-together in a Newmarket coffee shop where we discussed ways of promoting her book, Slaight told me her "real expertise" was "listening to kids with huge ears. Listening is as big as talking." "Kids don't think along lines of academic subjects," she told me. "Kids like what if questions, like 'what if a shark was in the lake.' And they like questions about superlatives, like 'what's the weirdest, biggest, ugliest, fastest.'" Slaight learned how to avoid "narrow channel," thinking from her days with *OWL* magazine, and learned from the kids "how to make the magazine theirs," so she and the Ladies of the Lake gathered 2100 questions that children from the Lake Simcoe area asked them. Of these, 200 were sent to 30 scientists, and the scientists' answers were translated into graphics and words children could understand. That is one way to make food relations or any other subject visible: let the students be the subjects as well as objects of the teaching plan.

Slaight was also influenced by the way First Nations people living on Lake Simcoe saw the lake. They did not see it as an inanimate resource, to be used wastefully or wisely, however humans saw fit. They saw the lake as a life force of Creation. They did not see it as an object of pity that had to be saved. This is why Slaight and the Ladies of the Lake go out of their way to insist that humans cannot save the lake; it must heal itself. They want people to love, enjoy and laugh in the lake so they can relate to the lake in a non-consuming way and go on from that starting point to protect the lake from having more pollutants dumped into it than it can ever possibly deal with.[11]

This is another order of thinking and seeing which students and teachers of food must grapple with because the place of food systems in the world cannot be seen by someone with a world view that separates good plants from bad plants, good insects from bad insects, good bacteria from bad bacteria, homo sapiens from all other living beings and forces, and food from land, water, air and biodiversity. That same narcissistic, human-centered view leads to a linear understanding of food. Even people who champion local and sustainable food systems sometimes fall prey to this linear view of life; that is why so many local and sustainable food groups adopt names such as "farm to fork" or "farm to school." But a moment's reflection leads to the view that life is organized around a circle, not along a line. The circle does not end the moment a human has eaten. Energy is neither lost nor created, the scientific principle of energy and thermodynamics goes, so the energy in food is carried on in other forms.

Once people at the school have finished eating, a sustainable system requires that the composted scraps, and even the humanure, complete the food lifecycle by returning fertility to the soil. If not, there's going to be trouble because pollution related to food is mainly a collection of right things in the wrong place—a landfill site instead of a compost heap. That is why composting belongs in all schools—not just to cut costs of waste disposal (actually waste making, since the waste is made by the work of putting it in garbage cans, trucks and dumps) but as part of the curriculum of teaching that food systems, like water cycles and all of life, are circular. A school-garden compost heap—and if someone is really daring, a composting toilet—can easily make the completing of the food cycle come to life.

The centerpiece of experiential teaching related to food takes place in school cafeterias and dining rooms. The modern food movement champions school meals featuring fresh, local and sustainable foods that taste great and provide the bulk of a day's essential nutrients. Whenever possible, the new model favors engaging students as producers, not just consumers, of these meals. Students contribute some of what they have grown in the school garden and also take turns serving as kitchen and serving staff. Not only do they experience food as co-producers, they learn employment-readiness skills (how to take instruction, work in a team, handle materials safely, work to deadline and so on) as well as career skills (the techniques of cooking and serving) that may well pay a student's way through high school and college, and maybe adulthood. There's a lot to be learned in such environments even if it's not in a regular classroom curriculum. It deserves to be classified as co-curricular and yanked out of the unskilled category of sheer consumption. Co-production and co-curricular go together.

It is also important to notice, since we are on the topic of visibility, that eating is seen as a skill set. The skill set is fast vanishing as a greater proportion of meals are eaten alone in cars, in TV rooms, at a work desk or while absorbed by a mobile phone. The meal table is historically where culture was passed on from one generation to the next and where people told stories, learned to speak up and express themselves, had courtesy, respect, consideration for others and politeness modeled for them, found out (hopefully) they belonged within a social support system. Meals were commonly preceded by some toast to health, and thanks to the people who made the meal possible. Whether the specific words of a grace is secular, non-denominationally spiritual or religious, the saying of grace is commonly when the food system is made visible with expressions of gratitude for all who contributed to the meal, As a public health worker, I was required by law to be totally secular and was very comfortable with this requirement of a public service. But when the occasion was right and the spirit moved me, I urged people to say a grace which I learned while volunteering at Sea to Sky children's camp on an island along the Sunshine Coast of British Columbia. It was written by E.E. Cummings:

we thank you for most this amazing day:
for the leaping greenly spirits of trees
and a blue true dream of sky; and for everything
which is natural, which is infinite, which is yes

Some forces, powers and connections best remain mysterious and invisible. But food badly needs to be made more visible, and good methods of teaching and learning can make a valuable contribution to seeing that through.

NOTES

1. Food's pre-eminence as a policy issue is partly due to the essential need for food and partly due to the "hidden driveways" and intersections food touches. The case for recognizing this centrality of food is made at length in three of my books: *Real Food for a Change* (Toronto, 1999); *The No Nonsense Guide to World Food* (Toronto, 2008, 2013) and *Food for City Building: A Field Guide for Planners, Entrepreneurs and Actionists* (Toronto, 2013).

2. Food denial within the global scientific community charged with reporting on climate change almost matches the global warming denial common within the fossil fuel industry. The Intergovernmental Panel on Climate Change treated agriculture and forestry and ignored food processing, distribution, preparation, consumption and disposal. See, for example, P. Smith et al., 2007: Agriculture. In Climate Change, 2007: Mitigation. Contribution of Working Group 111 to the Fourth Assessment Report of the Intergovernmental Panel on Climate Change. For a critique of this mindset, see, for example, T. Philpott, "A food/climate manifesto presents new visions for responding to climate change," *Grist*, 27 October 2008.

3. On food purchasing practices, see H. Friedmann (2007). Scaling up: Bringing public institutions and food service corporations into the project for a local, sustainable food system in Ontario. *Agriculture and Human Values*, 24 (3), 389–398. On programming, see http://www.newcollege. utoronto.ca/academics/new-college-academic-programs/equity-studies/ global-food-equity/; http://www.newcollege.utoronto.ca/academics/ new-college-academic-programs/newone-learning-without-borders/new- one-courses/; http://www.newcollege.utoronto.ca/academics/new- college-academic-programs/equity-studies/global-food-equity/ global-food-equity-2013-2014-activities/.

4. W. Roberts, S. Archibald, C. Colson, *Campus Food Systems: Sharing Out Project* (Meal Exchange, Sierra Youth Coalition, 2015).

5. B. Eastabrook, Tomatoland: *How Modern Industrial Agriculture Destroyed Our Most Amazing Fruit* (Andrews McMeel, 2012); Oxfam International, *Behind the Brands: Your Favorite Brands Care What You Think!* www. behindthebrands.org nd.

6. S. Leahy, *Your Water Footprint: The Shocking Facts About How Much Water We Use to Make Everyday Products* (Firefly Books, 2014).

7. Cited in www.pinterest.com/pin/65372632064826466.

8. N. Saul, A. Curtis, *The Stop: How The Fight For Good Food Transformed a Community and Inspired a Movement* (Random House, 2013).

9. See "Business and Technical Education in Toronto Schools, The Work Group Report," Toronto Board of Education, November, 1981.

10. In the interests of transparency, I acknowledge that I have joined Michael Sacco in an extended visit to the Indigenous Oaxacan village where he sources his cacao and also that I remain a close friend and advisor to him and am the godfather to his twin sons.

11. *Do Fish Fart? And Many More Amazing Questions and Answers About Lake Simcoe!* Ontario Water Centre, 2015. In the interests of transparency, I acknowledge that I provided consulting services to the Ontario Water Centre during the summer and fall of 2015, during which time I interviewed Annabel Slaight several times.

Glossary of Terms

Agency The notion of being an active agent in constructing knowledge and surrounding structures together with others. As such, it is the product of social processes and action, and an expression of personally meaningful orientation to surrounding realities and others. It can also be seen as a form of action challenging prevailing circumstances or interpretations.

Anticipatory socialization A sociological concept devised by Robert Merton to capture the new behaviours people engage in as they prepare to take on new social roles.

Autoethnography A reflective writing process whereby researchers seek to understand how their own lived experiences relate to the subject under study; an empirical qualitative method in which researchers engage in critical reflection of autobiographical and ethnographic stories, and bridge individual and collective experience, thus disrupting the often taken-for-granted norms of traditional scientific discourse and creating space for richer and more complex understanding of experience (Ellis 2004; Ellingson and Ellis 2008).

Banking system of education Pedagogy that preserves the status quo and lacks critical questioning; teachers are knowledge-holders and control the learning process and students are passive learners; assumes a dichotomous relationship between human beings and the world rather than a transformative relationship; approaches education as initiation rather than as liberation (Freire 1993).

© The Author(s) 2016
J. Sumner (ed.), *Learning, Food, and Sustainability,*
DOI 10.1057/978-1-137-53904-5

Behaviorally focused nutrition education Nutrition education that addresses a specific eating behavior (e.g., eat more fruits and vegetables, shop at farmers' markets, drink fewer sweetened beverages).

Citizenship education A course of study that provides students with the knowledge of the political, legal, and economic functions of adult society, and with the social and moral awareness to thrive in it (Citizenship Education, n.d.).

Closed-loop food system A closed-loop food system recycles waste into compost at the end of the production-consumption process, which then is used again for production. A closed-loop food system minimizes waste by eliminating the need for the landfilling of food.

Colostrum The first milk that is produced by the lactating mother shortly after giving birth. It is rich in antibodies so it helps protect the newborn from illnesses.

Community-based research (CBR) Research that involves a partnership of students, faculty, and community members who collaboratively engage in research with the purpose of solving pressing community problems or effecting social change (Strand et al. 2003).

Community-campus engagement (CCE) A form of engagement that encompasses **community-service learning** (CSL) and **community-based research** (CBR), as well as other forms of community-campus collaboration such as the role universities and colleges can play as 'anchor institutions' in their local economies (Dragicevic 2015).

Community food security A prominent alternative food movement or discourse based on issues of hunger and food security. It has been most notably described by Hamm and Bellows (2003) as a a situation in which all community residents obtain a safe, culturally acceptable, nutritionally adequate diet through a sustainable food system that maximizes community self-reliance and social justice.

Community food systems A popular alternative food discourse that purports localism and regionalism (place), with the addition of an emphasis on social health (space). Many refer to Feenstra's (2002) description of a community food system as a collaborative effort to build more locally based, self-reliant food economies—one in which sustainable food production, processing, distribution and consumption are integrated to enhance the economic, environmental and social health of a particular place.

Community food work A term related to Slocum's (2007) four approaches and social sectors associated with alternative food systems: farm sustainability, nutrition education, environmental sustainability and social justice. The integration of these processes and goals is discursively termed community food work.

Community-service learning An educational approach that integrates service in the community with intentional learning activities (Canadian Alliance for Community Service Learning n.d.).

Comprehensive school health An internationally recognized framework for supporting improvements in students' educational outcomes while addressing school health in a planned, integrated and holistic way. It encompasses the whole school environment with actions addressing four distinct but inter-related pillars: social and physical environment; teaching and learning; healthy school policy; and partnerships and services (Joint Consortium for School Health 2015).

Cultural work(ers) A term frequently used in radical education and critical pedagogy associated with Henry Giroux (1992) and the politics of difference. While generally used to refer to the contributions of artists and writers, Giroux extended it to include the performances of educators, asserting the primacy of the political and pedagogical.

Deskilling A loss of food knowledge from food skills to food systems understanding, which benefits agribusiness since much of the power in the current food system depends on consumer ignorance. A necessary and successful strategy to encourage consumers to disassociate the origins of food from its ultimate form, while simultaneously introducing highly processed and profitable goods that ensure control over food remains out of the hands of growers and eaters.

Ecohealth approach An approach to finding innovative solutions to improve the biophysical and social dimensions of human health and the environment that encourages participation from all sectors of the community in collaborative transdisciplinary initiatives.

Ecological sustainability Using natural resources wisely so that they can continue to be available for future generations.

Engaged pedagogy A pedagogical approach that empowers students and teachers, providing them with ways of knowing that enhance their capacity to live fully and deeply. This pedagogy is liberatory, healing, and connected to the lived experiences of the students and teachers, valuing expression and sharing. This can only be achieved through commitment by the educators to a process of self-actualization that promotes their own growth and well-being, in addition to that of their students (hooks 1994).

Food education Education on food and eating. It has traditionally been seen as a practice-based subfield of nutrition education to promote knowledge and skills about healthy and nutritionally balanced eating. Today, food education can refer also to education with broader aims, which are not necessarily connected (only) to health and nutrition.

Food enterprise A term that represents the neoliberal model of mono-cultural industrial food production, supported by global bodies like the International Monetary Fund and the World Trade Organization, as well as government policies of privatization and deregulation that support corporate concentration.

Food justice A discourse and movement developed in response to inequities in the food system.

Food literacy Keeping in mind that there are various definitions if food literacy, it includes the knowledge of food's impact on the individual, society and the environment as well as associated knowledge of cooking, producing, and processing food. Food literacy also involves the knowledge of the seasonality of food, where food comes from, how it arrived on our plates and where it goes when we are finished with it.

Food security A situation that exists when all people, at all times, have physical, social and economic access to sufficient, safe and nutritious food that meets their dietary needs and food preferences for an active and healthy life (FAO 2003). Considered by some as a reformist approach that does not challenge the structural underpinnings of the corporate food regime.

Food sense Making sense of everyday routines and habits that are a part of practical food-related activities in different situations, as well as the broader connections of these habits. Food sense can be seen as the outcome of food education according to its broad definition. Like the concept of health sense, food sense aims to detach from individual and knowledge-based definitions of food-related skills and to approach food education in a flexible and context-bound manner.

Food sovereignty Developed by the peasant movement called La Via Campesina, the term focuses on the right of peoples and governments to determine their own agriculture systems, food markets, environments and modes of production. Food sovereignty is seen as a radical alternative to corporate-led, neoliberal, industrial agriculture.

Food waste Any discarded organic matter that was intended for consumption by humans, regardless of its ultimate fate.

Global food system The interconnected, world-wide system that produces, distributes, processes, packages, markets, prepares and disposes of our food; typically the global food system refers to the system that is dominated by multinational agricultural companies that make inputs for producing food and multinational food companies that make highly processed food products.

Good food Food that is healthy, green, fair, accessible and affordable.

Good Food Box A volunteer-run program providing access to a box of fruits and vegetables to community members at a fixed cost on a bi-weekly or monthly basis. Bulk buying savings are passed along to participants. Good Food Box Programs in many areas prioritize locally sourced products.

Good food diet A diet made up of mostly 'good food,' which means food that is healthy, green, fair, accessible and affordable.

Good food education Learning environments, curricula, and experiences that encourage people to participate in and make progress towards a food system that produces food that is healthy, green, fair, accessible and affordable.

Health literacy The ability to obtain, interpret and use health-related information, as well as to interpret one's own and others' health. Health literacy is often described as an empowering skill that helps in coping with the complexities of modern societies. It is often also seen as a skill that enables the achievement of productive citizenship, personal life quality, and individual and social well-being.

Health sense The ability to make sense of everyday routines and habits that are a part of health-related activities in different situations. Health sense can be understood as an outcome of social processes and emphasizes the broader cultural and community surroundings in relation to health behavior.

Highly processed food Food that has been excessively altered from its natural state so that it has many ingredients, often refined from grains such as corn and soy, with the final product not resembling its base ingredients; highly processed foods are often made by multinational food companies.

Land Grant Universities President Abraham Lincoln signed the Morrill Act into law in 1862 providing a grant of federal land to each state to be sold in order to provide an endowment for at least one land-grant institution with the mission to teach and advance agriculture and mechanical arts (Mast 2012).

Local Food Act of Ontario Under the Act established in 2013, the Minister of Agriculture, Food and Rural Affairs for the Province of Ontario sets goals or targets for Ontario to aspire to in the areas of: improving food literacy in respect of local food, encouraging increased use of local food by public sector organizations, and increasing access to local food.

Narrative inquiry An approach to research that is both a methodology and a paradigmatic orientation to qualitative research in the social sciences and humanities that emerged in the 20th century. This approach might also be called "narrative" or defined as a particular branch of storytelling within the narrative method (see Clandinin and Connelly 2000).

Neoliberalism A theory of political-economic practices that emphasizes the withdrawal of government from services to promote the health and well-being of communities of citizens, and the substitution of individual responsibility and for-profit, commercial services (Koç et al. 2012).

Neophobia Fear of trying new foods.

Nutrition education Any combination of educational strategies, accompanied by environmental supports, designed to facilitate voluntary adoption of food choices and other food- and nutrition-related behaviors conducive to health and well-being...[and] delivered through multiple venues and involving activities at the individual, community, and policy levels (Contento 2015).

Nutritionism A paradigm that reduces the value and benefits of food to its nutrients, assuming that we eat only to promote physical health.

Participation A reflexive and dialogical relationship to surrounding circumstances that can be seen as a two-way learning process. A form of interaction and negotiation, in which intersubjectivity, competence, and shared responsibility is mutually recognized.

Personal troubles A sociological concept used by C. Wright Mills to capture the challenges individuals face when interacting with society.

Political ecology An approach to inquiry that aims to identify the influences of power in the construction and resolution of environmental issues.

Political ecology of education An approach to education that analyzes how public policies and economic incentives shape the content of sustainability education, environmental behavior, and our conceptions of the interrelationships between nature and society.

Practices Activities that take place in a specific location, indicating a reciprocal relationship between context and action. In reference to food education, practice-related learning activities refer to those including a concrete element of touching, tasting, preparing, or acquiring food items.

Praxis The process of reflecting on one's experience of a practical activity (practice) in order to improve understanding (theory), which in turn changes how one conducts one's practice in light of one's evolving understanding of it; commonly associated with Marxist, feminist, and postmodern critiques of knowledge production involving reflection, reflexivity, and deliberate social action (see Lather 1991). Freire (1993) described it as the transformative process of reflection and action.

Psychosocial theories Schemes or road maps of the interrelationships between an individual's behavior and social factors, such as motivation, beliefs, knowledge, and skills; these theories visually display how the social factors, often called determinants, mediators, or constructs work together to influence behavior.

Public issues A sociological term devised by C. Wright Mills to recognize that widespread social phenomena are rooted in the organization of society's activities and collective action; therefore the problems created by society must be solved by the collective, rather than the individual.

Retail modernization A process whereby retail markets undergo a process of modernization, industrialization and standardization. Retail modernization includes the transformation of traditional open market concepts into supermarkets.

Scholar activists Those teachers whose production of knowledge and pedagogical practices works with and serves progressive social movements (Sudbury and Okazawa-Rey 2009).

School food and nutrition policy Recommendations, guidelines or requirements that provide a framework by which schools can plan, implement, and evaluate food and nutrition-related actions using a coordinated approach that reflects current dietary guidance (McKenna 2010).

School meals Meals offered to students during the school day. The organization and contents of these meals vary considerably between different countries.

Self-efficacy Confidence in one's ability to perform a certain task (e.g., chop vegetables)

Sentipensante pedagogy (or 'sensing/thinking' pedagogy) A 'multi-human' approach that unites the poetry of teaching and learning with the rationality of teaching and learning. This pedagogy attends not only to our entire selves but also to all people; it excludes no one and nurtures all strengths, regardless of historical privilege (Rendón 2008).

Social justice The equitable distribution of wealth, resources, education, services, and opportunities in society.

Traditional knowledge The knowledge, innovations and practices of indigenous and local communities around the world. Developed from experience gained over the centuries and adapted to the local culture and environment, traditional knowledge is transmitted orally from generation to generation.

Transformative learning The process of effecting change in a frame of reference, occurring through critical awareness and reflection, discourse, and broader social engagement. Transformative learning asserts that it is this combination of outcomes that permits a change of consciousness. In sustainability education, a modified theory called transformative sustainability learning has been introduced, which involves learning through personal engagement that results in profound changes in attitudes around ecological, social, and economic justice.

Type 2 diabetes A disease that occurs when the body cannot properly use the insulin that is released (called insulin insensitivity) or does not make enough insulin. About 90 per cent of people with diabetes have type 2 diabetes. Type 2 diabetes more often develops in adults, but children can also be affected.

Urbanization A concept that refers to the growing number of people who live in urban areas.

Youth engagement The sustained and meaningful involvement of a young person in an activity focussed outside of themselves (Pancer et al. 2002).

References

Clandinin, D. J., & Connelly, F. M. (2000). *Narrative inquiry*. San Francisco: Jossey-Bass Publishers.

Contento, I. R. (2015). *Nutrition education: Linking research, theory and practice* (3rd ed.). Burlington: Jones and Bartlett.

Dragicevic, N. (2015). *Anchor institutions*. Atkinson Foundation. Toronto: Mowat Centre.

Ellingson, L. L., & Ellis, C. (2008). Autoethnography as constructionist project. In J. A. Holstein & J. F. Gubrium (Eds.), *Handbook of constructionist research* (pp. 445–465). New York: The Guilford Press.

Ellis, C. (2004). *The ethnographic I: A methodological novel about autoethnography*. Walnut Creek: Alta Mira Press.

FAO. (2003). *Trade reforms and food security: Conceptualising the linkages*. Rome: Commodity Policy and Projections Service, Commodities and Trade Division, Food and Agriculture Organization.

Feenstra, G. (2002). Creating space for sustainable food systems: Lessons from the field. *Agriculture and Human Values, 19*, 99–106.

Freire, P. (1993) [1970]. *Pedagogy of the oppressed*. London: Penguin Books.

Giroux, H. (1992). *Border crossings: Cultural workers and the politics of education*. New York: Routledge.

Hamm, M. W., & Bellows, A. C. (2003). Community food security and nutrition educators. *Journal of Nutrition Education and Behavior, 35*(1), 37–43.

hooks, b. (1994). *Teaching to transgress: Education as the practice of freedom*. New York: Routledge.

Joint Consortium for School Health. (2015). *What is comprehensive school health?* Retrieved December 13, 2015, from: http://www.jcsh-cces.ca/index.php/about/comprehensive-school-health

Koç, M., Sumner, J., & Winson, A. (Eds.). (2012). *Critical perspectives in food studies*. Toronto: Oxford University Press.

Lather, P. (1991). *Getting smart: Feminist research and pedagogy with/in the post-modern*. London: Routledge.

Mast, T. (2012). Morrill Act leaves long legacy. *Iowa State Daily*. Retrieved September 10, 2015. http://www.iowastatedaily.com/news/article_754cdcba-af28-11e1-aef2-0019bb2963f4.html

McKenna, M. L. (2010). Policy options to support healthy eating in schools. *Canadian Journal of Public Health, 101*(Suppl 2), S14–S17.

Pancer, S. M., Rose-Krasnor, L., & Loiselle, L. D. (2002). Youth conferences as a context for engagement. *New Directions in Youth Development, 96*, 47–64.

Rendón, L. I. (2008). *Sentipensante (sensing/thinking) pedagogy: Educating for wholeness, social justice and liberation*. Sterling: Stylus Publishing.

Slocum, R. (2007). Whiteness, space and alternative food practice. *Geoforum, 38*(3), 520–533.

Strand, K., Marullo, S., Cutforth, N., Stoecker, R., & Donohue, P. (2003). *Community-based research and higher education: Principles and practices*. San Francisco: John Wiley and Sons.

Sudbury, J., & Okazawa-Rey, M. (Eds.). (2009). *Activist scholarship: antiracism, feminism, and social change*. Boulder: Paradigm Publishers.

INDEX

© The Author(s) 2016
J. Sumner (ed.), *Learning, Food, and Sustainability*,
DOI 10.1057/978-1-137-53904-5